ALASKA MAN

A Memoir of Growing Up and Living in the Wilds of Alaska

A TRILOGY BOOK I OF III

GEORGE DAVIS & JILL DAVIS

© 2016 by Fly By Night Inc.

ISBN: 978-1548833510

George and Jill Davis
http://www.alaskawildadventures.tv

Dedicated to my oldest brother, Gregory Robert Davis. If it were not for him, none of this would have been possible.

"Good friends are like stars...You do not always see them, but you know that they are always there." - Unknown

George R. Davis & Greg R. Davis circa 1971

TABLE OF CONTENTS

Acknowledgements

GEORGE DAVIS ALASKA MAN

I would like to start off thanking my wife, Jill Davis, Alaska Woman. She earned this name spending twenty years with me adventuring and pioneering Alaska's savage, wild wilderness. She has been a driving force behind me in all of our endeavors, thriving, surviving, standing by my side through thick and thin in the unyielding and at times brutal territory that we call home. She was a key player in helping me write my Alaska Man novels and has been my loyal partner in crime.

I would like to thank all of my friends and family who stood behind me over the years and have enjoyed spending time with us on our adventures in the wilds of Alaska.

JILL DAVIS ALASKA WOMAN

I would like to give tribute to my husband, George Davis, Alaska Man, for taking me along on the most amazing adventures a person could ever dream of. We have been above and beyond Middle of Nowhere, Alaska. As you read Alaska Man novels you will come to find how unique Alaska Man is. I have never met anyone who had the range of talents and expertise in so many different professions. The pursuits we shared are commercial fishing, sport fishing, adventure guiding, flying airplanes, running jet boats, and running salt-water vessels all over, from Seattle to Alaska. I have seen copious amounts of wildlife, sea mammals, and birds that any average person never gets to see. I have gotten to see untouched wilderness and join George in pioneering Alaska's coastline from Haines to Cordova, which we named "The Lost Coast." Life is an adventure when you are with Alaska Man.

Lastly, I would like to thank my family and a handful of friends for putting up with my antics, mischievousness, and naughtiness. It is a curse that cannot be stifled. You either love me or hate me; most of the time it is both.

Foreword

I FIRST HEARD ABOUT GEORGE Davis, a.k.a. Alaska Man, while viewing an episode of the outdoor show *The Hunt for Big Fish* featuring Larry Dahlberg. My son and I hunt and fish worldwide, and we are always looking for that next great place. George and Larry were catching salmon sharks out of Cordova, Alaska. A phone number appeared at the end of the show. My son, who was only nine years old at the time, insisted that he wanted to catch a salmon shark with George. I called the number, and to my good fortune I was able to get in contact with him. We met up later that summer in Cordova. From that point on, George and I became great friends and fished together several times a year. We always had success in numerous fisheries. My son and I hold approximately thirty International Game Fish Association (IGFA) world records, most of them on a fly rod. One of our missions was to catch the world record Pacific Halibut on a fly rod. After George undertook the challenge, we accomplished the endeavor while out fishing on one of George's secret pinnacles on the Gulf of Alaska, using a twenty-pound fly line. It is the largest halibut ever taken on a fly rod.

George Davis is truly a remarkable individual deserving of the title "Alaska Man." He is a boat captain, pilot, fishing and hunting guide, builder, electrician, and plumber. You name it, George can do it. I think his wilderness prowess can be summed up by the comment my good friend Judge Anthony Black said after we fished with George at his lodge in Icy Bay, Alaska. "George Davis is the smartest man in the world!" Very few of us could live his lifestyle and survive in the wilderness where George calls home.

It is a world very few people ever see, let alone live in. He has built with his own hands three remote first-class lodges on Alaska's Lost Coast that are only accessible by bush plane or boat. We spent several evenings being entertained by George, sharing his astonishing stories of his adventures growing up in the wilds of Alaska. This led to him sharing his life story with the world with his Alaska Man novels.

Besides his career in commercial fishing, his lodging and adventure business is world class. It is impressive what he has accomplished in his lifetime, and he is still at it with his current businesses, Alaska Wild Adventures and Alaska Man Consulting. He is a true legend, and the real deal!

I am proud to have spent time with him and to call him my friend.

JIM SEEGRAVES

Jim Seegraves came to Alaska in 1969 with the US Army, and was the founding member and first president of the Alaska chapter of Safari Club International SCI. Since that time he has hunted and fished in Africa, Asia, South America, Central America, Mexico, Canada, and the United States. Jim was an assistant hunting guide in Alaska and has guided people from all over the world.

Jim knows intimately the world of hunting and fishing and was very pleased and flattered that George asked him to write the foreword to his book *Alaska Man*.

Prologue

I HAD BEEN WATCHING THE weather and thought I had a shot of making it back to camp before dark. I was already feeling anxious knowing that I had gotten a later start than intended and that I was probably going to have to land my plane in darkness. I knew without a doubt that I had to make it back to my set net camp where my brother Greg was waiting for me. Greg had throat cancer and this could very well be my last bear hunt with him. I fought to keep the Super Cub under control as I headed through the mountain pass. The wind was gusting up to forty knots on the upward side of the pass creating severe updrafts and turbulence. It was very difficult to keep the aircraft under control. I was visualizing what my good friend Iron Mike Ivers from Yakutat had expressed to me. Practice and get proficient at it. He told me to fly the mountain pass on clear days and mark the dead-end canyons on my chart. There are many canyons and crevices, and one wrong turn means death. Alaskan bush pilots call it cumulus granite. Now I was flying on the leeward side of the pass. I glanced at my instruments and was descending at 1000-1500 feet per minute. Even with the engine at full throttle and the trim set for the best rate of climb, I was still getting sucked down rapidly. I was hitting pockets of turbulence that would thrash the plane around like a kite. Looking out of the airplane window to my right, the mountainside loomed 300 feet off my wingtip. This was a bad situation. There was barely any visibility from the heavy snow showers, about a quarter of a mile at best. Sweat was pouring off of my brow from the tension of keeping my plane from crashing. My brother was waiting for me at camp, and death waited for me with open arms on the side of a mountain.

CHAPTER 1
NORTH TO ALASKA

I HAD DREAMED OF GOING to Alaska since the tender age of ten. My brother Greg, who was twelve years older, shared this vision of living off the land in the wilds of Alaska. I pored over books and photographs and wanted to learn how to hunt, fish, and trap just like the Alaska wild mountain men I had been reading about. It was all I could think about.

My father, George Davis Sr., owned a tool and die business in Michigan and was a private pilot. When I was twelve, I started flying with my dad. We would rent planes and I started learning how to fly. By the time I was fourteen, I was flying different types of aircraft three days week and put in as much stick time as I could. At fifteen I started taking lessons from an instructor.

Greg's work in construction made it easy for him to relocate and find work most anywhere. He finally made the decision to head north to Alaska, but, unfortunately, his first wife did not share his dream. Greg had to make the tough decision to make the trek to the last frontier alone. Later he met Jane, who shared his passion for the 49th state and they began the adventure to Alaska together.

Greg and Jane returned to Michigan two years later when she was expecting a baby. They talked with our parents about the opportunities in Haines, Alaska. Our dad was excited about the idea. I desperately wanted to attend the Air Force Academy, and then go into the United States Air Force to become a fighter pilot. My dad was all for it. However, my mother was firmly against it. I began talking more with my brother about life in Alaska. I was fascinated with the idea of living in Alaska already, but after listening to Greg's stories firsthand about living in the wild, fishing, hunting, trapping, and being a mountain man, I was consumed with the idea of living this kind of life myself. The loss of my aspirations of joining the Air

Force, combined with the timely arrival of my brother with tales of his life up north, could make my dream into a reality. I already had a thirst for adventure and a burning desire to go to Alaska. Now I was dead set on going to Alaska with my brother. Period!

Greg talked our parents into coming to Alaska with us to check out some property that Greg had found for sale. My dad, being an entrepreneur, he was interested to seeing in person what my brother was proposing. The adventure began. Greg and I jumped in his white Chevy van. My mom, dad, Jane, and newborn baby Dawn Rene traveled in our parents' four-door Oldsmobile and we all headed west for Seattle. We drove to Chicago, and then west on I-90 to Seattle.

When we arrived in Seattle four days later we stayed at the famous Edgewater Inn on the waterfront for three days while waiting excitedly for the Alaska state ferry, the *Malaspina*. The spectacular voyage up the Inside Passage from the Port of Seattle to Haines, Alaska, takes three days. The first port of call was Ketchikan, Alaska. The next stops were Wrangell, Petersburg, Juneau, and then finally Haines. After Haines the ferry goes on fifteen miles north to Skagway, then turns around and makes the same stops on the way back to Seattle.

I was thrilled to be taking this trip. The scenery was spectacular and at first taste I fell in love with Alaskan seafood. The ferry had a full-service restaurant onboard, and I was so impressed with king crab and halibut that I made the decision right then and there that crabbing and being a commercial fisherman would be something I would pursue along with the hunting, sport fishing, and trapping lifestyle. Haines is a beautiful, quaint little town that had a population of approximately 500 people at the time, which included the little native village of Klukwan twenty-two miles up the road in the Chilkat Valley right on the bank of the Chilkat River. Haines looks like something out of *National Geographic* with scenery like the Swiss Alps. It has sweeping views of steep rugged mountains, beautiful valleys, and swift rivers that flow into the sea.

When the Davis family arrived on February 7, 1971, Haines was buried under fifteen feet of snow. The town had been battling a wicked winter, and people were struggling to dig themselves out of back-to-back snowstorms. After checking into the Thunderbird Motel, Greg did his best to show everyone around his new hometown. Even some vehicles were completely buried, but that did not bother me. On the other hand, our mother, Alberta, who everyone called Birdie, was used to her creature comforts of fancy living in Michigan. She decided then and there that the small town *Northern Exposure* Alaska life was not meant for her. The first words out of her mouth were "When is the next ferry out of this godforsaken town?" At the ripe age of fifteen, I decided at once that I was going to stay in Haines with my brother Greg, his wife Jane, and their baby Dawn to live out my dream.

My father asked me if I was sure that I wanted to stay. He wanted to make sure this was the right decision I was making for myself. He told me he did not want to get a call from me in a few weeks or a month crying or whining to come home, and that if I did want to come back to Michigan, I was going to have to find my own way. If I wanted to make adult decisions for myself, I was going to have to take responsibility. I was dead set on living this mountain man lifestyle and I said, "Yes, for sure I am staying." Thirty-six hours later, after the ferry had gone to Skagway, it turned around and made its way back south to Haines. Mom and Dad were back on the ferry headed to Seattle where they would then make the trek back east to Michigan. Instead of being scared, a feeling of relief came over me. I knew in my heart this was home.

CHAPTER 2

ALASKA INITIATION

EVEN THOUGH I HAD DREAMED of living in Alaska, it was understandably a bit of a culture shock. Life certainly was anything but easy. It was a tough time of year to be looking for a place to live, but we ended up finding a small 28 ft. silver Airstream trailer in Port Chilkoot. It had one small bedroom and one small bathroom. I slept on the sofa under a cracked window covered in Visqueen plastic that let the snow blow in on me when the wind was really howling. In spite of all of this, there was no way I was turning back now. I was going to have to get used to these conditions if I was going to make a life here.

Port Chilkoot was a different part of Haines. It was actually a fort/base one mile south of town that was built back in World War I. It had barracks, military housing, and even a recreation hall that had a bowling alley and gym. The snowstorms kept coming and we kept getting hammered. I actually had to go to people's houses and dig out their front doors because the snow was so deep people were literally trapped in their homes with snow up to the windows.

Greg started a karate class. With his background training in the Army Special Forces Green Beret division, Greg excelled at karate after he got out of the military and became a black belt. I had been studying karate three years in Michigan prior to coming to Haines and had my brown belt. I helped him instruct the class. We taught in the basement of the local bowling alley and bar. Being only fifteen, I had to head off to school each day, which ended up being a very tough situation for me. Since I was from Michigan, the local kids considered me an outsider at first. I was not readily accepted and my head definitely was not on school. Instead of keeping my thoughts on books and class, I caught myself daydreaming about being out in the wilderness and starting my life of hunting, trapping, and fishing. I became close friends with a girl my age named Lisa, the daughter of my brother's good friend Ernie.

Being the new kid is tough enough, but being in an isolated place like Haines was even tougher. The Canadian border is a forty-two mile drive. It's 250 miles to the town of Whitehorse, Yukon. In another direction it is 330 miles to Beaver Creek, and then you enter back into Alaska from the Yukon. It's 585 miles to the town of Glenallen, 640 miles to Fairbanks, and 860 miles to Anchorage. The only other option for traveling was to take a ferry ride or fly a plane fifteen miles north up to Skagway or ninety miles south to Juneau.

Right off the bat the school tough guy picked a fight with me by accusing me of taking his schoolbook while we were in the library. This did not sit well with me and I stood up to him. I am not the kind of person who will take being bullied or intimidated. We got into a confrontation and I ended up fighting him. He threw the first punch and I blocked it, and then I counterpunched him once and knocked him flat on his ass. In one punch the fight was over. This landed me in the principal's office. I often ended up in that office and was sent home a few times. I was finally suspended for two weeks after getting into a fight with the principal for picking him up by the scruff of his suit jacket and hanging him from his mountain goat that was on the wall of his office. They called my brother at Snobble's Lumber Mill and he had to take off work to get me. Needless to say, he was pretty angry. Another big difference from what I was used to was the dating scene. In Michigan, dating was formal and I took girls out on dates. Boys were expected to have manners. In Alaska, girls were very advanced and went to parties with older boys. I had never had a problem finding dates, but in Haines, instead of making an effort to ask a girl out, I had numerous girls chasing me. My problems with the principal increased, and I ended up barely passing that year of school. I turned sixteen that March.

Greg and I went black bear hunting my first spring in Alaska, before fishing started. I had some money saved and had bought a used .375 H&H Magnum model 70 Winchester for $300. We went hunting May 10, almost two months after my sixteenth birthday.

We went out the Haines Highway looking on the slides and benches for bears. We could hike right up the bases of these mountains straight up from the side of the road. We drove about ten miles out the Haines Highway and spotted a black bear. We stopped, and then pulled over. I grabbed my gun thinking Greg was going to kill the bear, but that I would have my gun ready in case I needed to shoot for backup. Greg turned and said to me, "Do you want to take the bear?" I lit up with excitement. "Of course, I would love to take the bear!" Greg told me that he would back me up with his rifle. He told me to quietly get out of the truck, not shut the door all the way, as to keep the noise down. "Then we will find the best place to take a rest so you can get the best shot off." We got out and found a place where we could see the bear, and I found a big boulder to take a rest on. The bear was munching away on a dandelion patch on a bench about 500 feet above us. He asked me if I was ready. I said that I was. We had gone out the road earlier that week to the target range, and I was hitting bulls-eyes at, and over, one hundred yards with my .375. I was confident that I could pull off the five-hundred-foot shot. I got ready, looked through my scope, focused in on the bear, and picked a spot right behind his front shoulder. As he turned broadside, I pulled the trigger. I followed through and saw that I had hit the bear. I looked up, and the bear turned around, and started to go back up the mountain, then just fell down. I looked at my brother and he had a huge smile on his face. He grabbed me and exclaimed, "Congratulations, you just got your first black bear! I am so proud of you." I was overjoyed beyond belief. I told my brother that I was so grateful to be here, and I thanked him for bringing me to Alaska. He told me he was happy to have me here, and that family meant everything to him. He said that we were going to be a team from here on out. At that we got ready for the hike up the slide to take care of skinning and packing out the bear.

I was so thrilled to be living out my dream. We got up to the bear, and inspected the kill shot. Greg exclaimed, "Nice shot! Dead on the money. Now you have officially gotten your Alaska initiation." I was still almost in disbelief of what had just occurred. Greg told me to get my head out of the clouds, that we had work to do. I snapped out of it and started learning how to skin out this bear. I had grown up hunting in Michigan, but the biggest thing that I had killed and butchered was a deer. We skinned out the bear, and then we packed out the hide and meat down the mountain.

We got home and started to butcher and process the animal. The plan was to cut the meat into roasts, and then use the rest of it for sausage and jerky. It was really rewarding for me to go through this process of killing and butchering my own animal for the family. There is a satisfaction and pride in providing for the household. I could see that this would become an annual tradition for us. My mind was going nonstop that evening; I could not stop thinking about all of the adventures this life in Alaska would have in store for me.

Greg had already spent two seasons in Alaska and had been fishing with a local native family learning the ropes. I was eager to get my own commercial fishing enterprise going. I knew I was already getting ahead of myself, but I could not keep my enthusiasm under wraps. We excitedly got our commercial set net permits to fish for salmon. Greg was aggressive and hardworking, so we made the perfect team. Back then anyone could buy a commercial set gill net license. Later the law changed to a limited entry, meaning the state made a limit on the number of permits that could be issued for the different salmon fisheries. We outfitted a friend's unheated shop with a barrel stove and started building a wooden 16 ft. skiff, and added an Evinrude 50hp OMC outboard. We named it the *Last Chance*. We headed out to the end of the Chilkat Peninsula to Seduction Point with the building supplies in our skiff and enough rough-cut lumber to build a 12x16 ft. stick frame cabin. We brought out a little cast iron wood stove, a Coleman camp cooking stove, and lanterns. First we set up a mooring buoy and running line to anchor up the skiff out in front of our cabin. We made a set by tying one end of the net to a big rock right off the beach, and then stretched it out. The other end of the net had an anchor on the lead line and a big orange floating buoy on the cork line. The set is perpendicular to the shore. The top of the net floats with corks, and the bottom of the net is heavy with a weighted line called the lead line. Fish are ensnared usually by their heads or their gills in the mesh netting, hence the term gillnetting.

We set our nets strategically along the shoreline in the best possible place to catch schools of salmon. The first salmon to run are king salmon chinook, then the reds or sockeyes. We look for the best points where fish are going to be traveling through. Sometimes people actually fight over the areas that produce big sets. The areas that have good salmon runs are highly sought after. To keep catching fish we had to work the nets, keeping them clean of seaweed and kelp. We would also get the fish we caught out of the net and into our boat as soon as possible. If fish see other fish hanging in the net, they will dodge the net and go around it. We did not have ice, so we had to get the fish to the tender right away.

A few tender boats sat out in the peninsula. The cannery we sold our fish to kept a tender out on the fishing grounds to stand by near Seduction Point. We called the tender when our holding totes got full. The totes that we kept our fish in held about 100 sockeye, or 700 pounds. On a good day we would pitch off twice. The tender would weigh our fish and give us a fish ticket so that we could collect the money from the cannery when we got back to town after the opener. Tenders carried other supplies for fisherman on their boats, such as gas and groceries. We would buy supplies from them so that we could stay out fishing and not have to leave the fishing grounds to go to town. The openers ranged from three to four days a week. After the opener was over, during the closure, we had plenty of work to do. There was cleaning of the boat and totes. We had to repair nets that had been damaged by the fish, and sometimes by seals and sea lions. There was also maintenance to keep our outboard in good running condition. During the closures, we do what Alaskans call subsistence fishing. It is the same as set netting but you cannot sell your fish. The fish caught on the closures are strictly for personal consumption.

We used our subsistence fish for making fresh pack and smoked salmon for the pantry. We filleted and filled pint-sized Mason canning jars full of fish and then pressure-cooked them. It was our goal to put up thirty cases of pint jars a year. Fresh pack means pure fish with no smoke. We built a smoker and would do smoked salmon as well during the closures. We did our smoked fish in a variety of ways. We made dried fish and squaw candy. Squaw candy is a strip of salmon smoked and dried until fully cooked and hard like jerky. Some batches of fish we would only half smoke until barely cooked. Then we would jar this fish in a pressure cooker for the pantry and for gifts in pint and half pint jars. The jarred salmon would stay shelf stable for years, but only if it didn't freeze. If a jar of fish freezes, it turns mushy. We worked seven days a week during the salmon season. Three to four days fishing, then the rest of the week working on maintenance and putting away fish for the winter. We usually hit our mark of thirty cases of pint jars filled with salmon. We also put up berry preserves and had a garden. We canned up vegetables out of the garden as well.

All of this kept me pretty busy, but I did make time to get my sport fishing rod out. I would catch Dolly Varden trout near our set net site. I also learned how to troll for king salmon. I caught my first king salmon that spring, weighing in at forty-eight pounds. I became avid at bottom fishing for halibut, cod, and rockfish. We would put crab and shrimp pots out, and the catch was bountiful. I was always sport fishing while growing up in Michigan, and my thirst for sport fishing only increased after I was in this land of wild abundance.

The commercial fishing lifestyle is like farming and harvesting. You only have a certain amount of time available for catching and harvesting salmon and berries, so we worked as many hours as it took during these seasons to prepare for long, cold winters in Alaska. While we were fishing, Jane was taking care of the home. She learned the Alaskan way of picking berries and putting up preserves, such as salmonberries, strawberries, blueberries, raspberries, moss berries, wild currants, and high bush cranberries. We did the catching and filleting of the salmon, and Jane would do the jarring and cooking. We worked as a family team. Our salmon season ended after fishing for silver/cohos and chum/dogs, usually near Halloween.

Now it was time to get ready for trapping and the fall hunting season. I was ecstatic to be living out my dream. Fall moose hunting opened in September, and Greg and I both bagged one. Moose are very large game animals. When they are fully grown, a big bull can weigh on average 1500 pounds. When they are dressed out and all butchered up, we get an average of 500-700 pounds of meat from one moose. With all the fish and moose we put up, we had enough food so we did not have to buy any meat from the store. Trapping season started on November 10. We had a fifty-mile trapline in two different sections of the Chilkat Valley. On part of our trapline we used snow machines and on the other part we hiked off the road system on snowshoes. Greg had already put in two seasons of trapping and had learned a lot from an old-timer named Old Man Hepler. He had a grandson named Sonny who was about five years older than me. Sonny was in the army, and I was told that I would meet him this coming summer while we would be out fishing.

Greg was already partnered up with a guy named Ronnie Fisk who was a professional government trapper from Montana. I worked as a grunt for the operation just to learn the trade. We had about 200 traps to set. We trapped for wolf, wolverine, fox, coyote, lynx, marten, mink, land otter, and muskrat. Both of the trappers that my brother worked with showed him secrets that were not well known and produced major results. They used me a lot to hike in with snowshoes to higher elevations. I learned the ins and outs of how to be a professional trapper. I was in hog heaven and knee-deep in hides and furs. I was completely thriving while living life in the wilds of Alaska, and I had just completed my Alaskan initiation.

CHAPTER 3

SPRING SURPRISE

SPENDING THAT FIRST SEASON IN Alaska was a dream come true for me. Everything felt genuinely sublime. It was not an easy life, but I could not imagine living any other way. Greg told me that he was going to be working as an assistant guide for a famous big game guide, Duncan Gilcrest. An assistant guide helps master guides in the field with the hunt. This included setting up camps, cooking, helping spot and track animals, helping pack out animals, skinning and flushing hides, and tearing down camps. He was going to be working for him in May while hunting black and brown bears. I asked Greg if Duncan needed any help, as I was willing to do anything just to get my foot in the door. Duncan was a pilot and had a Super Cub aircraft. I wanted to continue flying and pursue getting my pilot's license. Duncan said that he could use my help, and I was on cloud nine.

Fishing started in June, so in between Duncan's hunts, Greg and I would work on getting our set-netting gear ready. The first thing we did was get our nets out of storage that we had put away the previous fall. In the spring we would fix and rebuild them like new for the upcoming season. Next we would get our boat in the water. Finally, we opened up our cabin and got that ready for the summer. Sometimes animals, like squirrels, would get in our cabin and we would have a mess on our hands. Everything was going smoothly so far this season. We worked for Duncan that spring, and we fished all summer and made a good living. I even got in a little bit of flying (stick time) in Duncan's Super Cub.

During the summer while we were out fishing, Thomas Williams's son Sonny came out. Thomas is one of my brother's native friends who had taught him a lot about fishing. His son was a little older than me, but we hit it off when we met. Sonny was just here on leave, visiting from the army, and had to go back. He was going to be done with his duty soon and moving back to Haines. I could tell we were going to have a lot of adventures together. Greg and I kept fishing, and Sonny went back to his station in Fort Lewis, Washington. Fall was fast approaching. While we were fishing for silvers, I got an urgent message from home. My mother had called Jane and said to have us call home right away.

All she had told Jane was that Dad was sick and in the hospital. Jane got a message sent to us via marine radio. As soon as Greg and I got the call we headed in and called home immediately. My parents and little sister Gina had moved lock, stock, and barrel from Michigan to central Florida. My dad had gotten into the building business. Now he was having a major health scare. When we called home and talked to my mom, she told us that Dad was in the hospital with diverticulitis. This particular condition of the intestines can easily kill a person if not caught in time. At any rate, my dad was sick and my family asked me to come back to Florida to help out. I did not want to leave Alaska, but I chose to go help my family. I got there in September and my mom put me in public school right away. It was a complete culture shock. I went from going to school in a town of 500 to going to a public school in the Orlando area with thousands of kids. The school was about 50 percent black and about 50 percent white. There were at least three gangs there. I even saw kids in the bathrooms shooting up heroin. There were a lot of bullies and a great deal of fighting going on.

Physical education (PE) was one of my most dreaded classes. I had become accustomed to Alaskan weather and it was already fall there, getting cold, and turning into winter. In Orlando, September was very hot and humid. We had to do major running in class, which made me miserable. After about five days in public school I was starting to get to know the scene. There was a particular gang in my PE class. The leader of the group was a bigger black kid who was always picking on people, but they constantly singled out a weaker nerdy kid in particular. I did not really want to get involved, but he was doing sick things to this kid that I just could not ignore. I started giving the bully dirty looks. I was in excellent shape from working out constantly, practicing karate, and living the Alaskan lifestyle. I was strong, but the kids in the gang meant business. They even carried knives and chains. We had just finished PE and formed a waiting line at the drinking fountain. I had been waiting for fifteen minutes and it was my turn to get a drink. I noticed out of the corner of my eye that the head gang member was coming at me. As I walked up to bend down to the fountain, the punk said, "Hey, white boy, you just lost your turn." He grabbed my shoulder from behind, pulled me back, and then bent down to drink. I turned and grabbed him by his hair. I slammed his face into the drinking fountain, pulled him back, and then backhanded him. I sent him flying to the ground. I quickly turned around and saw his main man, a white punk, coming at me and swinging a big roundhouse punch to take my head off. I quickly blocked it and gave him a four-finger thrust to his throat. That instantly dropped him to his knees, gasping for air. I swiftly bolted to the locker room, grabbed my clothes, and ran out of the front of the school and out to the highway to hitchhike home. I lived about eight miles from school. I got a ride most of the way home and immediately told my mom what had happened. I knew there was no way I could go back to that school without being beat up, knifed, or killed.

My parents agreed and found a private school to send me to called Platt's Academy. This was a really nice school that mostly had kids from wealthy families. The first friend I met was Martin. He was a 100 percent sunshine Florida boy from a rich family. His parents were in a business called Dare to Be Great, a company that specialized in inspirational conferences. Martin's parents were gone a lot and we pretty much had free rein of their 12,000 sq. ft. mansion. His family had a lot of cars, including a Cadillac limousine with whitewall gangster tires, two 750 RR Honda street racing bikes, and a lake house equipped with a speedboat and water skis. We were having the time of our lives using all of Martin's toys, as you can imagine.

My dad was on the mend. Since my dad was feeling better, I started getting jobs after school and on weekends working for different tradesmen. I worked for my dad's friend who did carpentry, plumbing, electric wiring, and finish carpentry. I stayed about six months in Florida. Even though I was having a fantastic time with my new friends and learning all these new trades, Alaska was always on my mind. After about six months, my dad and I got into an argument and he told me that Greg and I were the black sheep of the family and that we belonged in the woods, not society. I told him that he was right and that I would find a way to get back to Alaska immediately. I had had a taste of the frontier that had few limitations or boundaries. It was uncharted territory and a life of freedom from a structured society. A person could make a decent living off the land and sea. I felt that I was living a life of purpose and fulfillment in Alaska. I could live on my own terms. You got out what you put in and I could not imagine living any other way.

By early March I had $800 saved. I called my brother Greg and asked him if I could come back to live with him and Jane. He said that I could, and within a week I had my airline ticket and I was going back to Haines. My brother had already lined up a job for me at the sawmill where he was working. I started work the day after I arrived back in Haines as an off bearer. Greg worked as a sorter and operated a machine called a cherry picker.

My job included staying after work a half hour every day to change the saw blade for the next day. This started to get tiresome for Greg, who had to wait for me every evening, especially since neither one of us was being paid for the extra time. Greg would wait for me out in the cold and have to run his truck and heater. He wanted to just leave and go home. After about a month of this, Greg got burned out waiting for me in the parking lot when he could have been at home eating his dinner, so he told me to say something to the boss about it. After work the next day I approached the boss and said that if I had to stay after work, he should let me stay clocked in for the extra half hour to make up for my brother having to wait for me. The boss snapped at me and said, "Davis, you are lucky to even have this job!"

The next day we got to work early like always and were having a cup of coffee in the break room when the boss came up to my brother and me. He pointed at me in front of everyone and said, "Davis, I got a new job for you. Up on the hill shoveling sawdust."

I looked at my brother and he had a mean snarling look on his face. Shoveling sawdust was the worst job at the mill. I reluctantly clocked in and went up on the hill. I shoveled sawdust all day. I have to admit that it definitely was the most miserable job in the mill. I heard the factory bell ring. Thank God it was lunch hour! At lunch I sat with Greg and he told me, "To hell with this. We are quitting after the day is over." I was so happy, but I had a sinking feeling that Jane was not going to be pleased. Sure enough, Jane was pretty upset when we came home and told her that we had quit our jobs. Greg told us not to worry. He knew some people in town who wanted wanigans built on their trailer homes, so we already had work lined up. He told Jane and me that spring bear hunting was near and we would be working for Duncan again soon. I was looking forward to being an assistant guide in May. It was a relief not having to go back to that wretched job. I had gotten spoiled by the commercial fishing and trapping lifestyle. Working a so-called real job had left a bitter taste in my mouth. From now on I was going to do anything I had to do to work for myself or find jobs that allowed me to be in the wilderness. I just did not have it in me to take orders very well. I liked to be my own boss, my own man, and be in charge.

Duncan having a Super Cub was a big advantage for me. I was enthralled with flying. I was working towards accumulating flying time for my pilot's license. I already had about twenty-five hours of flying under my belt and was thirsty for more. To have the experience of learning from a skilled bush pilot was priceless. I did anything extra I could for Duncan in trade for getting to fly in the back seat of his Super Cub accumulating stick time. A Super Cub is a two-person front and back seat airplane that is frequently used in Alaska, flying on wheels or floats. They are superior planes for getting in and out of the Alaska bush and off gravel bars, small marginal handmade or natural airstrips, and the thousands of lakes and rivers. I got in five and a half hours of stick time in the Cub that spring. Working for other people in the wilderness was a lot different than your typical job. Being a packer for a big game guide allowed me to be in the wilderness doing what I loved to do and getting paid for it.

While I was hanging around the airport I found other people who owned their own airplanes and would trade me flying time for work. I met a friendly couple, Bill and Nelly. They were from Maine and had sold everything to move lock, stock, and barrel to Alaska. They were both retired certified flight instructors (CFI) and owned a tricked-out Super Cub. They had purchased a nice house on a large ten-acre parcel right on Mud Bay Road. It had a magnificent view overlooking the Chilkat mountain range and inlet, with the hanging Rainbow Glacier in view. Fortunately for me the house needed a lot of work and they were in the market for trading work for flying time. They wanted the whole basement framed in and a six-inch concrete slab poured for the floor. I did a partial trade with them. Bill gave me some incredible flight instruction. He was an exceptional aerobatics instructor and taught me how to perform a spin, falling leaf, and a hammerhead stall. I really believe the critical maneuvers old Bill taught me had drastically refined my flying skills. Besides the flight instruction, I even made a little pocket change.

CHAPTER 4

MAD TRAPPERS OF BEAR CREEK

SOON ENOUGH WE WOULD HAVE to start getting ready for fishing. I was primed and loving every minute of it. To my dismay, little did we know, but the drift gillnetters had been getting together during the winter and having secret meetings with the fish and game Board of Fisheries. We found out that they had succeeded in abolishing set netting. We knew that the drift gillnetters did not like set netting, but we had no idea they would be able to accomplish getting the whole fishery abolished in Haines. We were going to have change gears and get prepared to start drift gillnetting if we wanted to continue our commercial fishing lifestyle. A drift gill net is 200 fathoms long compared to a set net, which is only fifty fathoms. That year I got my first bank loan to get my own fishing boat. I found a custom heavy-duty, hand-built 19 ft. wood boat with a new 60 hp Evirude outboard motor for sale. I went out and looked at the boat and spoke with the owner. I really liked the boat and asked my brother to co-sign a loan for me. He said that he would and we went to the bank. I named the boat *Pisces,* after my zodiac sign. We acquired the nets that we needed and headed out for the drift gill net fishery.

This was a strength-building lifestyle. Most other drift gillnetters had a hydraulic reel on the bows of their boats. We had rollers and pulled 200 fathoms of net and lead line with the brute strength of our arms. We were known around Haines to be tough guys. The next year we were notified by the state of Alaska that drift gillnetting had gone to limited entry permit. That means the state issues a limited number of permits to people for the different fisheries based on a point system. Greg had accumulated enough points to obtain his own southeast Alaska limited entry drift gill net permit. I did not have enough points so I would have to buy my own permit from someone else, or fish as a crew member for someone who had been issued a permit. You can drift fish alone, but it is a lot easier to have an extra person called a crew member or deckhand. The crew member or deckhand usually got a certain percentage of the catch or a set day rate. Average percent of crew share is 10 percent after expenses. I was in such high demand that I would only work for a third. I stipulated that since I was such a valuable asset, I was worth 33.3 percent off the top, instead of having food and expenses coming out of my share. Sometimes I would negotiate and let the permit holder take expenses out of my share, but not always.

I started fishing for other people and then became my own captain, using other people's permits on medical transfers. If the owner of the permit has a medical problem they can temporarily sign over their permit for the season to another person and not have to sell their permit. Sonny got a drift gill net permit, and he and I sometimes fished together on the buddy system out on the fishing grounds. We would fish near each other, but if we were in different areas, we would report to each other how we were doing so that we would know where the most productive fishing was.

This season we had our hands full with a very competitive fishery. For instance, during one of the first openings, while fishing the boundary line, my brother and I were confronted by Wayne Alex. He was well-known for his hot temper and fast fist. We had been told that he was a former Golden Gloves boxer. Wayne pulled up to us yelling that we were too close to him. My brother had on a cutoff shirt and with his big twenty-inch biceps bulging, walked out on deck and said with a mean look on his face, "It's tough all over, buddy, tough all over."

Wayne sized up my brother and said, "Just stay away from me and we won't have a problem." Wayne just went back to fishing and did not pursue any physical confrontations, for now.

On one occasion, we were challenged at the dock by an ill-tempered fisherman. My brother had a tricky way of standing sideways half-cocked as he looked down and pulled out a cigarette. This was a way Greg would lure someone into sucker punching him. Sure enough, Greg was ready as he cocked his head to light his cigarette and the guy came at him with a punch. Greg immediately blocked his punch and came around with an uppercut to the chin. The guy flew off his feet and backward into the water. Greg leaned over and pulled him up out of the water by his hair and onto the dock. He was knocked out cold and looked like a dead seal. After that episode we did not get much flack on the fishing grounds or at the dock.

During the winter I did odd jobs like additions, shoveling snow, and cutting and splitting firewood. One of my favorite winter activities was trapping. My brother and I decided to go in as partners. We each got one of the first long, wide-track snow machines that came out to use on our trapline. We still had to snowshoe, but by using the snow machine we would cover a lot more area and make more money. Fur prices were really good at the time. If we made $10,000 to share, we would be doing pretty well. My best season was when Greg and I made $7,500 each after expenses.

While I was trapping with Greg, he and I were way out at our cabin up in Porcupine at Bear Creek. We had a sign made for the trailhead that read "The mad trappers of Bear Creek live here, beware violators will be persecuted."

There was a meticulous game warden who kept checking on us. He was kind of a nuisance to our operation, upsetting our trails and trapline. In fact, he was actually a hindrance to our trapping. We were not breaking any laws, but he kept disturbing the area to check on us. We were trapping up the Kluane River in the Porcupine and Bear Creek area. To trap this area we had to cross a peculiar two-log-wide bridge to get across the Porcupine River. If you did not balance on the log bridge just right, your snow machine would fall into the freezing river. This warden followed us fourteen miles back off of the main road and attempted to cross our tricky bridge. He did not balance his machine on the bridge and ended up crashing into the freezing river. We were in our cabin and heard someone call out. We looked outside and to our surprise it was the warden. We asked, "How the heck did you get out here?"

He answered, "By snow machine, then I tried to cross your log bridge and fell off into the river and walked from there."

We could not help but laugh. He came all that way to check on us and crashed his snow machine in the river. He was wet and freezing cold. We took him in and got him warm and dry. The next day we went out to see if there was any way to retrieve his snow machine out of the river, but it was frozen solid in the ice overflow. In these freezing temps, the shallow, fast-moving rivers freeze from the bottom up and the river keeps flowing on top of the ice, creating slush. We gave the game warden a ride back to town and at the same time got resupplied, and then went back out to our trapline. We continued business as usual. Two weeks later we heard a snow machine again. We wondered who it could be. It was kind of an unspoken trapper code that if someone had an established trapline, most people stayed clear. This made us curious as to who and why someone would be coming out to our cabin, especially after the warden had crashed his snow machine. Surprisingly, it was the warden again, and on a brand-new machine to boot. He was really proud of it, too. He looked arrogant and like he was feeling cocky, so I asked him if he wanted to race. He was all for it. I looked at my brother and smiled. This area was very dangerous and if you did not know every turn, you could easily crash. I jumped on my machine and said, "Get ready!" We took off from the log bridge and climbed up the old trail along a cliff side where there is a 300-foot drop off to the bottom of a river valley. We then circumnavigated across the Kluane River flats where you have to cross three spots of open water. You have to lean back on the machine and keep it wide open to ski across the open water. To my surprise, he was keeping up with me. We were neck and neck as we crossed the river flats and went up on an old logging road, which was up a steep hill where I had previously made a jump to make it across a gully. Unfortunately, the warden did not know that you had to hit this thing just right or you were toast. You had to stay on the far right side when you launched. We hit the ramp at about fifty miles per hour. The warden hit the ramp wrong, went airborne, and crashed hard into a thick patch of alders. I hit the ramp at the right speed and angle, and landed safely on the other side of the gully. I slowed down and turned around to see that the warden had crashed into the patch of alder trees. He had bent one ski and the windshield had gotten ripped off. When I got over to help him, I was glad to see that he had not hurt himself too badly. I am sure his pride and ego were damaged the most. He was very lucky not to have been seriously injured. I asked him if he was okay. He looked very crestfallen and told me he was just a little banged up, but was concerned mostly that he was going to be in trouble back at headquarters for damaging two expensive machines. I knew I should feel bad, but I found humor in the incident. I actually had a hard time not laughing in his face. I helped him get the machine out and he was able to slowly limp it back to the main road where his pickup truck was. I hoped that that accident would discourage him from making any more attempts to come out to our trapline. My brother kind of felt bad for the guy, but we were both happy to hopefully have gotten rid of him. We went back to trapping and ended up with a nice load of furs. We never heard another peep from anyone else the rest of the season.

CHAPTER 5

SPRING FLING

SPRING CAME TO THE HAINES valley. More and more people were moving to Alaska, and the population of Haines was increasing. Greg and Jane bought a few parcels of property in town. We lived on the piece that had a ranch-style house, with a big spot for a garden. Greg ended up building a barn and got his first horse. The other parcel of land was up for sale, and a family that had recently moved to town asked Greg about it. The Hartley's had moved to Haines and brought their granddaughter Debbie to live with them. I had seen their granddaughter working at the local supermarket in the produce department. When the Hartley's came out to look at the land I got to meet Debbie. She had caught my eye and I kept going back to the store so that I could ask her out on a date. I finally ran into her at work. I asked her out and she said yes. She asked what we would be doing. I told her that I wanted to take her with me black bear hunting and that we would then go trolling for king salmon. She thought that would be fun. I knew right then that she would be the kind of girl who could keep up with me. I picked her up and the first thing I noticed was that she was dressed appropriately for our date. Some girls would have declined that kind of date to begin with, much less know what to wear.

I took her out to my troll drag and we caught a thirty-eight-pound king salmon. While we were fishing, I spotted a black bear, and we went about a half mile down the beach to stay downwind of him. I beached my skiff and secured it with the anchor. The tide was coming in so it was perfect. Debbie got out and waited for me on the beach while I stalked the bear. I took a rest on a log and killed it with one shot. Debbie squealed in a cute way and congratulated me. I got butterflies in my stomach when she ran up and hugged me. I started to work on skinning and dressing out the bear. Debbie even jumped in and assisted me by holding its legs while I skinned and quartered it. I got the bear taken care of and stored it in the skiff. I gathered beach wood and made us a nice bonfire. Debbie had packed us a really nice picnic lunch. We had a wonderful time, and I knew that I would be asking her out again.

I dated other girls at the time besides Debbie, but she was special. Another nice thing about dating Debbie was that she worked at Food Center and was in charge of the produce department. She gave Greg and me the throwaway produce and milk for our little farm. Each spring we ordered fifty baby chicks for eating and kept twelve for eggs. We would also get two wiener pigs and raise them until November. It made a big difference in the flavor of our home-raised pigs, chickens, and goats to give them the produce and milk along with their feed.

When Sonny came back from the army, we became best friends. He was a Tlingit native and a true outdoorsman who had grown up in Haines. His dad was a full-blooded Tlingit and his mom was the daughter of Old Man Hepler who was from Michigan. Sonny and I had the same interests. During the summer we started organizing our winter trapping adventure. We planned to outfit Sonny's 29 ft. double ender, the *Ella Mae*, which had been given to him by his dad Thomas Williams Sr. The plan was to leave at the end of November and then come back in mid-February with a load of furs. Before we left on our adventure it had been snowing. It was the middle of November and Sonny had been driving on the road to Klukwan at night and in a blizzard. A cow and calf moose crossed the road in front of him. Sonny hit the brakes and tried to maneuver around the pair, but ended up clipping the calf. When Sonny got out to inspect the damage, he saw that the calf had a broken leg and the mother had run off. There was no way the calf would survive, so Sonny put it down. Sonny, being a true Alaskan, did not want the meat to go to waste, so he came to my brother Greg's house and told me what had happened and that he needed my help. Sonny and I went to the kill site and we loaded up the moose. Sonny asked me if we could hang it in my brother's shed, and said that he would claim the moose as a subsistence moose as a part of his native subsistence rights. I had no reason to think any differently since Sonny was able to shoot seals and sea otters as a part of his native hunting rights. We brought the moose back to our shed and hung it. We skinned it and peeled all the meat off the neck for a roast right away. The next day Jane made a wonderful pot roast with the neck meat by roasting it all day in the cast iron Dutch oven.

Sonny told us that he had to run to town, go to the store, and that he would be back later. The fish and wildlife protection officer in town was known to be a bloodhound detective. His routine included a drive every day to the Canadian border and back. That morning he saw the signs of the moose kill. He immediately started investigating, since it was not yet legal moose hunting season. He went to town and looked at every vehicle for any signs of damage. Sonny's truck had been cleaned but was still messed up. There was frozen blood water under the back bumper. The sun was out so the blood was dripping from under the bumper onto the fresh, white snow-packed road. The officer tracked down Sonny and questioned him. Sonny was wrong about being able to keep the moose as a subsistence moose, and that meant he had broken the law. We had the moose hanging on our property, which was putting us at risk of being in trouble as well. Sonny told the officer where the moose was hanging. Officer Roscovious came out and knocked on our door. Jane, being the polite and hospitable hostess, invited the officer to sit down with us and have some moose roast. He said, "Ma'am, that is not a legal moose."

"Oh," she said, looking quite embarrassed, "I was not aware of that."

My brother and the officer stepped outside and had a conversation. Sonny had taken full responsibility and the officer said that all he was going to do was confiscate the moose and give Sonny a ticket. Thank goodness. After the trooper left, I was in big trouble. My brother did not condone the breaking of ANY laws. He was an assistant big game guide and it was his responsibility to be ethical, enforce game regulations, and even turn in violators. I learned my lesson, and Sonny got an earful from my brother, too. He told us to make sure we didn't break any laws, especially around him. Sonny felt bad and apologized to him and Jane. He had to go to court, was fined, and had to do community service. Even though it was a game violation, the meat was put to good use. The judge ordered Sonny to butcher the moose and donate it to the Pioneer Home. The elders who lived there were more than grateful for the meat.

CHAPTER 6

TRAPPER'S NIGHTMARE

SONNY AND I DECIDED TO take his 29 ft. double-ender fishing boat and head out on a two-month trapping and exploring expedition. We left Haines and traveled ninety miles south down the Lynn Canal to Icy Strait, then headed west. We spent a month in Icy Strait out as far as Idaho Inlet and Elfin Cove trapping marten, mink, and land otter. We set out our shrimp and crab pots and feasted like kings on fresh venison and seafood. It was a blast going from one place to another, anchoring up in protected coves, taking the skiff ashore, and setting traps. After a month we decided to head north to Saint James Bay back up on the west side of the Lynn Canal, forty miles south of Haines.

We checked the weather on the marine VHF radio. It was calling for a storm front moving in right on top of us, so we anchored in a safe cove on the leeward side of Sullivan Island. The winds ended up increasing seventy-five to one hundred miles an hour. This persisted for weeks. The boat started freezing up. Sonny had fueled the Perkins diesel engine with #2 diesel, which would gel up if it started to get too cold. That was exactly what was starting to happen. Our only source of heat, an oil-burning stove, was also fueled by the same tank that the engine ran off of. It also started to gel up. We had a 14 ft. Monarch flat-bottom skiff with a 15 hp Evinrude onboard. We knew that we were going to have to go ashore if we wanted to survive. The engine and heater stopped running due to the gelled diesel fuel. The batteries on the boat that powered the radio also went dead. We could not reach anyone by radio, and no one knew exactly where we were.

We decided to take the skiff to the shore of Sullivan Island where there was an old fox farm. Back in the early 1900s it was a fad for people to raise foxes for their furs. The farms popped up all over Alaska and their remnants were scattered on numerous islands. Sullivan Island was seven miles long by one mile wide. The fox farm was an old abandoned two-story house. The windows were broken out and the house was in disarray. We had brought Visqueen and some old tarps ashore with us and decided that we would set up a tent camp in the kitchen of the old house. We had some rice, but our potatoes had frozen. We were in dire need of some protein. We were tough, but this was proving to be a pretty grave situation. We decided to go hunting to see if we could find a deer to eat for survival. Thank goodness we ended up killing one. We had our camp stove and plenty of fuel to cook with. As soon as we got the deer back to camp we started going to town skinning and butchering. We immediately started cooking up deer chops and devouring the fresh meat. After a huge meal, all we felt like doing was getting warm and crashing out. Being native, Sonny was allowed to kill seals, so the next day he killed some seals. We ate seal rib meat and seal liver, which has a lot of oil and protein in it. We ended up surviving off of deer and seal for over a month while we were waiting out this wretched never-ending storm. We kept thinking that the winds would subside and we would be able to go home at any time. No such luck. In the meantime, we had to bail the boat out with the hand pump once a day because it was leaking and there was no power to run the bilge pump.

We finally decided that we needed to call the Coast Guard. We had been contemplating the situation for weeks. We really thought that the weather would lighten up any day and we would be able to leave and get home on our own. We did not want to call the Coast Guard, but it was getting to the point that we did not have any other choice. We knew there was a Coast Guard light on a little island off the south end that always had spare batteries in it. The batteries could be used to power up our boat radio. We went there in our 14 ft. skiff and risked our lives in the big seas and winds to retrieve the battery out of the light. We brought the battery to the boat where we hooked it up to our marine single side band radio. We called "Mayday, Mayday, Mayday" for a rescue and were surprised that the station that answered was the Kodiak station. They were 500 miles from where we were in southeast Alaska. We gave them our location and told them what our situation was. They responded that they were going to dispatch the ninety-foot cutter *Sweetbrier* out of Juneau. Thank God, we were going to be saved!

We were still not out of harm's way. The weather was vicious with seas at thirteen feet, even on the inside waters of the Lynn Canal, and seventy- to one-hundred-mile-an-hour winds. When the Coast Guard got close, they pulled up to us and one of the officers told us that their plan was to throw us a towline and tow us back to Auke Bay, which was north of Juneau. To me that was suicide. I disagreed with their rescue plan and told them that there was no way this boat could be towed in gigantic seas without capsizing. They said we had the choice to come with them or abandon the boat. Sonny was adamant that he was not going to leave his boat. After that conversation they decided to tow us north up behind a bite in the Chilkat Peninsula called Paradise Cove, which was on the inside of Alexander Island. We decided to make a go of it. It was extremely dangerous, but we were willing to take the risk so that we did not have to abandon Sonny's boat. They threw us survival suits. There was not that much to them; they were more like wetsuits. Since our engine was not running we had to cut the anchor line and place a buoy on it. We cut loose and were on our way. As soon as we rounded the point protecting us, we hit fourteen-foot seas right off the bat. We went down in a wave, and when the boat reached the end of the towline, I suddenly felt a huge jerk that was so strong it felt like the boat might be torn apart. The towline went slack and we went sideways in the trough of the wave. The boat rolled upside down and the wheelhouse was under water in the side of the wave. Water gushed in the cabin and we thought we were going to be killed. The only thing that saved us was the boat's concrete keel, which had kept it from completely rolling over. I yelled to the Coast Guard on the handheld marine VHF radio they lent us, "Keep the towline taut and start towing us back. We'll never make it. Turn around NOW!" The boat turned herself upright again. The Coast Guard vessel got turned around with us in tow. Eventually, after a very rough, wild, and life-threatening attempt to get back home, we were headed back to the buoy that held our anchor. As we got near our buoy, the Coast Guard captain was screaming, the crew was screaming, and we were screaming. It was a three-ring circus! When we got back to our anchor buoy, we were able to pull it up and tie it back to our boat's existing anchor line. The captain's next step was to follow my first suggestion, which was to bring some #1 diesel fuel onboard the *Ella Mae,* along with a mechanic to help us fix our boat and get her back under her own power. After that we could follow the cutter instead of being towed.

They anchored their boat as close to us as possible and tied our boat to theirs. They lowered down #1 diesel, heaters, and a diesel mechanic to help us get the boat engine running. It took us about three hours. Working together, we got the lines bled of the gelled-up #2 fuel and then were able to put some #1 in the tank and fill the lines. We got the engine and the heater going in the boat, which would get our batteries charged.

They were nice enough to bring us aboard the cutter while the batteries were getting charged and the boat was warming up. They offered to feed us in the mess hall. We ate like kings. The cook fed us huge ham steaks, home fries, eggs, a big pile of toast, and strong black coffee. We were exhausted but wired out from the adrenaline After being so cold and hungry for so long, the food was delicious, comforting, and calming. We breathed a sigh of relief and savored the moment. I prayed to myself, thinking how grateful I was to be alive after this catastrophe.

The meal gave us the energy we would need to get us through the next part of this tribulation. Even though we hated to leave the warmth, safety, and food, we knew that we had to take one's medicine and go back onto the *Ella Mae*. From there we were going to cut loose and head for the Chilkat Peninsula. The plan was that they were going to follow us to Twin Coves. As we got underway, we looked back and saw that they were still on anchor. We were curious as to what could be wrong, so we radioed the cutter. They responded that their anchor winch had frozen up and were having difficulties. We were left to fate and knew there was no alternative but to keep going with or without the assistance of the cutter. We made our way one huge wave at a time north for Twin Coves, which would be a safe place to anchor. As soon as we got to the north end of Sullivan Island and out into open water, we hit sixteen-foot seas in a 29 ft. double ender. From the force of the waves, the engine would start dying as we were climbing, so I had to rip open the Perkins diesel engine cover and grab the hand injector. I had to manually inject fuel in to the engine while we were going up the wave to keep the boat running. When we were going down the wave, the engine would idle way up, which was unnerving but not as alarming as the engine almost dying. It was also nerve-racking that the Coast Guard cutter was not in sight. Our only chance for surviving this voyage was to stay focused on getting home. I pumped the hell out of the engine every time we climbed a wave and held my breath on the descent. This went on for seven hours until we reached the safe anchorage at Twin Coves. A feeling of relief came over us. We were still not home free, but better off than we were. Now we needed to figure out how to anchor the boat. Since we had left our main anchor back near Sullivan Island, we had to think of another way to secure the boat. Thankfully we remembered that we had four halibut anchors onboard from commercial fishing. They would do in a pinch. They had enough weight and bite that with the four of them fastened together, they would hold the boat.

It was fifteen degrees below zero and freezing spray had been hitting the boat. We were getting weighed down pretty heavily with ice, almost to the point of sinking the boat. The Coast Guard finally arrived and they sent four guys aboard to help us beat off the ice. They also sent us more food, which was much appreciated. The guys left our boat and got back on the cutter. As they were pulling away, they yelled down that they wanted their suits back. I went out on deck and had to jump up to get on the cutter to give them their suits and get our clothes back that they had laundered for us. In the process I almost fell off the rail into the freezing water between the boat and the cutter. The only thing that saved me was one of the crew, a big burly guy who grabbed me by the hair and kept me from falling in the water and being smashed between the two boats.

We were delirious from exhaustion and crashed hard. We rested that night and the next morning decided to make a go for Paradise Cove. At this point we could not stop; we knew we had to do whatever we had to do to get home. There were still huge waves out beyond the safety of the cove and as soon as we hit the open water, the boat went down a monster wave. It was like being in a head-on collision. All of a sudden, all we could see in front of us was blue water. The giant wall of a wave crashed onto the bow of the boat. It hit our boat so hard that it blew out one of the front windows of Sonny's boat. Water and glass gushed into the cabin and we screamed from pure shock. How could this get any worse? We would just have to hold on for dear life and keep our heading. We had to ignore the water washing in on us, and the damage to the wheelhouse, and just keep her heading toward home. We finally made it up to Paradise Cove and threw out four anchors to hold us. Thank God the end of this treacherous journey was near. We were exasperated and at our wits end. We both just wanted to get away from each other. As soon as we knew that the anchors were holding, we got our skiff off the boat and made it to shore. I was so happy to be on the mainland that I got down on my hands and knees to kiss the ground.

We hiked up a half-mile long snowed-in driveway to get to the main road. We were six miles from town on Mud Bay Road. A feeling of euphoria came over us as soon as we hit the main road. We were on easy street compared to the hell we had just been through. We could not stop smiling out of sheer happiness to be alive and almost home. We started to walk toward town. It was the middle of February, and snowy and cold. As we were walking along the road, out of nowhere came this huge, mean St. Bernard. The dog was growling and snarling at us. We were a sight to see. After everything we had been through, now this. I took out my bowie knife and pointed it at the dog and said, "Do not bite me or I will stab you!" and I meant it. I went at the dog like a charging bear. The dog backed down, thank goodness. After the dog ran off, along came an old army 4x4 truck that pulled up alongside us. It was an old-timer from town that I knew.

He said, "You boys look like you have been through hell and could use a lift. I'm headed into town for supplies. Jump in."

We said back in voices hoarse from yelling, "Sir, you do not even know the half of it. To top things off we just got attacked by a mean monster St. Bernard."

The old-timer started laughing and said, "Oh, that's my dog Zeus. He's harmless. Just a big teddy bear." We started laughing too. There was not much else we could do after all of that but laugh!

He gave us a ride home and, boy, were we relieved. We slept like boulders that night. Our work was still not done though. The next day we had to go out to check on Sonny's boat and somehow repair the window, at least something temporary to keep the wheelhouse from being exposed. We were going to have to get our gear off of the boat too.

Two weeks went by before we could get the boat back to town. Thank goodness that ordeal was over with, and the pact we had as blood brothers was still intact. Talk about a test of friendship.

Debbie was happy that I made it back alive, and we started dating exclusively that winter and spring. It takes a special kind of girl to keep up with me and my lifestyle. When Debbie went on a trip that March to visit family, I really knew she was the one. I knew I was in love because I missed her when she was gone. For someone like me that was a big deal. I spent weeks and months at a time fishing and trapping so I was not really big on attachment. I dated girls and had fun, but Debbie was different. She was the kind of girl you marry. I knew she was a keeper and that I wanted her as my wife. That April, after she got back, I proposed to her. I was nineteen, but very mature for my age. I had left home at fifteen, and even though I lived with my brother, I was treated as and expected to be my own man. Debbie and I had a small wedding ceremony on May 19, 1974.

Shortly after, I got a call from my dad. He had gone back to Michigan and was building a housing development. He asked me how it was going in Alaska. I told him it was going well and that I was living out my dream, but my brother and I had gotten into an argument over a piece of property and we were not on speaking terms. He did not even come to my wedding. I was ready for a change and something that would get me out of town for a while. What caught my attention was an offer from my dad that I could get into the building business working for him and could make a lot of money. I had my eye on a piece of land in Haines, and if I were able to make a nice chunk of money, I could afford to put a down payment on a piece of property for us. I talked to Debbie and she was all for making a go of the plan. We decided to go down to Michigan where I was going to make big money in the building business. I sold all of my traps, guns, and my truck. I then packed up and went to Michigan. When we got there, my parents were living in a three-bedroom condo. My little sister Gina was twelve years old at the time and my brother Ben lived nearby.

Lucky me, Debbie and my dad did not get along. My dad was really affectionate and he offended Debbie by being too touchy-feely. They had a weird relationship right out of the gate. I went right to work. It just so happened that the situation did not play out like I expected. The agreement was not the same as I had understood it before I had moved down there. I thought I was going to be working for him, but I ended up working for his subcontractor who was working on four big homes on farmland out of Howell, Michigan. I was working for seven dollars an hour in ninety-five degree heat and 90 percent humidity. I was thoroughly depressed and distraught. I had an anxious feeling that I would be trapped in a rut there.

Soon after I had gotten there, I was already trying to figure out a way to escape back to Alaska. The first thing I had to do was to make enough money to get us back home. For the time being I had to get a car. I found a Pontiac Catalina for a good price and bought it. I had to find us our own place. It was driving Debbie and me crazy living in a condo with my parents. I had some money left over from selling my belongings and was able to save a little money over the next few weeks, so we decided to go apartment hunting. We looked at a few places, and then in the parking lot I broke down and told Debbie that I could not live like this and had to get back to Alaska. I could not picture myself making a life down there even if it were temporary; I just could not risk being stuck in this miserable situation. Debbie agreed and we made up our minds to go back to Alaska.

I told my dad that it was not working out for us there and that his opinion of me being a renegade was correct. I was the black sheep of the family and I did not belong in society. I needed to live and work out in the woods. I called my brother Ben and told him about my decision. He suggested that I sell my car and said he knew of a 1968 Dodge pickup for sale for $450 that was in perfect condition. I immediately put the car up for sale and miraculously it sold the next day. Ben took me to look at the truck. We took it for a test drive and we agreed it was a sound vehicle, so I bought it on the spot. I built a three-foot by four-foot plywood box behind the back of the cab for our luggage. Debbie and I took off straight out of Howell, Michigan, and north to Canada without looking back. It took that whole ordeal to realize that Alaska was my home and where I belonged.

We drove nonstop and crossed the Mackinaw Bridge into Michigan's upper peninsula, and then into Canada to pick up Highway 1 that headed due west. It was a two-lane road across Canada to Winnipeg, then to Calgary, and then north to Edmonton. We picked up the Alaska Highway to Whitehorse in the Yukon, then to Haines Junction, and then finally south down to Haines. Since my brother Greg and I were still on the outs, I immediately went down to Front Street where the original old village was to see if I could find Sonny at his family's house. If he wasn't there, they would know where I could find him. He just happened to be there. I told him what had happened, and he asked if there was anything he could do. I asked him if he knew of any places to rent. He said that he did not know of anything, so he invited us up to his place, which was a small one-bedroom cabin about 16x24 ft. with an outhouse and outdoor plywood shower. It was in the village of Klukwan where he and my friend Lisa from school were living. He said that we could stay there until we found something. Unfortunately, we looked and looked, and could not find anything.

I needed to find work and fishing was already in full swing, so I looked around town for some kind of job. I walked into Haines Transfer, a freight and trucking company that would meet the state ferries and barges, and then offload and deliver the containers that had been shipped from the Lower 48 to Haines. These containers supplied the town with groceries, liquor, and hardware. Practically everything that came to town came by ferry or barge. I walked in and for once it was my lucky day. The guy I talked to said they needed a worker/driver ASAP and asked when I could start. I said, "Right now!"

He said, "Great, let's go down to the ferry and I will show you the ropes." He showed me how to load and offload a trailer one time and then said, "All right, now it is your turn." I had never driven a big truck like that before, but there was no time like the present to learn. I picked it up quickly. If I could fly an airplane, I could drive a truck. I started work right away, and Debbie found a job, too, at the other trucking company, Lynden Transfer.

We ended up eventually finding a nice duplex that had just been built and we were happy to move in. Even though the living conditions at Sonny's had not been that desirable, I did not regret leaving Michigan one bit. I was more comfortable in Sonny's cabin than in some condo with my parents. Even if I had had my own place, I still knew in my heart that I did not belong down there.

The owner of Haines Transfer was expanding and buying more trucks. I was getting extremely busy and could not find anyone around town to help me at the company, so I called a friend of mine from Michigan, Bob Trotter. I told him that we were very busy and I needed help up here. Besides the influx of business, the owner of Haines Transfer was a deteriorating alcoholic. Within two months of starting work, I had gotten the impression that Don had a severe drinking problem. Don gave me the reins to the company, and I was now in charge of most of the day-to-day operations. His problem got so severe that he ended up being medevaced out of town to a hospital for his uncontrollable drinking that was killing his liver, family life, and business. He spent two months in rehab while I worked my rear off running the company and drumming up new business. Bob came up to help and we worked great as a team.

One day I went down to the terminal when the ferry came in and was told that I needed to unload a ninety-foot-long rock crusher. The only way I could possibly unload the equipment was to jackknife the trailer and let air out of the tires. Even then, to move the crusher I had to call the office and have Bob bring me a cutting torch to cut a steel stanchion off the piece of equipment that was preventing me from getting under the ferry door with it on my trailer. After I maneuvered the crusher off of the ferry and into the parking lot, John approached me. He was a foreman for Alaska International, a big construction company that had come to town to resurface the highway from Haines to the Canadian border. It was the company that the crusher was being shipped to. John told me how impressed he was that I was able to jockey my truck and trailer on and off the ferry. He said that I had exceptional abilities as a driver and he offered me a job. He said that I would be perfect for the truck foreman position overseeing their fleet of twenty fifteen-yard end dumps and twelve big belly dumps. The position included being the main driver of the lowboy trailer that moved the heavy equipment to the different job sites. I told him that I already had a job, and that I already had plans to go fishing with Sonny. I thanked him for the offer and said I would keep it in mind. John told me that it was a union job, so if I did take him up on it, I would need to join the Teamsters Union. It was a good offer and I joined the Teamsters, so that in the future I would be able to get jobs driving trucks on union jobs if I wanted to.

Winter went by quickly and it was time to get ready for fishing. Haines Transfer was shut down by Don's family because of his drinking, and he went off to the hospital again for treatment. It was sad for me to see the thriving company go down the drain, but I had my own plans.

CHAPTER 7

SOCKEYE IN YOUR EYE

FISHING SEASON OPENED AND, SADLY, it turned out to be one of the worst sockeye seasons in years. Regrettably, fishing was so slow that we were barely getting any openers, and when we did, there was barely any fish. It was scratch fishing, meaning setting your net and barely catching any fish. There was no money to be made doing this all summer. I had only so many months in the summer to be able to support my family, so I decided to go see if I could get any work from John. I knew that the job he had offered me would not still be on the table, but it would not hurt to ask. He surprisingly had a driving job available and I snatched it up.

My first assignment was to head out to a gravel pit thirty-six miles up the Haines Highway toward the Canadian border where the company had twenty end dumps and twelve belly dumps staged. I drove out there in my Dodge, immediately hopped in a truck, and started work. After working half the day, I saw John show up at the job site. He waved me down, so I parked and got out to talk to him. I could tell by the look on his face that it was not good news. He came up to me and said, "I hate to do this to you, but the superintendent's nephew is coming. He told me you are off of this job and to give your truck to his nephew. Sorry, but if you still want a job, I have work for you building the water treatment road to Lilly Lake. It is a nasty older truck and not the most desirable job, but it is work."

I was pretty mad and disappointed, but I accepted the job. I was so mad about how everything was going that summer that I got in my Dodge at 36 Mile and when I got on the main road, I took my anger out on the truck and punched it. I drove the truck so hard that I blew up the engine. I did not realize that I had overdone it until it was too late. By the time I got to my house the engine was smoking, steaming, and knocking. I got out, opened the hood, and saw that it was blown. The only thing I could do was have it towed to Wallace's Garage. Thank goodness the owner of the shop liked Dodge trucks. I thought instead of fixing it, I would ask Wallace if he wanted to buy it. He asked how much. I told him $500. He asked, "Would you take $450?" I said, "SOLD!" I figured that even though I was out a truck, and really could not afford to have burned mine up, I still came out on top. I had bought it in Michigan for $450, drove it all the way to Alaska, then all winter, and sold it with a blown engine. I could not complain, especially since I needed the money to buy something else.

I got a ride out to the other job, and John was right, not only was it not pleasant, I was downright miserable. I was driving a wretched truck that was leaking steering fluid so bad that I had to wear gloves just to drive the truck, and still got fluid all over myself. It was old and nasty, and the hauls were only about a mile at a time. That only lasted a month, but I did make enough money to survive.

Fall was settling in and Sonny and I decided that after a season of scratching, we were going to go full steam ahead on seal hunting and trapping to make up for this summer's misfortune. That winter we got our grubstake together for the trapping season. We decided to go to a cabin out at Pyramid Harbor, which was on the west side of the Chilkat Inlet just south of the mouth of the Chilkat River. We hauled out a big load of gear and food in cardboard boxes with my 14 ft. Monarch skiff. There was an old cabin out there, but no wood stove, and the windows had been broken out. We knew of someone in town with an old cast iron potbelly wood stove that they were not using. They were willing to trade us some firewood for it, and we hauled it out to the cabin. We also put plastic over the holes where the windows used to be. We then flattened the cardboard boxes and stapled them up on the walls for makeshift insulation. It was a very small one-room cabin with a set of bunk beds. It was simple, but a decent place from which to stage our operation.

Once we got settled in, we worked out of our skiff, trolling the beach line when the water was calm enough, and used our snowshoes to hike up into the woods to set our fifty traps. We were mostly after timber marten, which were bringing a good price. We went back to Haines for Thanksgiving, and then out goat hunting. That winter we had gotten goat, deer, and moose meat for our freezers. That way we did not have to buy any meat from the grocery store. We stayed out at the cabin for two months and came back with a satisfying variety of furs ranging from marten, mink, and otter, to three wolverines, two wolves, and one big lynx cat.

Our next task was to sell our furs on the market. We headed to Anchorage in Sonny's truck to see David Green, one of the best and most honest furriers. He was really fair to us and always paid us generously. When we got back to Haines, we went on a major seal-hunting expedition. Sonny was the only one who was allowed to shoot and kill the seals, but in the partnership I came to the table with my skiff, and since I was running the boat Sonny could concentrate on shooting. I could also clean and cure the hides as my part of the deal. We got $30 a piece for the hides. After skinning the seals we would take the carcasses up to the native village of Klukwan and sell or trade them at five dollars for a small body, ten for a medium body, and fifteen for a large body. The native people would use everything. They would cut the two to three inches of fat off and render the fat and make oil by the gallon. They also ate all the meat and guts. Nothing was wasted.

While we were hunting, the fish and wildlife officer was always hounding us, even though we were not breaking any laws. The native rights act allowed natives to hunt seals and sea otters. Anyone else was forbidden to do so. I think that maybe the reason the officer was always after us was that he was convinced that I was shooting seals and sea otters. I never did any of the shooting, but I did carry a rifle in the boat. Sonny and I had the exact gun. We both loved the 25-06 Wildcat. We used this gun on all of our hunts. Everything I have ever hunted I have shot with my 25-06. We were out hunting one day and Sonny had shot six seals. As always, I had my 25-06 in the boat. I would look through the scope to see if Sonny had made the kill. It was also a good backup gun to let Sonny borrow if something were to happen to his gun. That way we could continue hunting and not have to scrap the day. This one day we were all done and heading back to the ramp. We spotted Officer Cane watching us from the shore. We were all legal, so we did not think we had anything to worry about. We pulled up to the ramp and Officer Cane was there to meet us. Right away he said, "Oh, I see you guys got six seals, huh?"

"Yes, sir," Sonny replied.

"So how many seals did you shoot, George?" he asked in a sarcastic tone.

Not surprised by his accusation I said, "None."

He came back with a snide response. "Oh, sure, c'mon just tell me. How many did you shoot?"

I said, "None, sir, and I am telling the truth."

He went on, and I could tell he did not believe me. He told me that he thought the law was unfair and that he believed that everyone should have the right to hunt seals. He asked if I agreed with him. I said I did not really have an opinion on the subject and that it was a native tradition that should be upheld for the natives. He said that he had an idea on how we could go about lobbying for rights for everyone to be able to shoot seals. He said if I agreed to admit that I had shot seals and let him write me a ticket, we could show how unfair the law is. I said "Are you crazy? Why would I want to admit to a federal crime and be in deep trouble?" He kept insisting that he would make sure that I would not get in trouble and that he would stand up for me. I just flatly told him that I did not shoot any seals and that I was not going to admit to something I did not do.

He finally said in a condescending tone, "Well, I see you have a gun, George. What caliber is it?"

I said, "25-06."

"Sonny, what kind of gun do you have?"

"25-06."

"Davis, why are you carrying a gun if you were not shooting seals?"

I said, "I look through the scope and watch to see if Sonny made the kill shot. Plus I love to watch the seal's head explode. It is also a backup gun for Sonny to borrow if his gun gets damaged," which was the truth.

I could tell he did not believe me, but he said, "Okay, boys, you are free to go, but Davis, if I catch you shooting seals, you are going down!"

Dang, I thought, *this guy is crazy and sounds like he has it out for me.* Later this assumption proved to be true.

That spring I fished for three weeks with Sonny and his dad in Taku Inlet down by Juneau, a hundred miles south of Haines, for the spring king salmon run, and then headed back to Haines for the start of sockeye season. Back then the commercial halibut season was open all summer, so when the salmon opener was closed, we would go to the dock, pull the salmon net off, and put halibut gear on and head straight back out to fish. We had a respectable season of fishing that year, especially compared to the previous year. I fished hard all summer and fall, and then I really lucked out on a moose that year. While we were out on a salmon opener fishing for chum/dog salmon near David's Cove on the Chilkat Peninsula, a cow moose came out of the forest and onto the beach. Right behind her was a beautiful four-year-old bull. We had my 14 ft. Monarch skiff with us, and Sonny's brother onboard as a crew hand. I had not found time to go moose hunting that year and it was the end of the hunting season. I really wanted to get a moose for the winter meat supply. Sonny and his brother told me they would take care of the fishing and that I should go for it. "Go get the moose!" they exclaimed.

I excitedly jumped in the skiff and went to the shoreline with my 25-06. The bull was standing right on the high tide line. The tide was low, but was about to switch and start coming in. I took a lying down rest. The cow and bull started to act spooky and turned to go back into the forest. I had one chance to take my shot and pulled the trigger. It was a 175-yard shot and I hit the bull right in the neck just behind the skull. The big moose dropped right there. I could hear Sonny and his brother Tony cheering from the boat 400 yards offshore. It was time for the real work to start.

I started dressing out the bull, and while I was doing that, the tide was coming in rapidly. Sonny and Tony were in the middle of catching fish, so they could not come to shore to help me. I had to use my own leverage, so I got the skiff pulled up to the moose. I turned the skiff sideways and took a long, strong beach pole and wedged it under the moose. The way the moose was lying on the beach I was able to use the pry logs with all my strength to move the beast onto my skiff. I have to admit that it was quite a feat! I put its head up on the bow and pushed off. There was not much freeboard, but I was lucky that it was flat calm on the water. The 15 hp motor was wide open and pushed me only about five miles an hour. As I weaved my way through the fishing boats, everyone waved and gave me a thumbs up. When

I made it to the boat ramp, I backed my F250 Ford pickup down to the skiff. I took the three-quarter-inch piece of plywood I always carried, and two 2x12's, and laid them from the bow to the tailgate to make a ramp. Then I hooked up my come-along winch to the front of the pickup bed and ran the cable out to the moose. I wrapped a noose behind its front shoulders and started ratcheting the moose up my ramp and into the truck. One hour later the bull was secure in the truck.

I drove out to my friend Uncle Terry's place and backed into his big shop. I tied a 4x4 ft. board between the hind legs, spreading them apart, and tied it to an overhead beam. Then I jacked the bull up until I could drive out of the shop. Now it was hanging there with its neck one foot off the ground and I would be able to skin it. The moose came out beautiful. I took my time and didn't make one hole in the hide. After I was done skinning, I took my razor-sharp handsaw and cut straight down the center of the backbone. The two half's hanging there looked just like a cow in a butcher shop. I age my meat in cold storage just like a butcher would. It is the best, cleanest meat a person could ask for.

CHAPTER 8

THE GARM:
WATCHDOG OF HELL'S GATE

BY THIS TIME I WAS seeking out the best offers for fishing. I was getting a real feel for the fishery and was always one of the top ten high-liners, someone who was top-notch, and brought in the most poundage during the fishery. This season I was thinking about a few different offers. One was from Tony Tang, the son of Marty Tang who owned the Pioneer Bar. Tony had just been in Seattle at the Radden boatyard building one of the first stern picker gill net boats that the company had ever manufactured. Mostly Radden had been building bow picker boats. I liked the idea of fishing on a brand-new boat that even had a shower onboard. He named the boat the *Garm*, after a Norse mythology creature that is a blood-stained watchdog that guards hell's gate.

There were a few offers on the table, but the one that appealed to me the most was from Tony. He said we could fish together and that he would give me 25 percent off the top. I took him up on his offer. Later, after I had accepted the offer, he disclosed to me that he was sick. He told me that he found out he had fibromyalgia (FM), a very painful disease. I was a little beside myself partnering up with him, but I knew I would still make good money and be fishing on a nice boat. One of the conditions of our agreement was that I would supply the net for the boat. I already had a brand-new net that matched the color of the water so the fish would not see it.

The first opener of the season was upon us and I was excited to start fishing. We picked our spot and set the net out as soon as the announcement came over the VHF radio. A trooper was on the fishing grounds making sure people did not set out early before the opening or that no one was fishing over the designated boundaries. It was the same trooper who was always giving me a hard time, Al Cane. It is common to be checked by the fish and wildlife troopers to make sure your net is legal, but usually you get checked while the boat is docked and in the harbor. I looked over and saw that the trooper boat was headed in a beeline toward us. *Oh great*, I thought, *now what?* As usual, we were not doing anything wrong. He came up to us with a pipe pole in his hand, a long aluminum pole with a hook on the end. I said, "Hello, Officer Cane, what can I do for you?"

He said, "Davis, I am here to check your net to make sure it is legal depth and length."

As he was talking he had grabbed on to my net with the hook end of his pole. Instead of hooking on to the cork line, he grabbed on to the web part of the net below the cork line. The current was moving pretty good and the wind was blowing at twenty-five miles an hour. Due to the weight of his boat, the wind, and the current, his hook started sliding. As it was sliding, it happened to be tearing the webbing of my net. It was like he had taken a knife and just cut the web away from the cork line. Furthermore, with his harassment, he was preventing me from fishing. We could see fish hitting the net and I yelled at him, "Hey, Officer, you are tearing up my net. Let go!"

He said, "Not until I check your net."

I was getting enraged. He ended up checking my net, but tore a huge hole in it during the process. I told him that this was absurd.

He said, "I am just doing my job."

I replied, "Yea, right, this is becoming harassment. You ruined my net and you are taking up my valuable fishing time."

He did not seem to care too much about what he had done and said, "Have a nice day," and left.

I told Tony that I knew there was a way you could get compensated for any damage a trooper had done to you or your equipment while out fishing. I pulled in the net and started repairing it so we could get back to work. It ended up costing me hours of fishing. The fishing opener only lasts so many hours at a time. When we got back to town, I filed a claim against the State of Alaska for $5000. I ended up winning in court and being reimbursed the full $5000 for the damages, and loss of fishing time. I was happy, but Al was probably not too thrilled. I am sure when troopers cost the state money, they get reprimanded. Maybe the guy would leave me alone after this.

During the next few openings, Tony's condition was worsening. Fishing became unbearable for him to continue. He came to me and said he was not going to be able to finish the season, but that he would let me fish the boat and permit for a one-third share off the top before expenses. It was up to me if I wanted to hire a deckhand. I decided to fish by myself, and at the peak of the season I would find someone to crew for me. Meanwhile, my brother and I had mended our relationship and were getting along really well. I asked Greg if he would like to make a little extra money during the season, and he told me that he thought that was a good idea.

There were certain sets near the boundaries that were highly sought after. To make it fair, the gillnetters had a meeting and decided that the rule would be that on those certain boundary sets, we would have a time limit of twenty minutes per set and then you had to pick up your net and wait in line for the next turn. Sometimes there would be a four-hour wait for a good set. I was not fond of waiting. I would rather be fishing. I found a way to set near the people in line without having to get in line. This really pissed off the guys waiting in line, especially since I was catching a lot of fish. They would come up to me in their boats and start yelling. I did not really care. I would fight anyone who wanted to challenge me. Even with my brother onboard they would yell, but when we were at the dock or in town, most guys acted like nothing ever happened.

Wayne Alex, who had already confronted us once a few years ago, was one of the guys yelling at us. Wayne came up to us while we were on the set and told me to move. I said, "I am not moving and if you have a problem with it, I will meet you at the dock after the opener."

He said back to me, "I will see you there!"

We kept fishing our spot and the guys kept fishing, taking their turns off the point. Greg looked over at me and asked me if I knew that Wayne had killed someone. I said that I had heard something about it, but did not know the whole story. Greg told me that while Wayne had been logging in Southeast, Alaska, he had been convicted of shooting two guys, killing one of them. Usually loggers spent months at a time out at remote camps without going to town. Most camps do not allow alcohol, so when they get

47

a break and get to go to town, they have a pocketful of cash and are ready to get drunk. Wayne had been at camp for six months when he got a break and went to Juneau. He cashed his check and was ready to party. Wayne went to downtown Juneau where there are about six bars in a two-block radius. He hit the Red Dog Saloon, known back then to be a rough bar. Wayne was a tough guy and could hold his own. He was having a hoot of a time ringing the bell, buying rounds for the whole bar. There happened to be two shady characters casing Wayne out. They saw that he was getting drunk and that he had a big wad of cash in his pocket. Meanwhile, Wayne wanted to leave the bar and go to a different one down the street. The two guys followed him out and shoved him into the alley. They then proceeded to pummel the living crap out of him and rob him of his money. They beat him so badly that any normal person would have been killed. But having been a Golden Gloves boxer and a tough logger, he could take a beating and survive. The attackers did not count on Wayne waking up. He did though, and he was irate and on the warpath. He was so furious that he went insane. He went home and got his .44 Magnum revolver, intent on finding the guys who had beaten and robbed him. He did not have to look hard. They went right back to the Red Dog Saloon thinking they were in the clear. When Wayne saw them, he pulled out his .44 Magnum and shot them both in the bar. The cops were called, an ambulance came, and Wayne was arrested. Wayne got a good attorney and when he went to court, he pleaded temporary insanity. The judge was lenient and gave Wayne one year in prison and took his right to own a gun away.

Wayne was known to be a high-liner and not afraid to fight anyone for crossing him on the fishing grounds. He was one of the fishermen who had been taking turns on the boundary set and getting angry at me for not waiting in line. Besides yelling at us in person, he got on the VHF radio and said, "The *Garm* is over the line, the *Garm* is over the line." I think he was hoping to sic the troopers on me. Even after knowing that about Wayne, I was not scared of him. After the opener I was prepared to get into a confrontation with him. I knew where he kept his boat docked and went to find him. My brother came along. Wayne came out.

I said, "Hey Wayne, here I am!"

He said, "Oh, yea?"

I said, "Yes, do you still have a problem?"

He smiled and said, "Oh, you mean about the fishing?"

"Yes," I replied.

He said, "No, I lost my temper. I do not want to fight you."

I said, "Okay then, it is all worked out?"

He said, "No hard feelings."

Wayne told me that he was not used to anyone challenging him and respected me because I stood up to him.

The summer was going nicely. We got an announcement from the fish and game department that they had gotten their allotment of fish needed for the fish run to sustain itself. Once there were enough fish that escaped up to the spawning beds, we were able to have more time to commercial fish. They were going to open up the fishing grounds that were normally closed off and let us fish all the way up to the mouth of the river. I headed right up there to secure my set. The first one to the grounds keeps watch over their spot. I was ready. As soon as the opener was announced, I set out off of the beach on the first point just below the river tidal flats. I actually shoved the bow of my boat up on the beach and ended up corking everyone off, in other words blocking them from setting and catching fish. I also set in a way that intercepted fish that would be going into their nets. People get pretty mad when this happens. There was a lot of money at stake and competitive fishermen were always out to try to catch the most fish. I set out, and instead of picking up and moving, I would just pull in half of my net and kept the other half fishing. Then run down to the other half and clean the fish out of it. I kept the net fishing without picking it completely up and moving. It was shallow there, and my lead line was actually caught up on a reef, so it was sort of like set net fishing, where one end would not move and stayed in one place and did not drift. This was really effective in mopping up all the fish. The other fishermen that came up to the boundary were livid. They were coming up to me yelling and telling me to pick my net up. I told them to, "Suck up a rope, I am not moving! It is tough all over, boys, tough all over." They thought I should pick up and give them a chance to set there. My net was actually hung up on a reef and if I picked it up, the reef would shred my net. I would run the net with my boat and just kept picking the fish out of my net. We were getting $1.50 a pound at the time for sockeye and they average seven pounds apiece. So in the twenty-four-hour opening, I had caught 1200 sockeye. I got an average of $10 a fish. I made about $12,000 in twenty-four hours! I was tickled pink, but some other fishermen were not too happy with me. *Too bad for them*, I thought to myself, *It is tough all over*. I parked my boat and went home with no regrets.

I went back down to the boat after taking a rest to do some work, and I noticed that there were bullet holes in my stovepipe. Someone had a serious problem with me. I was hoping the person would confront me instead of shooting at my boat. I looked at the holes and they looked like .223 caliber holes. I had an idea of who did it. I had gotten an Alaska Department of Fish and Game hat because I had been doing test fishing for them during the closures. I put on my fish and game hat, which was blue with a round ADF&G emblem in the middle, and went into the cannery store. I saw Coy Taylor in there. He said to me, "That patch on your hat looks like the perfect target for your head." I didn't even reply. I just up and punched him hard in the face. He got knocked back hard and was lying on the floor.

I said, "Your face makes the perfect target for my fist. You're probably the one who shot holes in my stovepipe, so consider us even and don't do it again."

I had a feeling that it was Coy who shot my boat because he always carried a .223 rifle in his truck, and after what he said it made me believe it even more. The rest of the season went on without any more major confrontations.

That fall I did a bunch of firewood cutting and chopping. I knew that my truck would hold exactly a cord of wood and that I had to get fifteen cords of wood every winter just for our house. While I was doing that, I would cut and chop wood for other people to make extra money at $75 a cord.

CHAPTER 9

TAKHIN OR BUST

WINTER WAS APPROACHING, AND MY good friend Harry and I decided to go on a two-month trapping expedition across the Chilkat River along the base of the Chilkat mountain range up the Takhin and Kicking Horse river valleys. Harry and I had been planning this expedition for several months. We went 250 miles up to Whitehorse, Canada, to go shopping. There was a 35 percent exchange rate at the time and we could take our American dollars up there and get an excellent deal on supplies. We would take our money straight to the bank and exchange it before we went shopping; otherwise, we found out that the local businesses would not give you the full exchange rate and you would get less for your dollar that way. We bought beans, rice, sugar, coffee, tea, flour, lard, a twenty-five-pound slab of good bacon, oatmeal, pancake mix, and an airtight, lightweight wood stove. From home we took a five-gallon bucket of dried fruit, dried fish, pilot crackers, some jarred meat and fish, and a bunch of other gear.

We started our trip by driving to a place called 10 Mile Steakhouse. It was a happening place during the summer but was shut down for the winter. It was a nice spot to park and to hike in to where we were going. From there we got our gear out and loaded it all in our plastic punt from our commercial fishing boat. It made a good sled and it would end up saving our lives. We had my dog Latcho, a Makenzie River Husky. I had gotten Latcho in Haines Junction, 159 miles north of Haines, from a trapper who trapped up in the Yukon by dogsled and pickup truck off the road system. His owner, Henry, said that Latcho kept fighting with the other dogs and so he was looking for a good home for him. That was perfect for me because we needed a sled dog for our trapping operation. We were going to be on snowshoes and cross-country skis the whole time and needed a dog to help pull the sled on the trapline every day. We had an 8 ft. oval-shaped plastic boat to bring with us. We filled the boat with our gear, food, and the airtight stove.

I was wearing a wool union suit, down vest, down underwear, heavy wool pants, bunny boots, and my heavy down parka with my lynx fur hat. From the truck we hiked in twelve feet of snow on our snowshoes. We headed across the frozen Chilkat River to the mouth of the Takhin, a beautiful fast-moving river that flowed out of the gorgeous Takhin Valley. We went seven miles up the right side of the river that had some open spots and we got to a point where we had to cross. We were only two miles from the log cabin that we would be using as our base camp.

We sent Latcho across the river so he would detect any cracked or weak ice. After coming back without incident, we decided that it was safe to cross. The dog went out in front of me first as I was pulling the punt ten feet behind me. Harry was behind the punt when we suddenly heard a loud crack, and I instantly fell through the ice into the river. The ice continued to break up around us. I frantically clawed at the icy bank, trying to climb up while kicking the water beneath me to push off the bottom, but with no luck. We were getting swept away downstream fast. When the ice broke, Harry fell forward into the punt and landed on top of the gear. I thought for sure this was it and asked God to help me. I was not just going to give up and die. Down below was a ninety-degree bend in the river, where I knew for sure I would be sucked down underneath the ice. I was kicking for the bottom. I had snowshoes on, which were making it extremely difficult for me to keep my head above water. With all my gear, I probably weighed 400 pounds. Since I was not making any headway trying to climb up the bank, I grabbed hold of the punt to see if I could climb into it with Harry. He yelled at me not to climb into the boat, that I would capsize it. I did not have a choice. We were approaching the ninety-degree bend in the river and I could see that if I did not get in the boat, I would be swept under the ice.

I was losing energy fast. The dog swam over to the bank and managed to climb up. I knew I had to make a move if I wanted to survive. I told Harry to lean back, I was going to get in the boat. He tried to argue with me and say it would capsize. I told him that I was getting in the boat and that it was my only choice. I told him to lean back on the count of three. One, two, three, and then I lunged with all my might up into the punt.

Harry leaned back and I pulled myself up and balanced myself on the bobbing punt with Harry and the gear that had already overfilled the boat. The boat swung around and we were approaching the bend of the river. If we hit it in the boat, we were done for. I told Harry, "I am going to try to make a leap for the shore." We were being swept around like a cork in the water and breaking ice. I jumped for the shore on pure faith and determination. Somehow I made it. I opened my eyes, and shockingly I was halfway up the bank. My snowshoes were making it very difficult to climb up the bank, but with sheer force and adrenaline, I managed to claw my way up. I even grabbed the rope and pulled Harry up to the shore. As soon as I got out of the water and stood in the open, I started to freeze. Harry only had wet feet. It was thirty degrees below zero and we were on a river flat without any protection. The wind was blowing fifteen miles an hour down the river, which made it more like fifty below with the wind chill factor. I was turning into a solid piece of ice on the riverbank.

We had ended up on the wrong side of the river to get to the cabin. We were only two miles from the cabin, but nine miles from the road where our pickup was parked. In the punt we had an airtight wood stove, into which I had packed a down vest. I tore off my down jacket that was soaked and put on the dry vest. I also had space blankets, which I took out and wrapped around me, but they were not helping me warm up at all. Building a fire was out of the question as we were too far from the woods and on an exposed river flat. I left my pants and wool union suit on. My one-piece wool union suit actually saved my life. I was starting to go into convulsions and hyperthermia was setting in. I found a dry wool beanie hat to put on and told Harry that we needed to get walking or I was going to die. Even though we were only two miles from the cabin, we were still on the wrong side of the river and there was no way that we were going to attempt to cross it again. I either had to make it to our truck nine miles away or I was going to perish. We left everything there and took off for the truck. We started hiking as fast as we could go. We made it to the truck and started it up to get the heater going. If it were not for my strength and conditioning, I could have easily met my demise. It takes more than strength to survive a near-death experience; it takes shear mind power not to succumb to the thoughts that creep in telling you that you are going to die. I did not let that happen. If anything like that started to happen, I immediately suppressed the negative self-talk. There was no way I was ready to cash in my chips just yet.

It was so cold that I could barely get my boots off, and there was ice inside of them when I finally got them off. We were pretty quiet on the drive home but decided that we had to make another go of the journey. We were not easily deterred. We went home, spent the night, regrouped, and started drawing up a new plan.

The next day we decided to venture out once more for the cabin. We believed that if we could find some trees to knock down across the river, we could fashion a makeshift bridge. We brought a big chainsaw with us and found a giant standing dead spruce tree a quarter mile from where the river broke. It was leaning out and half fallen already. We tied a line to the punt that was long enough to reach across the river. We dropped the tree across the river, and then crossed the log bridge. When we got across, we pulled the line we had tied to the punt and pulled the punt across the frozen river. Latcho crossed the frozen river in front of the log, but thankfully the ice did not break.

We made it to the cabin in the afternoon that was located right on the old Dalton Trail. We immediately got the little tin airtight stove out and hooked it up. I went up on the roof to fix the roof pipe and put the stove cap on. While I was up there, Harry was getting the fire going. He had grabbed a can in the cabin that said kerosene and poured some of it in the wood stove to get the fire going. Little did he know that it was a can labeled kerosene but someone had put Blazo fuel in it. As soon as it was lit, it exploded, and a flame shot up the stovepipe right past my head. It blew off the stove cap. I yelled, "What the hell, Harry?" He started laughing, and we figured out what had happened to the fuel. I suppose we were always finding humor in near-fatal incidents. We got a laugh out of it, and started unloading and putting away our gear and cooked some dinner.

The next day we set out some marten traps around the cabin and caught a marten the first night. We lucked out that there was a big, dead, standing spruce tree nearby to cut up and use for firewood. We decided to work around the cabin and then set out for intense trapping tomorrow. We would start our day by getting up at 4:30 a.m. and make a big pot of coffee and oatmeal. Getting ready for the trapline included getting our traps, bait, and the call lures packed. I had found a company in Montana, Big Sky Lures, that had the best urine to place in strategic locations to lure in animals into our sets. They even sold coyote urine by the gallon, which was very effective on the trapline. It worked great for covering up our human scent. A great bait that I used was fermented moose meat that I made myself. Every year when I got a moose, I would chop up the moose head and put the chunks in a five gallon bucket. I then let it ferment for months. It could be detected for miles and brought in all kinds of animals.

We would take off on snowshoes at 6:00 a.m. in pitch-black darkness and hike along the base of the mountains, setting traps south along the way to the Kicking Horse River where we kept our cross-country skis. Then we would head up the Kicking Horse Valley on the right side, which was about a 15 percent uphill grade all the way to the top of the valley to the Kicking Horse glacier. We set traps along the way in the timber. It was about a fifteen-mile round trip, and a physically intense workout. We usually would not get back to the cabin until about 7:00 p.m. every night. At that time of year it got light at 9:00 a.m. and dark by 4:00 p.m., so we were in the dark a lot using headlamps to see.

One day we decided to spend the night up at the face of the glacier. There was an awe-inspiring ice cave where we decided to set up camp and build a campfire. There were small flocks of ptarmigan everywhere. We shot some birds for dinner and had an amazing night. To top it off it was cold and clear, about twenty degrees below zero. The northern lights came out and it was one of the most remarkable displays that I had ever seen. The experience was so dramatic that it is hard to describe in words. The next day we hiked out and proceeded with our trapping operation. We got into a routine of hiking that route one day and then the next day we would head in the other direction up the Takhin River valley for eight miles.

When we got back to the cabin from trapping all day, it would be about forty degrees inside. Right off the bat we would get a fire going and eat some dinner, which would end up being at around 10:00 p.m. Sometimes when we got up, it would have snowed over three feet. It was harder to break trail, but once the trail was broken, it was smooth sailing.

About two weeks into our expedition, a stranger showed up out of the blue. We were in the cabin for the evening and cooking dinner when we heard something outside. Latcho was going nuts, growling and barking, so we shone our spotlight outside and saw someone. We called out, "Who is it?" He answered back, "It's Joe." We asked, "What the heck are you doing out here?"

Joe said he was curious about the area and wanted to come and check us out. We invited him in. He said that his feet were killing him and he took off his shoes. We saw that his feet were blistered up bad and his ankles were raw and bleeding. We asked if he was okay. He said that maybe he should not have worn new shoes, but he thought he would be okay if he could rest up with us. I got out my first aid kit and patched him up, whispering to Harry that this guy isn't going anywhere for a while. We figured that he must have seen our truck parked out at the parking lot, put two and two together, and followed our trail. It was well known that I trapped in the winter, and some people liked to hone in on others when they do well. It still kind of spooked us out a little. It was an unexpected surprise, but he had brought a pack full of goodies, including Scotch, cigars, and some baking supplies. Even though we were not too thrilled about someone intruding on us, it was nice to have some company. Joe's feet were pretty bad and he ended up staying at our cabin for five days healing up. While he was there he cooked for us. It was nice to come back from trapping to have a warm cabin and food ready. Joe healed up and then went on his way back to town. We were happy to have the area to ourselves again.

After we had trapped a large amount of animals and had their furs processed, we decided it was time to get some fresh meat. We had spotted a herd of mountain goats up the Takhin, but they were on the other side of the river, which meant that we somehow had to get across. We found a giant, dead, standing spruce leaning out over the river that was eventually going to fall over from erosion, so I dropped it with my chainsaw. It made the perfect bridge. The middle of the river was open and flowing, so there was no way we would have been able cross otherwise. This also opened up another area to trap. The goats were on the top of a ridge of timber about 600 feet up the mountain above a cliff. They would come out every day to the ridge and soak up the sun. The morning of the hunt we got over the river, and a nice looking goat was standing right up on top of the ridge. I found a log sticking up out of the snow to rest my gun on. It was a 300-

yard shot. I took steady aim for the neck and touched off the trigger. Down went the goat. It fell off the cliff onto a slide area that had scattered timber and came right down to the base of the valley floor.

Harry and I started to climb up to the slide area. It was very steep and the goat was about 200 feet above me. We left our rifles at the bottom because we were both packing pistols. I had my .44 Magnum and Harry had his .41 Magnum. As we were nearing the top, I looked up and saw goat legs walking through the woods. I heard Harry's gun go off and looked up to see this big mountain goat coming down the slide right at me. I had to jump out of the way as the beast went flying past me all the way to the bottom. I turned and yelled at Harry, "Thanks for the warning!"

He said back, "I did not have time, but you're welcome!"

When we got to the top of the slide, it was at the base of the cliff where my goat had fallen. There was an ice crevice so we had to put on our crampons to be able to climb over the icy rock ledge. My billy goat was lying wedged behind a giant boulder. It was a huge mountain goat with eleven-inch horns. It weighed about 400 pounds and we had a hard time getting him out, but we finally did and rolled him off of the edge. He fell all the way to the bottom. It was a wild ordeal.

We climbed back down to where Harry's billy goat was. It was fairly large, too, with ten-inch horns. We knew it would take two trips to get the goats all the way back to the camp, so we went to work and field dressed them out, quartered them up, loaded our packs, and took off. We would come back there the next morning for the rest of the meat. I laid all the quarters in the snow and covered them with the hide. The head was still attached, so I covered it up with snow in hopes that the wolves wouldn't get to it. When we arrived back at the cabin, Latcho was happy to see the fresh meat and us. That night we feasted on goat heart and liver. The next morning we got an early start to get the other goat. Luckily, no animals had found my goat. Everything was frozen stiff. We packed up and headed back for camp again with plenty of meat and more bait from the scraps.

We got to talking and we thought it would be fun to have our wives out. They were in good shape and liked the outdoors, so we decided to go to town and make a weekend out of bringing them out to our cabin and showing them around. They had a blast until it was time to head back. A warm front, a.k.a. a Pineapple Express, moved in and the temperature went from minus fifteen degrees up to forty degrees. Our trail went from a frozen walkway on top of fifteen feet of snow, to a soft slush puddle. You would sink to your knees with every step. It was very tough going, but we made it. Harry's wife was crying by the time we got to the parking lot. It was mean, but we laughed about it after they took off. We spent two months up there and ended up making out nicely. We caught over 100 martens, a lot of minks, twelve wolverines, four lynx cats, several foxes, and five wolves. It was a productive trapping season and we had an experience of a lifetime out there. Nothing could beat the feeling of doing what I love, the freedom, and independence of making a living out in the wilderness.

CHAPTER 10

MAYHEM IN PARADISE

JUST LIKE CLOCKWORK, WHEN IT got close to fishing season the offers started rolling in. As usual there were always drawbacks and risk, but I usually made out pretty well and evaluated all of the offers and picked the one that would suit me. I got a call from Dave Nanny and Steve Waste. They asked me if I would be interested in fishing their boat for 0.3 percent off of the top. Plus, this season I got word from the city and borough of Haines that they wanted me to build trails around the Haines area during the closures. The city told me I could work like a subcontractor, and had full control of whom I hired and what days we worked. I knew Harry would be great to have work beside me on the trail. Out of all the fishing offers I got, I liked the offer from Dave and Steve best. I was having a good fishing season fishing, and then I got $10 an hour to have fun building an impressive trail system for hikers. In addition to pay, we got a per diem to buy food for our job. We camped out overnight when we got a good distance from town, so we did not have to do a bunch of backtracking.

I hired assistants for the trail job. We found some eighteen-year-old high school track stars to work, knowing they were in good shape, but we really surprised them with our conditioning and training. We were in such good shape that we would hike up the trail packing a fifty-pound backpack and then drop and do twenty pushups. They were pretty amazed at how fit we were.

We spent the winters trapping and snowshoeing for miles. Then I spent the summers commercial fishing. This was keeping me in top physical condition. We had a lot of fun spending the closures out camping in the woods and building trails with chainsaws, axes, machetes, pulaskis, picks, come-alongs, and block and tackle sets. Harry and I would carry our .22

rifles with us to shoot blue grouse every chance we got. The grouse were everywhere on the mountain and are one of the most delicious eating game birds. We had store-bought food, but we loved wild game and hunting birds. I loved to cook them on a spit over the campfire, basting them with butter and honey. It was one of the guys' favorite meals too.

At this time we were working on the 7 Mile Saddle Trail. It started seven miles out the Haines Highway from town. It went straight up the mountain. Up at the top was a beautiful saddle-shaped valley with two small lakes in it. Once you were on top, there was a beautiful, long sloping hill going up the backside, and you could walk around it and end up on the ridge next to the top of Mt. Repinsky. The first part was really steep so we had to build switchbacks until we got up into the big timber. Then we wound our way up until we broke out into alpine. It was an absolutely spectacular view looking down on the Chilkat River valley and the Chilkat Inlet.

One day Harry and I decided to take our horses up the mountain since we had gotten the trail done all the way up to the saddle. In the evening, we took the horses out of the corral to get them worked out for the next day's outing. The next day we got the horses ready and decided to leave Sherman behind in the corral. He was our packhorse, but we really did not need him. He did hate to be left behind though, and usually found a way to escape no matter how we tried to secure him in the corral. We started up the trail and had to lead the horses up the switchbacks with a fifteen-foot lead rope. If you didn't stay far enough out in front of them, you would be stomped. Once we made it to the big timber we could ride the rest of the way. It was an amazing ride, and as soon as we were up in the saddle of the mountain, we rode all over and took in the breathtaking view of the area. It was literally a spiritual experience.

When we got back from the ride, Sherman was missing, but I had an idea of where he had gone. I had already taken off Sugarfoot's saddle, so I hopped on him bareback and rode off in the direction I thought Sherman had gone. I picked up his trail and was galloping wide open at about thirty-five to forty miles an hour. All of a sudden Sugarfoot saw Sherman out of the corner of his eye. He was hiding in the woods. When Sugarfoot saw him, he got frightened and panicked. He took a ninety-degree left turn into the forest and galloped out of control at full speed through the woods. I saw that we were approaching a big tree limb that would have hit me across the chest or head, so instead of being clotheslined, I went down to the right and got flung off. I bashed my forearms, right knee, and leg so hard into another tree that I went flying at least ten feet backward.

I was lying on the ground with my legs twitching from severe muscle spasms, and then felt the throbbing pain in my leg. It hurt so badly that I truly thought that my leg and knee were broken. I could not bend my knee and it started to swell up fast. Harry came over and helped me get up, and I was able to barely hobble around. The more that I walked on it, the better it got. With Harry's help, I managed to get up and get on the horse. It was very difficult, especially since I did not have a saddle on him. Sherman trotted over to us as if nothing had happened. I was furious, but held my temper. It would be easy to take it out on the horses, but they were just being horses. I got home, took off my jeans, and then wrapped and iced my knee. I probably should have gone to the hospital and been on crutches, but I was strong and stubborn. My knee was throbbing, but I had work to do and could not afford to miss out on making money. I had to go fishing, and I was not going to wimp out on the trail job, even with a sprained knee. I believe, also, that any regular person's leg or knee would have snapped by the shear force that I was hit with, but since I was so strong and was in such good condition, my leg did not break and I was able to do both jobs. I think by using my knee it was helpful in the healing process. At that time we were commercial fishing two to three days a week and working the trail job the rest of the week. After the fishing season was over, we continued to work on the trail job. We did our annual moose hunt and continued to traverse places that no one else dared to journey.

I wanted to go gold panning up in the mountains and thought that since my brother was a water witcher, he might use his gift to find gold. He would hold a willow branch in his hands and walk around in the woods, and the branch would bend down and the bark would actually peel off. We would always find water sources where his branch pointed. We wanted to test his skill on gold. I got some gold together and buried it in the yard to see if he could find it with a branch. As far-fetched as it may sound, he did find the gold without any assistance from us. I thought for sure that we had hit the mother lode. There were gold mining claims up by the town of Porcupine, a small gold mining town where people were still out there scratching out some gold. Mostly miners were making enough to eek out a humble living. In its heyday there were up to 5,000 people living there. I thought we had a good chance of becoming rich. We did stake a claim and tried our luck at gold mining, but we did not make enough to make it worthwhile. Greg's abilities were not really strong enough to find enough gold to make a lucrative living, at least not that we knew of. We were not really patient enough to put a lot of time into something that did not pay off fairly quickly.

There was a small community of miners and trappers in the town of Chicken, up on Taylor Highway. There were two old-timers up there that made a decent living mining and trapping. Everyone has it in their mind that gold mining is glamorous, but really most of the guys that do it full time on a small level are just making a living. Everyone in the area knew Fred and Henry. They were good guys who everyone liked. There were always newcomers to the area thinking they were going to come out there and strike it rich. Most of them come and go pretty quickly. My brother and I saw some new folks in town and heard that the new guy and his wife moved to Haines from California. When they had heard about good gold claims on the Taylor Highway between the little towns of Chicken and Eagle, they got big ideas and had big plans. They had heard that the old-timers that partnered up did pretty well up there. Maybe they thought they would follow suit. They got a claim and ended up moving there.

I was in town at the hardware store when I overheard some people talking about a murder up at the gold claims near Chicken. I asked what happened. The folks at the store told me that the Californians shot the old-timers and claimed it was self-defense. The husband said that they went up to the miners' cabin to talk about mining claim rights and that Fred and Henry shot at him and his wife. When the trial occurred, all the information about the shootings became public information. We found out that both miners had been shot, but Henry had survived and crawled to the town store in Chicken. He lived long enough to explain that the Californians had ambushed him and his partner. The miner told the clerk that one guy came up to the door and knocked. Henry answered the door and Fred was looking out the front window. Henry said that the guy who had knocked on the door immediately pulled out a .45 semiautomatic and shot him at point-blank range. Henry told the clerk that there must have been someone else off in the distance, because the next thing he knew Fred had been shot through the window. The Californians left the scene, thinking that the miners were both dead. Henry woke up in shock and managed to crawl to the store. The clerk immediately called the troopers. Henry died before they arrived, but had lived long enough to tell the clerk what had happened.

In court the Californians testified that they approached the cabin and were fired upon first by Henry and Fred, and that that they were completely innocent of any crime. They claimed that they killed them because they got shot at first. It was well known around town what had happened and people were in disbelief because Henry had made it out to the store and was able to tell someone that it was foul play. They were charged with murder, but the jury acquitted them due to the lack of evidence and the fact that the couple from California both testified that the old miners drew first. The husband testified that he saw Henry with his own eyes with a gun and that Henry had shot at him. Was it just a coincidence that the Californians ended up taking over the old boys mining claims? I did not trust them one bit.

The husband later became a village public safety officer (VPSO) back in the town of Haines. A VSPO is not a full-fledged police officer, but they do carry a gun and use a police patrol car.

Not too long after the trial, my full-blooded Tlingit friend, Ross, got in a tussle with the VPSO. Ross was unique because he had bright red hair. He had grown up in Haines and was a state champion wrestler. He was really strong and was built of pure muscle. He was not very tall, about five foot seven and weighed 220 pounds. When Ross drank he would go nuts. He already had a reputation of getting into bar brawls with three or four men at a time. He had a crazy girlfriend, too. When they drank together, they would fight like cats and dogs and get physical. One night Ross and his girlfriend were out drinking at Duke's Bar. They started to argue and got kicked out. They continued their argument in the parking lot. As usual, they started hitting each other. The VPSO just happened to be on patrol that night and saw them arguing. It was getting physical, so I imagine that the VPSO thought he should get involved. Instead of trying to break up the argument, the officer thumped Ross on the back of the head with his billy club. Ross was stunned. He was not sure what had happened and he instantly went ballistic. He started beating the VPSO not knowing who he was or what was happening. During the tussle, the officer pulled his gun. He was in plain clothes, so Ross just thought he was a civilian. Ross took the guy's gun out of his hand and pistol whipped him, and then knocked him down and got on top of him. He was so blinded with rage that he ended up gouging the VPSO's eyes out and beat him to a bloody pulp. By the time he calmed down and realized what he had done, he panicked. He had just beaten and assaulted the VPSO. Ross had been just stunned by the blow to the back of his head and did not realize he was not just defending himself against someone, but attacking him. He got in the officer's car and fled. He drove out toward Mud Bay Road. He got some crazy idea of finding Harry and me, maybe because Harry and I were always in the woods and knew how to get to remote cabins. Ross wanted to hide out and he tried to come out to our house. There was no way that we were going to help him be a fugitive, but I did feel bad for him. Someone spotted the car heading out of town toward Mud Bay Road. The one Alaska state trooper stationed in Haines, Walt Ormeson, got the call and jumped in his car to pursue Ross. He raced out Mud Bay Road and caught up to him about four miles out of town. Ross ran off the road and tried to flee into the thick forest, but Walt pulled a gun on him and said, "Halt or I'll shoot!" Ross surrendered.

When Ross was arraigned, they charged him with first-degree mayhem, which is a lot different than assault, because he had injured the VPSO so badly. From Ross gouging his eyes, he was blind in one eye and mostly blind in the other. To make matters worse, he was charged with assault on a police officer. The court does not look too kindly on people who assault peace officers. The court threw the book at Ross and gave him twenty-eight years in prison, with first chance of parole after serving fifteen years. Ross never made parole. He ended up doing the full twenty-eight years.

I always had an opinion about what had happened to the VPSO. I felt that he might have gotten his injury due to testifying in his trial that he saw the miners with his own eyes pull out a gun and shoot at him and his wife. It was very unfortunate what happened to Ross, but it was also shameful what happened to the innocent miners who got murdered.

CHAPTER 11

MACHETE MAN

THAT FALL WE WERE GOING to move up to Mosquito Lake Road where my brother had been living for the past few years. I had the rent paid on my current house through the end of October. We had all of our belongings packed and had moved most of everything to our new place during the first two weeks of the month. I had been renting my present house from Mrs. Dorvel. Her and her husband were getting a divorce and the house was going to be tied up. I was happy to be moving because the family that had been living down the road from us was strange. The husband had been convicted of murdering Frank Burlet several years ago and he had been put in a mental institution, only to return to Haines all these years later. He still seemed to be mentally ill. He claimed that the killing was an accident, but he also pleaded that he was mentally ill. They found him not to be of sound mind. Instead of going to prison, he went to a mental institution for his sentence. He got out fifteen years later and came back to Haines. When he got back, he moved into an abandoned cabin down the hill from me. I was not too thrilled about having a murderer living down the hill from me.

Debbie and I only had a few boxes and two cords of firewood that I needed to move to our new place. We went on a drive and decided to make a run with a load from the house. We pulled up in the driveway and I backed up my pickup truck to the woodpile. I looked up and saw someone in my second-story bedroom window. I recognized that it was the guy who had been living down the hill. I got out of the truck and told Debbie to stay put. I strapped on my .44 Magnum. As I was walking up to the front door, it flew open. It was him, and he had a .357 pistol in his hand. He did not point it at me, he was just holding it down next to his leg. He told me that Mr. Dorvel told him that he could move in and that no one was supposed to take anything from the house. I said, "You must be mistaken, because I have my rent paid until the end of October. As you can see, I still have my personal effects here and I came to get them and my firewood."

He said, "No one is taking anything."

I told him, "I am taking a load of firewood right now!" I was already backed up to the firewood pile and wanted to take a load because it was thirty-five miles to my other house. From the woodpile I yelled at him, "I'll be back for the rest of my stuff and nothing had better be missing!" I kept watch, loaded my truck with wood, and then left.

I immediately went to my brother's house and told him what had happened, and that I needed his help. Greg grabbed his .41 Magnum, with which he was a crack shot. We drove back to my house and I opened the door while my brother covered me. We stormed in, and crazy guy pulled his gun on us. We pulled our guns and I told him he had better put the gun down on the floor and kick it toward us. So he did. We picked up his gun and backed out of the house. We were concerned that his wife could be upstairs with a gun ready to shoot us. We left and decided to get the state trooper who lived in town and tell him what had happened. We found the trooper, and after we were done, he said, "I am going to go get this guy out of there, and I will shoot him if he pulls a gun on me. That guy sounds crazy!" So we all three went back to the house. The trooper knocked on the door and when the crazy guy answered, the trooper handcuffed and arrested him because he was not supposed to be in possession of a firearm. The trooper told the family that they had to vacate the premises, so they did. I was able to finish moving my belongings out of there with no further incidents. We heard that he got shipped off to another institution. I was glad that he left town, as he seemed to be a danger to the community.

His girlfriend, who he had a child with, moved into town and got a job at the Thunderbird Motel. They gave her a room to live in while she worked there. The weirdo ended up coming back sooner than I imagined. It was only about a month later that we saw him around town. He walked around town with a trench coat on, and stalked his girlfriend and child. He was creeping around the school and had been caught making his hand into a pistol, pretending to shoot at people. My friend who worked at the Pioneer Bar called me one evening and told me that he was in there with his trench coat on and acting weird. Some friends told me that the weirdo had told people he was going to shoot me if he got the chance. I was also informed that he was carrying around a machete or a gun in his coat. When I got the call from my friend at the bar, I got Harry and we went to the Pioneer Bar. Harry knew the guy had been making threats on my life. We walked in and sat down at the opposite end of the bar from the weirdo. We watched as he pulled out his hand and made it into a pistol. He pointed it at my friend who was bartending and pretended to shoot her. Then he swung around and pointed his finger pistol at me and pretended to shoot. Harry and I got up and walked up to him. I grabbed one arm and Larry grabbed his other arm. We dragged him out the back door and into the alley. I pulled his trench coat off and sure enough, he was carrying a machete. I started to punch him. I told him, "You made a big mistake creeping around the school and threatening kids, and then going to the bar and acting like you are going to shoot people, especially after I heard that you told people you were going to kill me." I punched him some more in the face and pummeled him pretty hard. I said, "You need to leave town. I heard your girlfriend does not want you around either. No one wants you around!" Harry and I left and went home. A few days later we heard that the crazy machete guy went to the Thunderbird Motel and broke into his girlfriend's room. He became unhinged and chopped the room to pieces with his machete. They called the police and they hauled him off for good this time, and he never came back.

CHAPTER 12

CAW LITUYA

THERE WAS AN ANNOUNCEMENT THAT there would be a seventeen-day halibut longline opening. I saw Wayne Alex in town and he asked me if I would be interested in fishing for him on his 58 ft. combination fishing boat the *Pacific Belle*. The crew would consist of Wayne, Sonny, Harry, Tony, Sonny's brother, two greenhorns from California, and me. I told him I was interested and would get back to him. I talked to Sonny and Harry and they were onboard with fishing the opener, so I called Wayne and told him, "Done deal." I found out that Wayne had made some arrangement with the greenhorns that they would work for half a share each on the *Pacific Belle* to get experience. They started helping from the beginning by getting everything ready for the season, including the three weeks it took to build the sixty skates with all new hooks and line. Wayne had all the latest state-of-the-art electronics installed on the boat and had me work with the installer to learn the system. I was hoping we would get at least 50,000 pounds of fish, which would net me about $10,000.

When the opener was announced, we went west from Juneau around the north end of Admiralty Island through Icy Strait to Elfin Cove, a tiny boardwalk village on the edge of Cross Sound and the Gulf of Alaska. Everyone at Elfin Cove said we were nuts because we planned on heading out on the open ocean to fish, even though there was a storm forecasted to hit with fifty- to sixty-knot winds. That would be the equivalent of eighty-mile-an-hour winds. When there is a big storm on the ocean, you can get rogue waves and up to fifty-foot combers. Wayne decided to head out anyway to fish the Fairweather grounds off the northeast Gulf of Alaska. We arrived at the fishing grounds and set our gear. We were fishing fifty miles offshore, below the mouth of Lituya Bay and straight off Cape Fairweather looking up at 15,300 ft. Mt. Fairweather. Sonny and I were at the helm. It wasn't long after we got our gear set out that the storm started picking up. It was hard to work in fifty- to sixty-knot winds, and within seven hours the seas were building to twenty-four feet with an occasional monster thirty- to forty-foot rogue wave. Sonny and I were the most experienced crew members besides Wayne. We had to jog the boat into the waves for twenty-four hours straight. There was no other place we could go. We were stuck out on the Gulf of Alaska fifty miles offshore with no protection. We decided to have our survival suits and raft ready to go after a day and a half of getting beat to pieces. It finally calmed down enough to get the boat in to Lituya Bay, an incredible place that had been carved out by a receding glacier. The native tradition is that Caw Lituya lives there. The Caw is an evil spirit that mainly takes the form of a land otter. Lituya Bay is where one of the world's largest tsunamis took place on July 9, 1958. At the head of the bay there was a massive landslide. When the earth broke loose from the mountainside, millions of metric tons of land came crashing down into the narrow deep water bay, creating a 1100-foot tidal wave.

We got to the mouth of Lituya, which has about a quarter mile wide sandbar. The safest time to attempt entry into the bay would be at high water slack tide. We would have to time the breakers just right to get into the bay from the ocean, especially in these rough water conditions. A person has to be careful not to attempt to go in after the tide switches to an outgoing tide. To get in safely, we had to watch the waves and surf the boat in on one of the waves. We watched the sets of waves and picked one to ride, and made a perfect entry into Lituya Bay. As soon as we got into the bay, we set out shrimp pots. We were relieved to be in the safety of the bay and out of the storm but were a little creeped out about the Caw. Sonny was superstitious and acted worried. I hit the rack and yelled to him, "Don't let the Caw Lituya get you in your sleep!"

He yelled back, "Not funny, George, the Caw is real and I hope he gets you in your sleep for mocking him." The next morning I woke up in one piece with no evidence of being attacked by the Caw.

We had let the pots soak overnight. After breakfast, we got our gear baited up and ready to go. After we got the gear stowed, we went to pull our shrimp pots. As we pulled the pots onboard we saw that they were loaded. When we took inventory of our catch, we counted fifty-seven monster spot prawns. That equaled about six to a pound. We were going to have a feast fit for kings tonight! They were huge, like baby lobster tails. That afternoon we headed back out into the Gulf of Alaska, set out, and picked up our gear again. We thought for sure that by setting out 10,000 baited hooks that we would have at least 15,000-20,000 pounds of halibut, but unfortunately we only caught 5000 pounds.

Sonny and I talked it over with Wayne and told him we should head west and fish off of Yakutat. He was still recovering from hard-core seasickness and told me that I was in charge, and to set a course for Yakutat and wake him up when we got there. The whole crew was seasick, except for Sonny and me. The greenhorns proved to be worthless and had such severe seasickness that they could not even get out of bed the whole time we were fishing. It was an eighteen-hour run to Yakutat, and I woke Wayne up when we got to our destination.

Our next fishing area was thirty miles offshore of Yakutat Bay. We set out our gear here. When we started pulling our gear, we were getting mostly starfish, so we went in closer to the shore and fished a spot that looked good on the chart. The greenhorns were sick and puking their guts out the whole time. We fished the whole seventeen days and only caught 20,000 pounds for the entire opening. The *Vagabond Queen*, a beautiful boat out of Hoonah, Alaska, had gone inside Glacier Bay, the place where Sonny and I had told Wayne to fish in the first place, and caught 60,000 pounds.

After the opener, Wayne told us to head to Yakutat harbor. We got in to Yakutat Bay and Wayne told us that he was going to get rid of the greenhorns. We got to the dock and Wayne told the two guys to get off the boat, they were fired. They said, "What? No way, we don't want to be left in this miserable place."

But Wayne said, "Yes way," and grabbed them by the scruff of their necks and literally kicked their butts off the boat and onto the dock. He gave them each a check for their work and included extra money to buy an airline ticket back to California.

Even though Yakutat is small, it has daily Alaska Airlines jet service. During World War II the military built several runways along Alaska's coastline and had built a 6000 ft. airstrip there. We told Wayne that we wanted to go to town, which was a three-mile walk from the dock. Wayne said the people in Yakutat were evil, and that they hated everyone. He told us that if we went in to town, we had a good chance of getting in a fight or being killed and eaten by the savages that lived there. He said that he was not even going to stay tied up at the dock and was going to anchor up in Monti Bay.

He told us there was a sandy beach in Monti Bay right in town and that we could take the little punt in after we got the boat safely anchored up out in the bay. We got into Monti Bay and dropped the hook. He tried to warn us again before we left that we should not go into town. We told him not to worry, we could take care of ourselves. How tough could they be? Sonny, Tony, Harry, and I took the punt to Sandy Beach, and pulled it up the beach so that the tide would not wash it away. We started walking toward town where we knew there was a bar on Main Street called the Glass Door. Yakutat was a small village of about 500 people with mostly Tlingit native people living there.

On the way to town we ran in to a guy propped up on a guardrail. As we got closer we saw that he had been beaten up. I said, "Hey, what happened to you? Are you all right?" He said he had just come from the Glass Door and that a bunch of mean-ass prejudiced natives had jumped him and beat him up. He told us that he was off the Delta Western fuel barge that had came to town to fill the tanks at the fuel dock facility. He advised us not to go to the bar unless we wanted trouble. Sonny, along with Harry and I, never backed down from a fight, and we really wanted to have a drink after the hell we had just been through on the boat.

We headed on into town to the bar, and walked in and found a booth. The bartender came over and was very pleasant while taking our drink order. Suddenly, I noticed that all eyes were on us and we were getting a lot of nasty looks. We knew right then that these guys were looking for a fight. I looked straight at the biggest, meanest guy and asked him, "What are you staring at with your ugly face?" He did not answer, so I said that it looked like they had a problem and asked if they would like to go outside and solve it right now. The big guy walked over to me and introduced himself as Big Terry. We shook hands and he asked if he could buy us a round. I said "Certainly," so we had a few drinks and some laughs. We actually gained some knowledge of the area and had a good time. After a few drinks, we headed back to the boat. Wayne had already gone to bed and was crashed out and we all followed suit.

The next day we headed back out into the Gulf of Alaska, and then set sail back to Juneau. The price of halibut was three dollars per pound, and after everything was said and done, we made $6500 apiece for our crew share. We were disappointed. I wished we would have gone fishing on Sonny's boat in Glacier Bay, instead of going on Wayne's boat.

A few weeks later the Department of Fish and Game announced that they were going to have a three-day opening in May. Sonny, Harry, and I got together and decided to go out on Sonny's boat the *Ella Mae*. We put fifteen skates of gear onboard and headed south down the Lynn Canal for the Excursion Inlet cannery store. We bought bait and then headed out past Pleasant Island north to Glacier Bay. We arrived there three days early, so we went way up inside to an incredible place, Hugh Miller Inlet, and set out shrimp pots. We caught some nice spot shrimp and found a spot to anchor up behind a point, and then started baiting up our hooks.

Just for fun I took some monofilament sport fishing line off my reel and wound it up into a ball. Then I took a twenty-four-ounce lead cannonball, wrapped the tangled mono around it, put a couple of baited treble hooks in the ball, put it on a swivel, put a leader on it, and then used my sport halibut rod to fish the mutant mess. We were anchored in sixty feet of water. It didn't take long for my gear to hit the bottom and I began to feel something pulling at the bait on the other end, so I slowly pulled it up. There was a big blue king crab on the ball! That is how plentiful the fishing was there. You could even catch crab on a sport rod. I cooked us up a fabulous dinner that night of crab and shrimp.

The opener started and we set out our gear. When we picked up all our gear, we ended up loading down the boat. We filled it to the top of the hatch, and then deck loaded the boat. We figured we had about 14,000 pounds onboard. Loaded to the gunnels with only six inches of free board, we headed back to the Excursion Inlet plant to offload. Thank goodness it was calm weather. We were worried that if there had been rough seas, it would have been too dangerous to attempt the run. We were blessed with beautiful weather during the whole trip, and we made it back to Haines safely with a pocketful of money.

Harry's wife, Kathy, had inherited the original three-story log house that her grandfather Chief McCray had built eight miles out at the end of

Mud Bay Road. The house had not been maintained and needed total refurbishing. The chief had also built a nice little one-bedroom house 300 feet behind the big house. Harry asked if Debbie and I would be interested in renting it. He said that if I would help him fix up the big house for him and Kathy to move into, he would take my hours of work off of my rent. I talked to Debbie and she was all for it.

Harry and I would work twelve to fourteen hours a day fixing up the big house. We got the house comfortable and they moved in. Harry liked it, but Kathy liked living in town next to her parents. She only lasted a few months out there and then insisted that they move back to town. They would come out on weekends but were not there very often. Harry and Kathy asked us if we wanted to move in because they did not want the place to sit empty. We took a look at it, and even though it was a big house and was going to take a lot of firewood to heat, we fell in love with it.

Once we got moved in, we discovered that the old Fisher wood stove really didn't put out very good heat, so I bought a brand-new large earth stove. It was a phenomenal airtight wood stove. I wanted to make a double-barrel stove for down in the basement and remembered seeing different sizes of quarter-inch-thick flume pipe up in Porcupine at the old gold mining camp. I went up there and got one piece that was the size of a fifty-five-gallon drum, three and a half feet long, and a second piece about the size of a thirty-gallon drum and three feet long. I took them to my buddy's welding shop and we welded ends on them. We then took a cutting torch and cut out the holes for the door and eight-inch stovepipe. After I got the stove fabricated and installed in the basement, I took old metal roofing and enclosed it all around the stove from the floor to the basement ceiling, and then cut out a 3x4 ft. hole in the floor and put a steel floor grate in so all the heat was channeled upstairs. I could put three-foot logs in this bad boy, stoke it up, and it would burn for twenty-four hours.

We worked on the place every spare chance we had, plus we had a huge garden and a smokehouse going. One of the things I enjoy most about Alaska is that there is so much to do and so much daylight in the summer that you don't want to sleep!

That summer Sonny got jobs hanging nets, charging $500 per net. Sonny would hire me to help him and I would make a few hundred dollars for every net we hung. Debbie learned how to mend the nets and became very fast and sought after as a first-rate net mender. Debbie ended up being very good and was charging $15 to $20 an hour, and had so much work that she had to turn people down. Fishermen were begging her to mend their nets. Sonny and I knew how to mend, but we were not as fast as Debbie. I ended up having to plead with her to mend our nets. She told us jokingly that she should be charging us!

I fished intensively because fishing season is only so long and you have a short amount of time to make your money that is supposed to sustain you for the winter. Of course I supplemented my income with other jobs during the winter, but during the fishing season I went all out to make as much money as I could.

Our son Jason was born that July on Friday 13, 1979. When we found out that Debbie was pregnant, I got a custom-made Case XX buffalo knife from my knife collector friend. I bought the knife for the son I knew was coming. When we brought him home I put the knife in his crib. I knew that he was going to take after me and become a woodsman and commercial fisherman.

Sonny and I were fishing out by Alexander Island in the upper Chilkat Inlet. It was a miserable damp, rainy, and foggy night, but we were slaying the fish. There were big tides running, which meant a lot of currents and tide rips. We were setting our net out at the south end of the mile long island and drifting very fast up toward the north end. We would start hauling in the net at the halfway mark, and by the time we picked the fish and got the net back in the boat, we would be near the boundary line.

It was now 1:00 a.m. and we were picking up our set. We were fishing near the boundary and all of a sudden I saw a spotlight shining on us. I wondered what the heck it could be. I had a floodlight onboard and shone it out where the light was coming from. It was a person in a skiff. I shone the light on shore where the boundary was to make sure we were behind the marker. Sure enough, we were a good distance from being over the line. We continued to haul the net in the boat and were picking fish like wildfire. We were going fast to make sure to get the net into the boat before we drifted over the line. We were almost done and had about twenty-five feet of net left to get in the boat when the light started coming toward us. We kept working because we did not want to drift over the line with our net out. There were fish in the end of our net and we had to keep stopping the reel and pick the fish out. The person in the skiff got close enough for us to see that it was the fish and game officer. He yelled at us to stop. We stopped and asked what the problem was. He pulled up closer and tied on to our boat. He said that we were over the boundary line. I immediately pulled up my spotlight and shone it on the marker and said that we were not. He argued with me and said, "Yes, you are. I am going to take you both to the dock, write you a ticket, and confiscate your boat, net, and fish."

I said to him sternly, "No, you are not! If you want to write us a ticket then go ahead, but you are not taking us anywhere." As I was saying that, Sonny hit the hydraulics and sucked up the rest of the net on to the reel without picking the fish out. We were drifting faster toward the boundary line, especially with having the other boat tied up to us.

He said back to me in an elevated tone, "Are you threatening an officer?"

I said, "No, I am just stating the facts. You are actually causing us to lose money by harassing us and causing us not to be able to fish."

He said, "Fine, I will write you the tickets then."

Officer Cane told us that he would be at the dock when we were done fishing to give us our tickets. We were pretty worked up over this guy accusing us of fishing over the line and wasting our time. He was also keeping us from fishing, plus his threat of seizing the gear and handcuffing us was unnerving. We went back to fishing. Sure enough, when we got to the dock, he was there to give us our tickets. There was a court date set in front of the local magistrate. I was aware that a person could request a district court judge to hear your case if you wished. I was thinking that would be a good idea.

Sonny and I talked about what had happened and decided that we would just tell the judge the truth and that we were not guilty. The bad thing was that the officer had given me the impression that he did not like me, and I had a feeling he thought I was a lawbreaker by the way he treated me when I was helping Sonny with the seals. It was not good when an officer had it out for you. I have experienced many things over the years, including numerous officers lying in court to persuade judges and juries to get convictions against innocent people. I was hoping this would not be the case with our upcoming hearing. When we went to the hearing, the officer had a storyboard and all kinds of diagrams set up in the small courtroom. I kind of had a bad feeling about the whole thing. I decided that I wanted to have my hearing in front of a district court judge instead of the local person they had elected as the town magistrate. The magistrates in small towns usually do not have any legal experience and are easily persuaded by law enforcement.

The officer got to tell his side of the story, which was completely fabricated. He actually said he could see up on the mountain above the marker and showed on the map where he had been during the day. He said he was up there to get a bird's-eye view of the boundary line. Then he said he got in his boat and watched us fish, and that he looked up and saw that we were fishing over the line. That could not be true. It was rainy and foggy and you could not see the mountain from where we were, so I knew that there was no way he could see us. I had referenced the boundary marker from where we were fishing and we did not drift over the line with our net in the water. We did drift over the line with the officer onboard, but we had already pulled our net in. The officer said we were guilty and then it was our turn to talk.

They told Sonny that the repercussions of being found guilty of this violation was up to a $36,000 fine and a year in jail. Sonny was scared because he had two prior fishing violations. The officer made him out to be a criminal. Sonny panicked and said he was pleading no contest. I pleaded innocent and said that I wanted my case to be heard in front of a district court judge. There was no need for Sonny to plead his case since he had pleaded no contest. They threw the book at him because of his two prior convictions. He got a $12,000 fine and a suspended one-year jail sentence. He had to pay half the fine right away, and if he received any kind of violation in the next two years, he would have to do a year in jail no questions asked.

My hearing came later. They flew in a district court judge and the district attorney. I did not have the money for an attorney so I went to the library and read up on maritime law. I read that when you are a crew member on a boat, the captain's word is law. That meant that even if Sonny was found guilty, if he was the captain and he got the ticket, I should not be held responsible as a crew member. I was preparing to use this law to prove my innocence. When it came time for my hearing, I brought the maritime law book. I saw the district attorney before the hearing. He looked scary. He was about six feet tall and was a true albino. He had stark white hair and beady red eyes, with very thick round glasses. When he looked at me, it sent a chill up my spine. He was very intimidating, and I was not easily intimidated. I sat on my side of the courtroom and waited for the judge to come out. The State of Alaska had the judge and DA flown to Haines just for this hearing. I believed they would be pressing hard for a conviction. The fish and game officer was sitting across from me with the district attorney. The judge came in and called us to order. We stood up and I gave my plea of not guilty.

Officer Cane used the mountain for a reference to the so-called incident. He said he witnessed us fishing over the boundary line. The judge asked if I had anything to say and I replied, "Yes, Your Honor. The incident occurred at one o'clock in the morning in the dark." I had the weather report printed out showing that there was a low ceiling with rain drizzle and fog, and I told the judge that there was no way the trooper could see us from the mountain. I had the maritime law book with copies of the pages of the law I would be referencing. I handed my evidence to the prosecutor and the judge. Then I said, "Your Honor, besides those facts I handed you, I would like to say that I am a crew member on Sonny's boat. Even if he pleaded no contest, I am not guilty of a crime. Sonny was the captain in charge of when the net was set out and when we picked it up. We were not fishing over the line, but if we were, he is responsible. I have here the pages in the maritime law book that states 'the captain's word on a documented vessel is the law.' The captain can even wed people on his boat if he wishes. When we fish, I do as I am told by the captain."

The judge said he would like to hear from the prosecutor. The DA stood up. He looked very proper in his suit and fancy bow tie. He had a very good demeanor in the courtroom. He started out with, "So, Mr. Davis, you say that the captain's word on the boat is law. Am I correct?"

I said, "Yes, sir, that is correct."

He came back with, "Well then, you would obey your captain's orders?"

I said, "Yes, that is right."

Then he raised his voice, pointed at me, and said, "If you were in the Vietnam War under the order of your superior would you gun down innocent civilians?"

I loudly said back, "Yes, I would obey my officer's orders. If not, I would be court-martialed and executed for treason!"

I looked at the judge who looked disturbed. He slammed his gavel down three times very hard and said, "Case dismissed!"

I was relieved. I looked over at the DA and Officer Cane. They gave me dirty looks. I gathered up my papers and books and walked out of the courtroom. The DA and Cane were in the hallway near the exit. As I walked by them, the DA snarled at me, "Davis, I had better not catch you in the my courtroom again."

I told him, "Do not worry, I don't plan on it," and smiled. Then I walked out the door. It felt good to win, especially since we were innocent. After this incident I was very cautious when I was fishing and hunting. Every year I read the rules and regulations and made sure I was always abiding by the law.

There was a nice small meadow system at the base of the mountain just 300 yards behind our house where I was planning to hunt to get my fall moose. These meadows were the perfect habitat for moose to eat and bed down. Every fall moose would come right through here, but only stay for a week or so and then move on. I would check for signs to know when to hunt. I made a simple tree stand of two boards twenty feet up a fairly big spruce tree so that I could glass the whole area.

Moose season opened, and I had come in from fishing and went straight out to the moose blind. I was sitting twenty feet up in my tree blind when I heard something in the brush behind me. I looked and saw a cow moose coming out of the forest. A calf and a big bull moose followed her. I got really excited. Holy smokes, I was expecting that I would have to shoot a moose from a distance and then pack the moose back to my house. Now there were three moose walking directly toward me. I tried to maneuver myself to see if I could get off a shot. I had my single shot 25-06 Browning, but could not position myself to shoot one of the moose with my rifle. All three moose were now directly below me. I pulled out my .44 Magnum pistol that I always carried and cocked the hammer. The bull moose's ears pricked up like a horse's ears, and I shot it directly below me in the top of the skull. The bull instantly dropped and the cow and calf went running off. It was a fifty-inch bull, perfect eating size. I was happy to get my fall moose on opening day, and lucky enough to get him right behind my house.

Now the work began. It was getting dark already and I went back to the house and gathered my gear. I grabbed my come-along, Coleman lanterns, flashlights, 4x4 ft. post, galvanized tub, and razor-sharp handsaw, and walked back out to my moose blind. I needed to be alert and prepared for a bear that might be on the kill as well. Lucky for me I did not see any sign of bear, but I would be keeping a close eye out. I tied the 4x4 ft. post to the back legs of the moose. Then I lifted the moose up with the come-along until its head was off the ground and its body was hanging in the air. I skinned the moose and then cut the head off. I placed the galvanized tub underneath the moose, made a small incision down the belly, and peeled the guts out into the tub in one action. This way everything stays clean and none of the guts get on the meat. Not many people keep their meat as clean as I do. I think that is a big reason people do not like wild game. It's a must to take care of your meat properly by getting the animal bled well and cooled down fast, and then aged in a cool, ventilated place. I used a razor-sharp saw to cut the body/brisket in half right down the middle.

I went back to my house and got some coffee, a thermos, and my chocolate-covered coffee beans. I had decided to go back into the field to guard my moose. There was about an 80 percent chance that if I did not go back, a bear could easily be on my moose. It was a cold, clear night. The stars were out and the temperature was about thirty-six degrees, perfect for cooling and hanging the meat.

The next morning I called my friend Lee and offered him a quarter of the moose to help me pack it out. We packed the four sections of the moose back to my house. It took us two trips each. I hung my moose in the meat shed. I like to hang and age my wild game for fourteen to twenty-one days before butchering it. That way the meat cures and tenderizes. I took the beautiful hide and got it tanned into rawhide. My friend Buckskin Jack made a heavy-duty, moose-skin jacket for me with a thick double collar. He even made custom buttons out of the round part of deer antlers.

I worked for the Alaska Department of Fish and Game as a Tech 3 doing fish and habitat surveys, catching salmon fry and smolt in fish traps, writing down data, and putting microchips in the king salmon smolt's nose. I got Sonny a job working with me. We mapped out every river and tributary flowing into the Chilkat and Chilkoot valleys and their drainages. We would start at the mouth of a river or tributary and work our way upsteam, with every 100 meters or 328 feet being a section. I hand-mapped and surveyed these areas to collect data to find out where the available spawning, rearing, and available habitat areas were. I did this during the months of April and May, and then picked it back up in the fall from the middle of October to late December.

During the first week in December, Sonny and I decided to hike up to Devils Elbow on the Tsirku River to look for open, backwater slues, which were the perfect rearing areas for most salmon. The snow was deep so we had to wear snowshoes. We took a shortcut two miles through the forest and came out above Devils Elbow. Suddenly, we came along a beaten-down bear trail that headed out to an open meadow at the base of the mountain. You could see the evidence where this giant brown bear had killed a full-grown moose in the meadow, and then dragged the whole animal three benches up the mountain to it lair. Its tracks were huge! We followed the trail all the way up and found its den underneath a giant, old-growth spruce tree. It had eaten the entire moose. All that was left were a few bone scraps and chunks of fur. We could feel an eerie presence, as if the bear was hiding and watching, so we hightailed it out of there.

We got a lot of work done on the project, and Sonny and I were held in high regard at the office. We worked all winter and then in the spring on the project.

This spring, Steven Waste contacted me and asked if I would be interested in fishing his new 42 ft. combination vessel that he had bought. He wanted me to go down to Petersburg, pick up the vessel, buy all brand-new halibut gear, get rigged up, and go halibut fishing. I liked the offer and took him up on it. I asked my brother Greg if he wanted to go with me and be my crew. Greg was all for it. We made ferry arrangements to travel from Haines to Petersburg. When we arrived, the boat was in exceptional condition. We spent a week there buying all new gear, and tying up all the ganions and hooks. Finally, we were ready to set sail northwest to Fredrick Sound, around the south end of Admiralty Island crossing over to Baranof, and then going all the way up Chatham Strait to Icy Strait.

We spent the night on Baranof Island and took a dip in the natural hot springs. It was a real treat. After our outing we headed up the strait to Chichagof Island and then to Tenakee Inlet where we went to the Tenakee hot springs. We had a campfire and cookout with some interesting hippies that we befriended. The next morning we headed north again to Icy Straights and then across to Excursion Inlet to get ice and bait. We fueled up and headed west for Glacier Bay. We had done research around Glacier Bay with our sport rods and discovered that there was halibut everywhere. When we laid down the commercial gear, we got 10,000 pounds right off the bat. We were loaded down and had to run back to the cannery to pitch off. We headed back to Glacier Bay, picked up the rest of the gear, and got another 8,000 pounds for a total of 18,000 pounds. It was a great trip and we ended up catching one monster halibut that weighed 335 pounds even after gutting it.

Greg had been thinking about moving north to the interior, halfway between Tok and Glennallen, near Chistochina, which was 525 miles up the road north of Haines. Greg went up there and looked at some property. He ended up liking it, sold his commercial fishing permit, and moved there lock, stock, and barrel. Greg had been an assistant big game guide and was looking at buying an outfit up there that he could do big game guiding out of. He found a piece of land and asked me if I was interested. I took Debbie up there, but she did not like it and neither did I. I came to find that I needed to live near the ocean. After Greg moved up there and got settled in, I wanted to visit him at his new place. I asked Harry if he wanted to go with me. He did, and said that he wanted to check out some property up there. I told Harry that if he wanted to come with me, he had to leave his marijuana at home because I was not going to have anything illegal with me, especially going through borders and customs. Harry was a really big pothead and was always smoking weed.

I told Harry we should take my truck. I had a custom-built 1974 Ford pickup truck with a high performance 429 engine with a high-rise Edelbrock manifold, dual twin point ignition, Hooker headers, and a cherry bomb exhaust with a custom camshaft. My truck had some serious power. I always loved Ford trucks, and they had always done really well when I used them for all my crazy off-road adventures out in the extreme wilderness.

We got up to Beaver Creek, 330 miles from Haines, which was at the Canadian border twenty miles from U.S. Customs. We both had long hair and looked like hippies. We got through the Canadian border with no problems, but when we got to U.S. Customs they made us pull into the search area. They asked us to get out of the truck, so we did. I was just hoping Harry did not have any pot with him. They tore my truck apart and searched everything. They actually said, "Okay, where is the pot?" We told them that we did not have any. "Oh, sure," they said. So they asked us to empty our backpacks and we did. Still nothing, except that I had a bottle of vitamins. They saw the vitamins and really thought they had found something.

The one border patrol guy says, "Hey, Joe, I think I got something," and flicked the vitamin across the room and Joe caught it mid air.

Joe then said, "I am going to go analyze this."

So Joe went in the back to test my multivitamin. Joe comes out from the back and Henry asked what it was. Joe answered, "Multivitamin." Henry was getting sore because he was convinced we had pot or drugs. We definitely looked like pot-smoking hippies with our hair and clothes.

Henry said to us, "Okay, boys, empty your pockets," so we did, and I did not have anything but a can of Copenhagen. Harry emptied out his pockets and he had a pack of Zig-Zags. Henry and Joe were ecstatic!

They said to us, "Okay, just tell us where the dope is."

We told them, "Sir, we do not have any dope."

They continued tearing apart my truck. Finally, Joe and Henry said, "Okay, Harry, what are you doing with Zig-Zags if you do not have any dope?"

Harry looked them straight in the face and said, "I roll Copenhagen and smoke it!" I could not help but start laughing. They never found anything, so they had to let us go. As soon as we got a fair distance from the boarder Harry told me to pull over so that he could pee. When he got back in the truck, he was holding a bag of weed. I was so pissed. He could have gotten us arrested, and my truck confiscated. Harry just laughed and said that it was no big deal, it was just pot. I guess since it was not his butt on the line he did not really care. I told him to keep the weed hidden because my brother was straight, and Harry promised he would. We got up to my brother's house, and had a good visit. He showed us a few primo pieces of property. Harry and I both thought it was beautiful country, and had fun looking around. It was nice up there, but I knew my home was near the water. Something inside of me did not feel right if I was not living near rivers and the ocean. My home was near the water.

CHAPTER 13

FIRE DOWN BELOW

HARRY CAME OUT TO THE house and said that he wanted my help with the roof. The house already had comp rolled roofing, but he had gotten some cedar shakes that he wanted to cover the roof with. I noticed that they were not treated, and I told Harry that we should treat the cedar shakes or put metal or comp roofing on. The nice thing about metal roofing is that everything slides off, and you can also hook up a rain catchment system. At the moment the house only had gravity feed water that had little to no pressure. Harry disagreed with me and said it would be fine, so we roofed the cabin with the cedar shakes. Since we had moved in to the big house, Harry and Kathy had rented out the little cabin to a friend of ours, Filbert. He was a big burly guy and a survivalist who liked to shoot guns, hunt, trap, and reload bullets. These were hobbies that we all shared.

It was a beautiful May spring day. I asked Debbie if she wanted to go for a drive. Jason was going to be three that July and Debbie was four months pregnant with our second child. She thought that would be nice to go for a drive and enjoy the day. We jumped in the truck and headed out. I got about two miles down the road from the house, out near Cannery Cove, when a feeling overwhelmed me. I had a distinct message come into my spirit. It was almost like someone was talking directly to me. The voice of intuition was telling me to turn around and go home now. Debbie looked over at me and she could tell something was wrong. I told her that I just got an overwhelming feeling to turn around and go back to our house. Debbie agreed that if it was that strong of a feeling, we should follow it. I immediately turned around and started driving back toward our house.

As I pulled up in the driveway I saw Filbert coming out of our house with an armful of my guns. I was wondering what was going on. As soon as I looked up, I could see that the roof near the chimney was on fire. There must have been sparks coming out of the smokestack that had caught the dry cedar shakes on fire. I immediately jumped out of the truck and see that the fire was spreading fast. All we had for water was gravity-fed running water, which was not flowing fast enough to really do anything substantial to slow down the hot fire.

Filbert and I broke windows, and then we went inside and started throwing my belongings out the windows. Debbie started moving stuff away from the front of the house because the fire was starting to burn so hot that anything that was close to the house was getting scorched. During all of this frantic and chaotic mess, I looked up and noticed some people who I did not recognize helping us. Later we found out that they were a family on vacation in Haines out on a drive on Mud Bay road and saw us frantically trying to salvage our burning house. They came up to us and did what they could. I could swear they were angels. Eventually it got too dangerous, and we had to stop going inside. We had a Birman Siamese cat named Scrapper. We thought we had secured Scrapper, but the cat kept escaping with all of the chaos. Debbie, Jason, Filbert, the family that was helping, and I stood there and watched the rest of the house burn. It was a very hot fire and it burned the house completely to the ground. The volunteer fire department came out, but it was way too late to do anything. My wood-burning earth stove was sitting there glowing red hot. I was looking at it, wondering if it could be saved once it cooled down. All of a sudden out of nowhere, one of the firemen blasted it with the hose, and it buckled and completely cracked in half. We were only able to save about a third of our belongings.

There were a lot of sentimental things lost in the fire, but when it was all said and done we were looking for Scrapper. We searched everywhere and discovered that he had gone back into the house and burned to death. Another thing that I lost was my expensive Nikon FS1 camera with a 300mm telephoto lens, a 2.8 wide-angle lens, and a 35-55 mm lens. I had four boxes of pictures and slides that were irreplaceable. I was so sad about my camera, photos, and slide collection that I thought I might have lost my motivation to take pictures again.

Harry and Kathy came out with her parents. Instead of being compassionate, they acted very cross toward us and blamed us for the house burning down. They accused us of being negligent. The reason the house burned down was the cedar shake roof that I had advised Harry not to put on. Honestly, that was the least of my worries right now. We were homeless and I had a three-year-old and a pregnant wife to take care of. I needed to find a place to live immediately. Fishing was going to start soon and I already had a deal with the owner of the *Garm* to fish the boat for the season. I called one of my friends that had a shop and asked if I could store my belongings there for the time being. Thank goodness he said that I could. At least I had gotten that taken care of.

I looked all over town for a place to rent, but could not find anything. The only place we could live was on the 41 ft. commercial fishing boat the *Garm*. Debbie was pretty disappointed, as was I. We knew that there was no other option and that we were going to have to make the best of it. I made a harness for Jason with a life jacket and I would tie him off while I was fishing. He was a little wild man. Jason was so full of energy that he climbed on everything. To make matters worse, Debbie had a bad case of seasickness. She would get sick even while we were tied up in the harbor. Debbie, Jason, and I lived and fished on the boat all summer in miserable conditions. We hoped something would come available at any time, but it was not until October that we found a place to rent. My friend Bob Becker told me that he had a place that had recently become available. I was unbelievably happy. Debbie was eight months pregnant and this could not have come at a better time. Our family was really burned out having to live together on the boat all summer. We were so excited to be moving into a real place. We got moved in to our new home out on Small Track Road on October 15. About two weeks later, on November 2, 1982, my son Adam was born.

CHAPTER 14

ALASKA GIRL

EVEN THOUGH MY SON HAD just been born, Sonny and I had already made plans to go trapping together. The plan was to build a trapper's cabin on the Endicott River. My friend with a lumber mill told me he would give me a really good deal on demential lumber if I brought him logs in the round. I had been clearing some property and had some nice trees to bring him. We got the wood to my friend and he milled enough demential lumber for our 12x16 ft. cabin. I had gotten a 19 ft. aluminum square stern Grumman canoe, and we were going to bring my 12 ft. Sears Gamefisher skiff with us. We would use the *Garm* to haul everything out and anchor up. Then we would use the smaller boats to shuttle supplies to the beach. After we were done unloading we would anchor my big boat in a protected cove for the duration of our expedition.

Excitedly we headed south to Sullivan Island. From Sullivan Island ten miles to the south was where the Endicott River comes out of the mountains. There used to be a small logging operation out there, and there was even a small airstrip. There was no protected cove for anchoring so we had to anchor the boat right off the beach where the cabin would be going up. The north wind was slowly picking up and we were anchored 200 yards off the beach with no protection. We left the boat running. Diesel boats can run for days without stopping. We made a catamaran out of the two boats and started loading lumber and supplies on the catamaran. We made trip after trip. After a night of working nonstop we had the supplies hauled to shore. The next mission was to get the supplies from the shore up to the building site. The wind started picking up at daylight. The seas started building up fast. We never would have accomplished the job if we had waited until morning.

When we started on the cabin, we worked like wild men. We used nine posts to build the foundation two feet off of the ground so we could store supplies underneath the platform. We also needed to secure under a tarp what we could not fit under the cabin. The north wind was picking up rapidly and we needed to get back to the *Garm* and anchor up in a protected cove. We dragged the canoe up the beach to a secure place in the trees. The big boat was sitting 200 yards offshore on an anchor jerking up and down in seven- to eight-foot seas. We had to get through four- to six-foot breakers crashing on the beach to get out to the boat on the Gamefisher skiff. We got swamped and were soaking wet after two attempts to get the skiff off of the beach. After the first two tries, I had Sonny get in the bow with a paddle. I got behind the stern and walked out into the breakers up to my chest, pushing the skiff while Sonny was paddling. Then I quickly jumped in. Sonny paddled vigorously and we finally got the skiff through the beakers out far enough to put the outboard down and start the motor. We headed out to the *Garm*.

We got the skiff pulled up to the boat that was lurching up and down. Sonny was able to grab onto the rail and jump onboard. I quickly threw him a line and he tied the skiff to the big boat. I grabbed the rail and pulled myself over. We both had an extreme adrenaline rush going, and as the big boat came down on a wave, we gave a giant pull and miraculously got the skiff pulled onboard. We pulled the anchor and headed for a safe cove behind Sullivan Island ten miles to the north, the same place we were anchored during our earlier episode when we had to get rescued by the Coast Guard. We dropped the hook and made a sigh of relief. I asked Sonny if he was up for an Alaskan Heater. This was a drink we invented when we were out hunting and trapping, that became a tradition. An Alaskan Heater is strong coffee, Baileys, Kahlúa, and a shot of brandy as a floater on top. We sucked down a few of these toddies, and crashed out.

We woke up early the next morning and noticed that the engine sounded weird. After an inspection we concluded that there was a blown cylinder. I had a mechanic friend tell me that there is a trick where you can pinch off the fuel line to the injector on a bad cylinder and the engine will still run fine. The north wind was now howling at gale force, but we had to get the boat back to town, so we took off on five cylinders back to Haines. We were getting beat to pieces bucking into twelve- to fourteen-foot seas with freezing spray and icing on the boat. It was a long grueling twelve-hour run, but we made it back safely. We asked Sonny's brother Mark to take us back down to our cabin site with his 38 ft. fishing boat the *Sockeye King* when the weather calmed down.

A few days later the winds subsided and Sonny's brother Mark took us and more supplies ten miles from our camp. We dropped our 12 ft. Sears Gamefisher in the water at the south end of Sullivan Island and skirted the beach line ten miles south to our new camp under construction. It was November 10 and we wouldn't be going back to town until Christmas. The weather was clear and cold, with lows in the twenties at night and upper thirties by day. We got all the gear set up and organized, and we were ready to build. We worked without stopping and drank a lot of strong coffee. We had our 12x16 ft. cabin completed with a fire going in the wood stove thirty-six hours later. There were two big spruce trees twenty feet in front of the cabin, twelve feet apart, so we built a giant enclosed 12x20 ft. front porch to use as a shop and workstation. A friend had given us a lot of clear plastic corrugated roofing that let in a lot of light. Now we had a nice 12x20 ft. shop for our fur operation. It was the perfect place to skin and work on our furs and traps. My dog Jake the Fake was with us to help with the trapping operation. We would have Jake pull the sled on the trail for us. Jake was a mixed breed: three-quarters black Lab and one-quarter St. Bernard beast. We hiked up the Endicott every day. We were mostly targeting martens, which were bringing in an average of eighty dollars apiece.

We had gotten out to the camp in November and now it was already February and toward the end of our expedition. We were in the middle of our daily routine when all of a sudden we heard a helicopter. We had not heard a peep from anyone all winter. I recognized the helicopter to be a Hughes 500. We had just come back from our trapline and pulled the skiff up on the beach. We got out and were curious to see what the people in the helicopter wanted. When they hovered above us, they ended up blowing our skiff out into the water. I looked up at the chopper and waved my arms at the pilot and pointed at our skiff drifting away. The pilot used the helicopter to blow our skiff back onto the beach. We secured the skiff with our anchor and headed up to our cabin. The helicopter landed but kept the engine running. Two people walked up to us. I recognized their green forest service uniforms. There was a lady and a guy. I noticed that the female agent was very attractive.

She started to ask us questions. She wanted to know if we had gotten permits to build the cabin. We said, "No." Then she asked if we knew that we had built our cabin on forest service land. We said, "No," and that we thought we had built the cabin on state land. She told us that they were going to have to write us a ticket and that we were going to have to tear the cabin down because it was built on forest service land without permission.

We were devastated and tried to plead with them that it would be a shame to have to tear down the cabin. If she was correct, and we were assuming she was, we told her that we would relinquish the cabin to the forest service and that it would be an asset for them. They would be able to use it and also rent it out like they did on other forest service lands all over the state. She emphasized that they wanted us to tear it down and said that we even needed a permit to have a tent camp there. As we were talking, I kept looking at her and thought that I recognized her. I started really looking at her and asked her if we knew each other from somewhere. She told me that she had never met me before. I told her that she looked undoubtedly familiar, and that I was positive that I had seen her before. She was really attractive, and it was driving me crazy wondering where I knew her from.

Then it hit me. I said, "I know where I have seen you. You were a *Playboy* centerfold. That was a really sexy spread. You were looking very seductive near a fireplace, and you were laying on a bear rug, with a flannel shirt lying next to you, and they called the spread "'Alaska Girl.'" Sonny started laughing, and she was obviously embarrassed. A lot of people really frowned upon *Playboy* and the models who posed for the magazine. She was quite flustered, and sternly told us to give them our addresses and that they would be sending us official tickets by mail, that would accompany a court date. We gave them our addresses, and they were on their way and flew off. We were thoroughly disappointed. Trapping season was coming to an end and we were running out of supplies. Now the Forest Service was kicking us out of our cabin. Besides kicking us out of the cabin that we paid for and built, they were making us tear it down, and writing us tickets.

Sonny chewed tobacco and he had now run out of it. He had become pretty grouchy. We were also out of whisky and brandy. We started arguing with each other and decided we needed to get to town. Even though it was unpleasant weather, we decided to go for it. We got in our canoe with a 15 hp motor and headed for Haines. On the way to town the seas built up to ten feet. It turned out to be really dangerous. I kept seeing flashes of newspaper clippings that showed two young men found dead. I could not ignore my intuition. We had the dog with us and he was really scared. Sonny was yelling at me to head across the bay. I said, "No! Let's go back to the beach." Right then we took a wave and it swamped the boat. We had not made it out very far from the beach, which was covered in ice and snow. The dog jumped out of the canoe and almost capsized us. I jumped out of the canoe into the water to stabilize the boat so that it would not turn over. We made it back to about ten feet from the beach and looked for a decent place to land the canoe. As soon as we got close enough, Sonny got into the water and pushed the boat up on the beach, which consisted of rocks covered in solid ice. The dog had taken off on a dead run while we were maneuvering the canoe on the rocks. There was no stopping him. I yelled and yelled, but he never even looked back. I gave up on the dog and we got the canoe pulled up the beach above the high tide line. This situation was bringing back memories of when I fell through the ice on the Takhin and almost died.

I saw some spots where the wind had blown the snow and there were patches of dry beach grass. I knew I had to get a fire started quickly. I gathered handfuls of dry grass. When I lit the dry beach grass, it worked as a fire starter. We gathered beach wood of all sizes, anything that was dry, and built a huge bonfire. We got warm, and the fire was burning so hot that we even got our clothes dried out. I talked to Sonny about how dangerous the situation was, and that we already had four friends die by capsizing in a boat. The best decision was to wait for the seas to calm down. He agreed and said that we really should not be out in this kind of weather in a canoe. After the tide had switched, the winds calmed down, and now it was marginally safe to make a go for it. We got back into the canoe and headed out, with no sign of my dog, Jake. We took off and made it to Cannery Cove where we had parked our truck. We finally got back to town and took a much-needed break.

Two weeks went by and all of a sudden Jake the Fake showed up on my doorstep. We found out that the dog had gone south to some people's property that had a homestead and raided their food supply. Then he ran to Pyramid Harbor and crossed the Chilkat River. All in all, that crazy dog did about a hundred-mile trek. I was not even really happy to see him. Jake had abandoned us out in the wilderness and caused a big problem when he ate the homesteaders' food that I had to replace.

We were ready to go back at it after a two-week break. We got geared up, got Sonny's boat, and went back out to get our gear. After that we had to tear down the cabin. We had to go to court and we each ended up getting an $800 fine. Even though the fine was a blow, we still made out pretty well trapping that winter.

CHAPTER 15

THE DEADLIEST CATCH

THIS SPRING THE OWNER OF the *Garm* took his boat out to the Alaska Peninsula to fish a False Pass fishing permit. That meant that I needed to find a new boat to fish. I looked around town for a dependable person whose boat I could fish for the season. There was a guy in town named Johnny Roth. I got a message to Johnny that I was looking for work. He said that he was looking for a fishing partner, and he asked me to come up to his house and talk. He was not known to be the best fisherman, and he was kind of a backwoods hillbilly. His house and yard looked like a garbage dump. He was a talented boat builder though. That winter he had hand built a 41 ft. stern picker and had a brand-new engine put in it. It was a pretty nice boat and he offered me a third share off of the top before expenses. I told him that one of my stipulations was that I was in charge of where and when we set the net. I was a really good fisherman and I was always in the top ten high liners of the fleet. He agreed. He kept his boat on a trailer twenty-seven miles from town instead of in the harbor. He had a crazy vision that a tidal wave was going to come and that he would survive because he would be able to get into his boat.

We headed out for the first opener. I did not realize that the windows in the cabin of the boat did not open, Johnny was a chain smoker, and I hated cigarette smoke. He smoked about five to seven packs a day. I had to stand outside most of the time just to breathe. Johnny always made the coffee, and it was what you call cowboy coffee. You could easily stand a spoon up in it. I tried to drink a cup and immediately got a gut ache. He kept the same pot of coffee on the stove for days and just kept adding water and coffee to the pot.

Despite the smoking and coffee, the fishing was going pretty well. We got 100 sockeye the first set, then 200, then 250. We were up at Point

Sherman and the fishing went dead. I told him we should go back to Seduction Point on the Chilkat side. My friend Bob Becker was up there and Johnny was starting to get under my skin. For now I told Johnny that I wanted to set off of my spot I called the circle jerk set. I call it this because the current pulls the boat and net around in a circle. He agreed and we got 100 fish on the first set, which is pretty good. I came inside from standing outside all day fishing and looked over at Johnny. He was washing dishes in a bucket. I thought, *That looks like the bucket we crap in.* The boat did not have a toilet and it is common practice to go in a five-gallon bucket. I asked Johnny, "Is that the same bucket we crap in?"

He said, "Yes, it is."

I yelled, "Johnny, that is SICK!"

He joked back, "Oh, it's no big deal. It all goes in and comes out the other end."

We were up in the circle jerk set and Johnny told me to come into the cabin. He needed to tell me something. I said, "All right, Johnny, what is it?" I was still feeling disgusted and nauseated.

With a really serious look on his face he said, "George, I had a vision you put my boat up on the rocks."

That was all I could take. I threw my hands up and said, "Johnny, I had a vision. I quit, and you are taking me over to Bob Becker's boat the *Nellie Bligh*, and I am jumping off of your boat on to his!"

He said, "What?"

I said, "Yes!"

I snatched the mic for the marine VHF and called Bob on the radio and asked him if he needed a crew member. He told me to get my ass over there. Johnny reluctantly took me over to Bob's boat. When I got onboard and my pack was stowed, I looked on the stove and Bob was cooking up deer steaks, onions, and potatoes. I was starving, and it was a relief to get off Johnny's boat. I came at the perfect time. Bob had gotten all the permits and had started a fish processing plant to process and sell his own fish without selling to the cannery.

He offered me 40 percent off the top if I fished his boat. For this crew share I had to gill and gut all the fish, keep the fish on ice, and bring the fish to his plant from the boat. I could hire a deckhand if I wanted or do all the work myself. I decided to do the work myself for the full 40 percent. Bob had even gotten his own ice machine to keep me supplied with plenty of ice. It was backbreaking work, but I was making really good money. Bob bought big freezer units to keep the flash-frozen fish in containers that you could put in a container for a truck. At the end of the season he had his freezer truck containers filled with a nice custom product. I had a pocket full of cash. He got on the ferry and took the fish down to Seattle. He sold to restaurants and set up stands off of the side of the road for top dollar.

That next winter I was thinking about who to approach about finding work, and Don Turner came to mind. He had a 55 ft. steel boat and two sons, Donnie Jr. and Lloyd, who worked the vessel. The father used the boat for crabbing and salmon trolling. During the winter they used the boat for crabbing, then they took off the crabbing gear and outfitted the vessel for power trolling salmon. I asked the dad for the winter crabbing job. He said that he had heard that I was a great worker and would love to have me onboard his boat. The older son, Donnie, was a diesel mechanic and together we worked on the boat that winter, taking the engine apart, and rebuilding it. Then we installed a water circulation pump in the fish hold. Crabs need constantly circulating water to keep them alive. If crabs die, they immediately release a poisonous toxin that can kill you if you eat them. There have actually been deaths caused by rotten crabs that had been left in the fish hatch. The dead crabs made a deadly gas, and when the hatch was opened, the people that breathed the gas died.

We worked for two months on rebuilding the engine and installing the single banger Italian Ruggerini motor. Then the three of us worked together and fixed the 125 crab pots. We totally went through all the pots and made them like new and the engine was completely gone through and rebuilt. We were going to be fishing for brown king and tanner crab. This fishery lasted ten weeks starting January 1 until March 15. The dad told me that his older son Donnie was the captain, but he wanted me to oversee everything and take over if they were doing anything that would get us injured or sink the boat. The sons were only twenty and twenty-one years old. I was twenty-seven and had a lot of experience. These young men were very messy and did not eat very good food either. They mostly ate junk food and Pop Tarts. I had to have good food to eat while I was working. Since we had a freezer full of deer and moose meat, I cooked real meals for us. I could not stand the messiness, so I would end up cleaning up all of the time, but I was hoping they would take the hint and clean up after themselves. They never did. I suppose being on a crowded boat and living in a mess did not bother them, but it drove me absolutely crazy. Especially because of how hard I worked, but I could not live in filth, so I grudgingly cleaned up the boat enough so it was not a complete pig stye.

After the boat was loaded with crab, we would pull all the gear and head to Pelican to sell our crabs. It was a ten-hour run that was always at night in the darkness. I would stay up all night on wheel watch, even after fishing non-stop all day, because I did not trust them to run the boat. I would rather run the boat and know I was safe than trust my life in their hands. I would have to say that crabbing was one of the toughest jobs I have ever done. Donnie would run the boat when we were pulling the pots. Lloyd and I would take turns coiling the crab line. Every two pots we would trade from coiling to running the hydraulics. We would pull and reset all 100 crab pots every day. We would find a spot that we thought would have crabs and set out a string of ten to twenty pots along a bench, then come back the next day and pull each pot and sort the crabs. We then baited the pots and got them set out again. If we didn't do well on a pull, we would stack the pots on the back deck and go make a set elsewhere. When we filled the crab tank full, we would run 140 miles to Pelican and pitch off our load, then head straight back to the crab grounds. We filled the boat about every two days and would make the ten-hour run to Pelican. We could have sold to closer processors in Juneau or Hoonah, but we had a deal with the plant in Pelican. They paid us an extra ten cents a pound, and for the extra fuel it took to run there.

It was usually very rough crossing Cross Sound on the Gulf of Alaska. It was normal to run into twenty-five- to thirty-foot seas. One bonus of the job was that anytime I wanted, I could take a crab out of the tank to eat. We kept a pot of water on the stove for steaming king crab. While we were fishing it was a quick, easy, and delicious meal packed with protein. Eating a crab leg would give me an energy rush. We welded a little bracket on the side of the exhaust pipe on the little single cylinder Ruggerini diesel engine that we had mounted on deck just behind the wheelhouse. It ran 24/7 as our circulation pump for the crab tank. We had a little saucepan with butter in it for our fresh, hot steaming crab. It was a heavenly treat to be able to eat fresh king crab out on deck while working. Grab a crab leg, break it, walk by the butter pan dip, and munch the fresh white meat slathered in butter! That is one food I could never get tired of eating.

When we were done fishing we would have a cocktail. The boys would have a wine cooler and I would have whisky and a beer. It is no exaggeration that crabbing is one of the hardest and most dangerous jobs out there. We fished in rough water and had freezing spray on the boat. We would constantly have to knock the ice off the boat with baseball bats.

While I was crabbing I earned a 15 percent crew share off the top. I could have hired another deckhand if I wanted to, but 5 percent would come out of my share. I chose to just work harder and keep the money. I did really well fishing with them for eight winters straight. In the 1970s and 1980s me and my friends fished in Glacier Bay. It was a very rich fishing ground and we always caught a lot of halibut, crab, and shrimp up there. We had discovered the place was full of fish. I liked to head there for ten days before the halibut opener to sport fish, testing different areas inside the bay. I would always throw out a few shrimp pots and feast on monster spot shrimp. I also knew how to catch king crab on a hook and line. I had my hibachi barbie onboard so we would eat like kings and have a blast. A few days before the halibut season would open, we would start baiting hooks and staging the gear to set out on opening day. After all the gear was set, we would go back to the first skate that we had set and start hauling in the gear. As we hauled in the gear, hooks were being baited again, and if we were catching fish, we would set it right back out. Fishing is a dangerous profession, but living the life I desired and making the amount of money I was earning made it worth the risk for me.

CHAPTER 16

FLYING HIGH

WHEN THE FISHING SEASON WAS over, I was hanging out at the airport at my friend Ernie Walker's shop. Ernie was a pilot, and A&P mechanic. He had two shops, one for stripping and painting airplanes, and one for mechanical work. I would do work for Ernie and he would give me flying time in his Cessna 150. It was a kind of a thrasher, but a good plane for learning. I flew with Ernie quite a bit. Besides the trainer plane, he had a nice 170 B Cessna tail dragger with big flaps. We did all kinds of winter flying in it, and even landed his plane on frozen lakes in front of glaciers, practicing ground loops. His shop is where I first met Iron Mike Ivers, who I later became very good friends with. Mike had his own air taxi in Yakutat called Gulf Air Taxi, and had brought a Cessna 207 over to have a complete annual inspection done on it. Ernie introduced us and then they talked for a few minutes. When I met Mike I could tell he had a toughness and ruggedness about him. I suppose he probably lived up to his nickname, Iron Mike. Mike said he wished he had more time to shoot the breeze but that he was in a hurry and had to get back to Yakutat. Before he left, he told me that if I were ever in Yakutat to stop by his air taxi and say hi. I told him that I would and had heard good things about the fishing and the flying in the Yakutat District. I told him I had been there commercial fishing, but would love to do some flying out that way. He shook my hand firmly and said he would show me around if I came over. He yelled out at Ernie to take good care of his plane, and Ernie promised that his 207 was in good hands. After he left I started trying to figure out a way to make it to Yakutat, and take him up on his offer.

I worked on planes with Ernie doing annuals, and then a plane came through the shop for a paint job. Ernie asked me if I wanted the job of stripping the paint off of it. I did not really want to do it, because it was a very nasty job using toxic liquid goop that you brushed on, waited a bit, and then you scraped the paint off. I told him that I would do it even though it was an awful job. I could be coerced into doing almost anything to get stick time.

That spring Ernie got called by the logging company to pick up a Cessna 185 on straight floats. He asked me to go with him down to Wrangell, and fly it back to Haines. There was a strip of compacted, hard snow with a layer of powder off the bank of the Chilkat River right next to the Haines airport. As we were getting close to Haines Ernie told me that was where he was going to land. He landed the floatplane on the snow. It was a thrilling experience and being able to land in snow was a unique skill. We taxied the plane close enough to the road where we could back Ernie's custom float plane trailer down to load the plane, then tow it to the shop. We did the annual on the plane, and then a week later we launched the plane in the middle of the night. We towed the plane on the trailer through town, backed it down the ramp, and put it in the boat harbor. Next morning we fired it up, taxied out and took off. We did a thirty-minute test flight, after everything checked out. We filed a flight plan and flew it back to Wrangell. I was thirsty to get any kind of flying experience that I could.

It was the first week in March and I was at Ernie's shop when a young lady pulled up in a little Chevy S-10 pickup with a camper on the back full of gear. We figured she had just come off the ferry. The young lady came up to us and introduced herself as Helen. She asked if anyone had a flight school there. Ernie started to talk with her. I lurked around in the shop trying to hear every word of their conversation without looking too nosey.

She asked why there were no flight schools around. Ernie told her that flight instructors were few and far between. Ernie was curious why she was asking. Helen said, "Because I am a flight instructor from Washington state and always wanted to see Alaska, so I packed my truck and got on the ferry. Now I am here and looking for a place like this to open a small flight school."

I overheard Ernie saying he thought he would be interested in pursuing the venture with her.

She asked, "Whose 150 is that?"

Ernie told her that it was his. Helen asked if he might be willing to use it as a trainer plane. Ernie had already told me how great it would be to have a flight school in Haines, and he told Helen that he would like to use the 150 for a training plane. He told Helen that he was very interested, and invited her into his office to talk further about the details. Helen and Ernie ended up working out a deal to start a flight school. I knew that I wanted to be their first student.

I took flying lessons from Helen in Ernie's Cessna 150 every possible chance I had. I soloed in only five hours. It takes most pilots twenty hours. I had soloed and was on my own in the plane, and got a taste of absolute exhilarating freedom.

My friend Donnie Jr., the captain on the crab boat, and his dad Don both wanted to learn to fly. They ended up taking lessons and they both got their pilot's license. They loved flying so much that they bought their own plane. They found a completely tricked-out Cessna 170B in Montana that had a bush stall kit and heavy landing gear. The engine had 180 hp with a constant speed prop, instead of 145 hp. We had a lot of fun flying around in their plane.

Word got out and I got three more people to sign up for flying lessons. Helen had nine students within a month. We got to know each other pretty well that year. She knew that I wanted to get a Piper Super Cub and asked me if I would like to go in partners with her on a plane. I was blown away, and said, "Are you kidding me? Of course!" Without hesitation, I jumped on the opportunity.

We were always looking in *Trade a Plane*, which is a newspaper-type flyer that advertises planes for sale. We found a cherry tricked-out 1947 Piper Super Cruiser PA-12 for sale. It had been completely rebuilt like new with a Piper Super Cub PA18 150 hp engine, heavy-duty landing gear, and tail feathers. The PA-12 is very similar to a Super Cub. The only difference is the fuselage. Right behind the pilot seat they widened it so it had a side-by-side back seat. If you take one and put in the bigger 150 hp engine, tail, and landing gear, they make one heck of a bush plane. Cubs are very popular in Alaska for the reason of being able to get in and out of tight areas, and being very durable when using it on remote unapproved bush landing strips. This particular plane was a one-owner aircraft. The owner had a custom rebuild on it from the frame up. It was just like a new plane. It even had a factory-new engine and a brand-new prop, not an overhaul. The owner was asking $22,000 for it. This was a great deal for that plane. I was definitely in! Helen and I flew commercial back east to Elmira, New York, picked up the plane, and flew it back to Alaska together. It was a sweet plane. We had good weather for the trip and it took us five days of flying to get home.

I wanted to start flying the Cub, so we were flying together a lot. Helen told me that if I could fly the plane from the back seat, she would turn me loose and solo me in the Cub. They say if you can fly a tail dragger from the back seat you can fly anything. After seven hours of flying with her in the Cub, she told me she wanted to see me do one flight around the patch with her in the back seat and then I would be ready to go on my own. She got out of the plane and we switched seats. I taxied out and took off. It felt really weird being in the front, so I did a big two-mile wide circle and came back around and lined up and landed on runway 08. We taxied over and I dropped Helen off. She said, "You are on your own now."

I was nervous, but excited. I taxied out and lined up on 08. I was so used to her being in the back seat, and having her 200 pounds of weight in the tail, that when I flew by myself from the front seat of the plane, I almost nosed it over on my first takeoff. I was holding full nose down trim and elevator to get the tail up, but with just me in the front seat, that tail came up fast and I was in the air swiftly.

Helen and I really hit it off and we became good friends. When I was not working, I would spend every spare minute I could flying the Cub.

CHAPTER 17

WESTBOUND TRAIN

GREG AND I HAD ALWAYS talked about going to Yakutat. More and more people were moving to Haines and it was getting more and more crowded. It went from being a quaint, quiet little town of 500 people to being a bustling town of 5,000 residents. People were developing property and we could barely trap without seeing other people. Greg found a set net permit for sale in the Yakutat district that came with a cabin and said we should go check it out.

The Yakutat district had a lot of benefits, such as 200 miles of fishing grounds. If you owned a permit, you could fish from the Alsek River all the way up the gulf coast to Cape Suckling. In some areas of Alaska, when you buy a set net site, you can't move. In this district you can move to any river in the area that the Department of Fish and Game opened. There were all species of fish in these rivers. King, sockeye, chum, silver, and pink salmon. For sport fishing there was also trout and steelhead in the rivers. Another unique thing about fishing in Yakutat is that you can fish up to one mile offshore in the ocean from the mouth of the river, and in Yakutat Bay you can fish with a seventy-five-fathom-long net called a bay net.

We flew out and checked the cabin site over. We had already spoken to a few people who had permits and they highly recommended the fishery. We even stopped in the Gulf Air Taxi to say hi to Mike and tell him what we were up to. Mike was happy to see me, and welcomed my brother and me in. Mike said he did a lot of flying for commercial fishermen on the remote rivers, and even had his own fishing permit. Mike told us that because of running his air taxi he did not fish as much as he would like, but he enjoyed it when he got a chance. He told us that his son Wayne commercial fished and made a good living at it. Before we left the office Mike told us that if we ended up coming back to fish that he would like to do the flying for my brothers set-net operation. Greg told him that there was no question that he would be flying with Gulf Air. After we left Yakutat, my brother ended up buying the permit with a cabin site on the Italio River. I was fishing the drift gill net fishery in Haines at the time, and then on the closures I would fly to Yakutat and fish with my brother. I loved the new area and really wanted to get my own permit to fish there. His cabin site was located in a spectacular area with forty miles of Yakutat forelands stretching from Yakutat Bay to the Alsek River, and about a fifteen- to twenty-mile stretch of sandy, hard-packed beach line between the mountains and the Gulf of Alaska. There are thousands of acres of giant, old-growth timber and beautiful wetlands, with long stretches of beaches with sand dunes covered with wild berries. The scenery of the Fairweather mountain range is absolutely breathtaking.

While I was fishing with my brother, I met the Miller family, who had a set net site up the beach from Greg. Doug, his wife, and his daughter were down there fishing. They had a valuable operation, that included a nice cabin, skiff, nets, and Doug also had an airplane. He was a pilot and A&I mechanic. I came to find out from the daughter that Doug had cancer and the family was selling the permit, plane, and set net site. It was sad that they had to sell it, but it was a good opportunity for me to get this permit. It would be perfect. My brother and I could fish together, and I would be able to fly the fish out. We could make a lot of extra money utilizing the plane and hauling fish.

That season the openers in Haines were getting shorter and I was able to fly over to Yakutat more often and fish with my brother. I decided that I really liked the area and the fishing was good. On top of it, there was a good market for hauling fish with Doug's 206 that was for sale with the deal. I talked to Doug and his family about purchasing the outfit. I had $4000 saved in cash. I offered them the $4000 as earnest money to take the permit off of the market. They agreed to sell me the cabin, permit, skiff, and gear for $40,000. They told me they would include the airplane for another $20,000. I thought it was a very good deal and was excited to sew it up. Helen and I were partners on the Cub and I asked her if she would be interested in partnering up with me on the flying end of the operation in Yakutat. She said that she would like to check it out, so I took her over there on a trip. She really liked the area too, and said that she would like to partner up with me on the deal. My offer to her was this: I was going to apply for a state loan for the permit that fall, and then we would become partners on the planes. She could make money hauling the fish with the plane. I would own the permit and cabin outright. She thought it was a fair deal and we shook on it.

The rest of the summer was going fantastic. Fall silvers started to show up on the Italio River where our set net camps were. I had flown out to fish with Greg, and he told me that there was something he wanted to show me. He took me outside where the light was better. There was something on his neck. It was a weird bump on his throat. I told him he should get it checked out right away. Greg was pretty tough and stubborn and thought it was no big deal. He did say that after fishing was done in October he would get it checked out at the clinic. But in one month the lump grew from the size of an eraser head to the size of the end of a thumb. I knew it was serious and was scared that it was cancer. Greg went to the doctor after he closed up his camp and found out that it was cancer, a very dangerous and serious cancer. I was completely devastated. I had all these plans with my brother and could not believe this was happening. Jane and his kids were distraught. Greg had smoked a pipe for years and where the lump was located happened to be on the side of his throat where the pipe had been sitting in his mouth all of those years. Meanwhile, I had already given the money to the Millers for the permit and was approved for the state loan, so I decided to follow through with my plan.

The doctors put Greg on chemotherapy for a month, and then I had Greg stay with me. I put him on a super health food program. Debbie and I were really into organic and holistic health food. We had been reading books about the healing factors of massive doses of vitamin C, and eating organic food. We worked together on giving Greg a program of barley greens, wheat grass, and 30,000 units of vitamin C. We bought cases of cabbage and carrots and juiced them up for him. The doctors still wanted to treat him with chemotherapy and zap the cancer with radiation. Greg stayed on my program for twelve weeks and when he went back to the doctor, amazingly the tumor was gone.

I had to go crabbing that winter and Greg went back home to Chistochina. Before I left for fishing, I drove to Anchorage with him when he went in for a checkup. They did tests and did not find any cancer. It was a miracle, but the radiologist was not convinced that Greg was healed. He told Greg that he was not out of the woods yet and that he should get treated with radiation. That would be sure to kill any cancer cells that might still be in his system. The radiologist actually told Greg that not getting the radiation would be like walking into a grizzly bear's den without a gun. Even though Greg's health was showing major signs of improvement by the day, the doctor insisted on continuing the treatment. I could not understand why they would want to continue treatments and advised Greg not to do it, since there was not any sign of a tumor. Jane had been pressuring Greg to get the treatments, and with what the radiologist told him about the bear den, Greg decided to take the recommendation of the doctor. I was in disbelief. I thought Greg was healing. When Greg made up his mind there was not much anyone could do about it. I tried my best to talk him out of it, but there was no changing his mind.

As soon as I was done crabbing, I raced the 525 miles up north to Greg's house to see how he was doing. When he came out on the porch, I got a good look at him and could not help but start crying. He looked terrible. He looked like death. He looked like he had aged twenty years in two months. I tried to hold back my tears, but as tough as I was, I broke down. When Greg showed me his mouth and tongue, I could not believe my eyes. His tongue was black and burnt from the radiation and split down the middle. Greg was a big, strong man, but he had lost at least thirty pounds in two months, and I could tell he was in severe pain.

It was March now and normally it was a time of year that I looked forward to. Greg and I had been going bear hunting with a friend of his from up in the interior. We had a brown bear hunt planned for May. We had already planned on going to the Italio camp in April to get everything opened up and ready for the season. I flew the Super Cub up to Greg's house in April to pick him up, and we flew out to the Italio. We got to camp and got all settled in. Greg and I went out to the beach dunes and were looking up at Mount Fairweather enjoying the dramatic view when Greg got all choked up. He looked at me and started crying. He said he was not ready to die. At forty-two years old he was too young, and he had so much that he still wanted to do. I could not help but get choked up as well, and I tried to assure him by telling him to keep the faith and that it was going to be fine. I knew right then that it was probably going to be our last spring bear hunt together.

Charlie would be coming in about ten days and we had a lot of work to do opening up the camp. We got the ATVs going, went beach combing for glass balls, and looked for bear signs. Finding Japanese glass floats was one of our favorite pastimes out at camp. It was like treasure hunting, and finding one was like finding a piece of gold. We found some nice logs on the beach to cut up for firewood. The beaches on the Italio were phenomenal. The ocean beaches on the coastline are nice, hard-packed sandy beaches. We went about five miles west to the Dangerous River. I had a 16 ft. flat-bottom riverboat and I used 2x12 ft. planks for loading and unloading ATVs on the skiff. We drove the three-wheeler into the boat and took it across the Akwe River and then unloaded it. When we got to the Akwe Spit, we drove my twenty miles east to the Alsek River.

We found numerous Japanese glass balls and a lot of strange, random debris that had washed up on the beach over the winter. The Japanese fishermen used glass balls to float their nets before we started using corks. There are all different kinds of floats. Large ones were about the size of a basketball, and some were bigger than that with netting still on them. We found a lot that were the size of a small apple. Others were grapefruit size, and some the size of a tangerine. Some of them had special symbols stamped on them. I found out the stamps meant different things, ranging from belonging to a certain fishing fleet or the company that made them. Some even came from the imperial royal fishing fleet. Those would usually be a special magenta color.

Now that we had everything shipshape, the plan was for me to fly back to Haines, get my Cub, and come back to camp. Charlie was supposed to fly to Yakutat, where we were supposed to pick him up. I only had a small window of time to get the Cub. There was a weather front moving in, so this would be my only chance to get the plane before the storm hit. I got in my 206 and flew to Yakutat. I got on a jet to Juneau and from there I had to fly Haines Airways, but everyone called it Haines Scareways. These flights usually ran late and, low and behold, my flight was delayed for about an hour. There is not much daylight and it gets dark early. I knew it would be marginal getting back to camp with little or no daylight left.

I got to Haines and Debbie was at the airport to meet me. She knew I would be hungry so she brought me a pizza from our local pizzeria. I threw the pizza in the back seat of the Cub, kissed Debbie goodbye, and did my preflight on the plane. I did not have time for any chitchat. I needed to get going ASAP. I could see the sky was getting dark and a storm was moving in rapidly. The wind was already gusting at thirty miles an hour out of the southeast. I got in the plane, called flight service, filed a flight plan, and took off on runway 08 into the wind. I did a right downwind bank and was headed westbound with a thirty-mile-an-hour tailwind up the Chilkat Valley. I headed for the mountains. I looked at my watch and said a little prayer for the Lord to watch over me and protect me on my flight. I knew by now it would be dark by the time I made it to the Italio. I might even have to keep flying east and land at the Yakutat airport where there would be runway lights. I would have to make that decision when I got there. I already had an anxious feeling from getting such a late start out of Haines, and knew I was probably going to have to land my plane in darkness. I knew though that this would be the only shot I would have to make it back to the Italio before the predicted storm. This could very well be my last bear hunt with my brother who was very sick with throat cancer, and I would do everything in my power to get there.

I fought to keep my Cub under control as I headed through the mountain pass. The winds were gusting at forty knots on the upward side of the pass, creating severe updrafts and severe turbulence. I had the throttle pulled back to almost an idle and was getting sucked up almost into the cloud base, and it was very difficult to keep the aircraft under control. I was visualizing in my mind what my good friend Mike Ivers had told me.

He said to practice and get proficient at flying the pass on clear days, and mark the dead-end canyons and crevices on a chart, because one wrong turn could mean death. Now I was flying on the leeward side of the pass. I glanced at my instruments and was descending 1000-1500 feet per minute. Even with the engine at full throttle and the trim set for the best rate of climb, I was getting sucked down rapidly. I was hitting pockets of turbulence that would thrash the plane around like a kite. Looking out the airplane window to my right, the mountainside loomed 300 feet off my wingtip. This was a bad situation. There was barely any visibility because of the heavy snow showers. When there was visibility, it was about a quarter of a mile at best. Sweat was pouring off of my brow from the tension of keeping my plane from crashing. My brother was waiting for me at camp, and death waited for me with open arms on the side of a mountain.

I made it to Gateway Knob, which was at the confluence of where the Tatshenshini River dumps into the mighty Alsek River, suddenly the weather broke open. The snow stopped and I had a 1700 ft. ceiling with ten to fifteen miles of visibility. The valley opened up, reducing the turbulence from severe down to moderate. I let out a huge sigh of relief, grabbed my water bottle, and guzzled some water. I followed the Alsek River down to the Gulf of Alaska and turned due west along the coastline where I could see the white surf breaking. It was now getting dark with only twenty-five miles left to go. I knew Greg would have lights set up for me as a threshold. Sure enough, when I was about ten miles out, I could see ATV lights. Greg had two three-wheelers sitting twenty feet apart with the headlights pointed down the airstrip. The red taillights were my threshold. The wind was twenty miles an hour on my tail so I flew downwind, looked at the setup, and did a nice easy standard rate turn back for the strip. I got lined up and touched down right between the ATVs. I knew I had just cheated death. I was excited to get unloaded and tie the plane down so I could have a celebration shot of whisky! Greg came over to the plane and gave me a big grizzly bear hug and told me how glad he was that I had made it.

Charlie arrived the next day on Alaska Airlines. By afternoon the severe storm front had passed. I wanted to stay at camp so we decided to get him a charter flight out with Gulf Air instead of me flying to town to pick him up. When Mike landed at the strip, we got him unloaded out of the plane, and carried his gear up to the cabin. I was going to cook us some moose steaks that I had brought from home. Charlie was ecstatic. Our cabin was pretty rustic, a modest 14x24 ft. framed-in plywood shack. I had wires going to the generator so we could run lights. I had flown down a standard-size household propane stove for cooking. There were four bunks in back. In the main part of the cabin I had built a little table with bench seats, and had a wood stove for heat.

After Charlie got settled in, we joined him for a few Scotches by the campfire and told bear stories. I went inside and seared up some moose steaks in the cast iron skillet and made some baked potatoes. The next morning we were going to head out for an early morning glassing of the dunes for big brown bears. Greg told us he was going to hit the hay and he went to bed. Charlie and I stayed up. I waited awhile and let Greg get to sleep, and then I came right out and told Charlie I needed to ask him a serious question. I said, "So, Charlie, in your honest opinion, what are my brother's chances?"

Charlie hesitantly responded, "I cannot really say."

I came back and said, "Come on, Charlie, just give me your opinion with your experience. What do you think?"

Charlie hemmed and hawed and then finally said, "He is not doing well and does not have long. Six months at the most."

My heart sank. At least he was honest. I knew then that I needed to make the most of our last few months together. I needed to think about the next day and concentrate on getting a bear.

Greg and I got up early and made coffee and breakfast. Charlie joined us. Charlie had brought some interesting reading material with him. His radiology books with weird pictures of anatomy. One in particular had women's breasts. We teased him and asked him if he wanted to borrow one of our *Playboy*s. He laughed and said no.

I decided we should go out hunting. Charlie said he wanted to stay at the cabin, but that I should go glass for bears, and if I saw something, to come back and get him. I wanted Charlie to come with me, but he was dead set on staying at the cabin, so I took my three-wheeler to where I had my skiff secured in the river on an anchor and pulley system. I got in my skiff and headed up the river to a beach dune that was a good place to glass for bears. I got up there with my binoculars and started glassing. All of a sudden I saw Big Red. He was a monster bear that had been living down on the Italio. He was an old bear with very red fur, so we named him Big Red. Big Red was a smart bear and we usually only saw him in the summer when it was not open for hunting bears. I believe that animals have a keen sense of when hunting seasons begin and end. Bears do not get big and old by accident. They are very smart and they mostly only come out at dark during the spring and fall hunting season. It was pure luck that I happened to see this particular bear. Of course, Charlie was not with me. I stealthily snuck back to my skiff and then as quietly as I could ran my skiff back to where my three-wheeler was parked. I raced back to my cabin where Charlie was reading his breast book. I came in out of breath and told Charlie that I saw Big Red and that he was stupid for not coming with me! So Charlie hurriedly got his gear on and grabbed his gun. Greg came along as well, and scolded Charlie for not taking the hunt more seriously.

We got to the skiff and then out to the dunes and to our glassing spot. Big Red was nowhere to be found. We took the skiff over to where I had spotted Big Red. We saw where his tracks had come down the bluff and crossed the river into the dense woods. "Well," I said, "that is probably the last time we are going to see him. Nice going, Charlie! You were in the cabin reading your titty book and missed your chance at a trophy bear. It is only once in a blue moon that we see Big Red, especially during hunting season."

Greg agreed and told Charlie, "You really screwed up by not going with George this morning."

We could tell Charlie felt bad. We ended up hunting for the next ten days, and did not see any bears worth shooting. We made the most out of the trip though. That area of the coast is beautiful, and we went beach combing and found Japanese glass balls, which is a treat that not many people get to experience. We also went fishing up the river and we caught some nice trout. Soon enough it was time for Charlie to go back home, and Greg and I to finish getting ready for fishing. I knew my brother was in severe pain, but we had a good time regardless. I also knew in my heart that these were the last few months that I was probably going to spend with Greg, so I made it a point to have the best time possible.

CHAPTER 18

FACING THE INEVITABLE

I KNEW GREG WAS IN too much pain to fish, and not long after Charlie was gone, Greg approached me and told me that as much as he did not want to, that he had to go home. We were silent and an overwhelming sadness came over me. I told him that I was distraught, and torn up inside. He tried to tell him not to worry that he had come to terms with the situation and that it was just a part of life. I told him that I would see him at the end of the season, and to be strong. We hugged and he told me to be strong, and that he was looking forward to me coming to visit him after fishing.

Greg went back to Chistochina and stayed home. He stayed on very powerful morphine painkillers, just to endure the pain that he was in. I knew that I would have a break in the beginning of August before silvers started showing up, and that would be a good time to go see Greg. I had made arrangements with my dad, and he had gotten an airline ticket to come up from Florida. My dad had found a medical doctor that had developed an innovative experimental cure for cancer that was new then. It was a black serum with electrolytes in it, and Dad told me that he would be bringing the medicine with him. Our dad and my outcast brother Barry flew to Haines, and I was there to meet them at the airport in my pickup. Dad looked at the truck and told me that he thought it would be more comfortable for us if he rented a car, instead of driving the 550 miles to see Greg in my standard Ford pickup. I agreed, and I took him over to the car rental place and we found a four-door sedan. After renting the car, we started our trek. On the way to Greg's we had to go through the Canadian border, and then back through customs to enter the United States. When we went through customs, the border patrol went out of their minds when they saw the vials of serum in a suitcase. My brother Barry was a real hippie-looking character with big, curly, afro-like hair, and freaky bulging eyeballs.

He was the oddball of the brothers because the rest of us were really handsome, but he was sort of ugly, and strange.

The border patrol found the suitcase and was convinced that the serum was some kind of drug and that we were dealers. They were also suspicious because my dad and brother had Florida drivers licenses. My dad went ballistic on the staff and lost his temper because we were all emotional about Greg dying. We were afraid the Canadians would confiscate the serum, and then we would not be able to get it to my brother. Finally, we got the scientist on the phone who had created the serum, and he explained to the border patrol exactly what it was. It was two hours of complete hell. We were lucky to get ahold of him on a landline. We finally got released from the border office and were on our way to my brother's house.

I came to find out that Barry had been on drugs down in Florida, and that he was a hard-core cocaine addict. I caught him snorting coke, and I was furious when I found out. We could have all been arrested. I did not even tell my dad or he would have totally lost his temper and who knows what would have happened. With everything going on I did not have it in me to get into an argument with Barry over it.

It was an emotional arrival at Greg's house. My dad gave Greg the serum. Greg looked terrible and I could smell death in the air. I was used to seeing Greg as a big, strong man, but now he that was so thin and sickly looking it was tough to take for all of us. We had our visit and tried to act normal, but it was very difficult. My other brother Ben flew up from Florida to see Greg also. After the short visit, my dad and Ben had to get back to Florida, and I had to get back to Yakutat for silver fishing. My brother Barry was on the outs with his wife and offered to stay and help. Greg agreed to sign his permit over to my brother for the season on a medical transfer. Barry said that he would go back to Florida and tell his wife it was over, and then come back to Alaska for the season. When I left Greg, I had a feeling that it would be the last time I would see him alive. I left with a heavy heart, but there was not much I could do. The facts were that Greg was dying, and I had to make a living. I flew back to the Italio and brought my brother back up to fish Greg's permit under the condition that he stay off of drugs. I had too much on the line to risk getting my aircraft taken away or being in any kind of legal trouble. I could not believe how thoughtless and selfish Barry was to bring drugs with him from Florida and put us all at risk. It was hard for me to leave, and I hugged my brother and did not want to let go. It was hard for me not to start crying, but I choked back the tears and had to be strong. I told Greg that I would be back in October and to get better. He said that he would be there waiting for me. I left with Dad and Barry. It was a pretty quiet drive back to Haines, but thankfully we did not have any problems at the border.

Barry got back to Alaska after making a trip to Florida. He was a total cheechako greenhorn. He was also a city party boy and tenderfoot. I had to teach him everything about Alaskan life, and literally how to work. To get back at my brother for the stunt he pulled with smuggling the cocaine kit through Canada, I wanted to play a prank on him. On the flight over from Haines to the Italio, I was telling him all about Helen, my pilot friend. I told Barry that she was a hot babe and that they would hit it off. My brother was all excited. When we arrived at camp, he was in for a big surprise. Helen was pretty, but she was tall and weighed about 200 pounds. She was very strong, but I told my brother she looked like a Playboy model. She was anything but. She was an excellent pilot and a hard worker, but kind of animalistic. I think you kind of have to be that way to live the kind of lifestyle we were living. Helen greeted us when we arrived at camp and had a wonderful fried chicken dinner ready. My brother gave me a dirty look when he saw Helen in person. She was a little different than I described her. Barry was a pretty shallow person, so it did not surprise me that he thought that Helen was not pretty. The icing on the cake for my brother was when Helen actually ate the cartilage right off the pieces of chicken and sucked vigorously on the bones. I thought it was funny, but Barry was not amused and had a disgusted look on his face. He pulled me aside after dinner and told me that he could not believe that I told him that she was a hot babe. I said did he really think some Playboy model-looking girl would be living in a rustic cabin at a commercial fishing site with no running water? She was a really strong, young lady that worked hard and was also a good friend and my partner. I told him that he had better treat her well and not be so superficial. I believe it would have been a total distraction to have some hot-looking girl down there. My brother would probably not get any work done. That was what we were there for anyway and we did not need any distractions.

We were in the middle of the silver season in September when a severe storm hit the gulf coast. Rain was blowing horizontally, and there had not been much flying going on. This storm was happening during our fishing opener. There was a quarter mile visibility, drizzle, and fog. We just happened to be at the cabin after checking our net and all of a sudden we heard a plane. It was Danny Farmer who was a member of the Remis/Smokestack family and a friend of mine. He had risked flying down to my cabin in this severe weather and in my gut I knew it had to be bad news. When he got out of the plane, the look on his face told me that he was here to tell me something important. I had a feeling it was about Greg. Danny approached my brother and me with a somber look on his face. He said, "George, I have bad news. Your brother passed." He gave me a hug. Barry and I started to tear up and we invited Danny inside, but he said he needed to get the plane back to town.

Danny took off and Barry and I went inside and shed some tears and mourned the loss of our oldest brother. We had a toast in remembrance of our brother Greg. It was a very sad day, but a relief in a way because we knew how much pain Greg was in. When the opener ended, I flew to town and called Jane. Jane told me how Greg's life came to an end. She told me that he was in so much pain he had to go to the hospital. He was too sick to stay at home. She said he read the Bible and prayed a lot. He was kept loaded up on morphine for the pain. He did not want to be on any kind of life support or revived if he were to die. He just wanted to let go. He spent two days in the hospital and was lying in bed with Jane at his side. She said he sat straight up in bed and said to her, "I love you, I love God, but it is time for me to go." Then he exhaled and died.

My brother was cremated and he wanted his ashes to be spread on top of a bench at 10,000 feet on Mt. Sanford. We had a famous bush pilot from Haines, one of the Ellis brothers, fly up there and drop his ashes out. I could not leave my commercial fishing operation to attend the memorial so we had our own memorial for Greg at our set net camp. Greg was so much a part of my life. It was a very sad time for me. Everyone goes through loss, but Greg was so young and I always thought we would grow old together. I thought our kids would grow up together, and we would be alongside each other for years to come.

I finished the rest of the season. Barry helped me close up the camp, and then he flew back to Florida. I went back to Haines to get ready for crabbing. As I was flying back over the mountains, I said a prayer for my brother. I missed Greg tremendously. I had to be strong though, and stay strong. Jane was having a very difficult time. All of her family lived in Michigan, and we were the only family she had in Alaska. Even then, I lived 525 miles from their house. She also had four kids to take care of by herself. They had no savings or life insurance. The only thing they had was their property and set net permit. I had a talk with Jane and told her that if she wanted to sell the house and move back to Haines, Debbie and I would help her out. We could also find someone to fish the permit. They did not outright own it and had a loan from the state that they had to make payments on. Jane was so distraught she could not deal with everything. She wanted to be close to her family so she packed up and took the kids down to Michigan.

Jane sold everything of Greg's, including his traps, guns, and anything of value. I was out fishing at the time and was so sad because my brother and I had a lot of things that we had bought together. The only thing of my brother's that I got from Jane was his .22 Ruger pistol that we used while we were trapping. Jane let the house, property, and permit go to the state. What a shame. I was really saddened by the whole ordeal, but it was because she did not have any help. I did offer to help, but I was always out fishing. I really wanted to see them stay and the kids grow up in Alaska, but Jane could not handle everything by herself.

The next spring was my second season herring spotting and I took the Cub to Sitka. I had flown over 700 hours the previous year in the PA-12. Wayne Alex had called me and asked if I would be his spotter again, and I jumped on it. Spotting for herring is very dangerous and is considered one of the most dangerous jobs besides commercial fishing in Alaska. It was a way I could make a good amount of money in a short period of time. This season there were about thirty airplanes spotting within a two-mile radius. I spent seventeen days in Sitka and flew thirty hours during the opener. I put Wayne's boat on some good sets. One set weighed in at 220 tons. That season our crew share was $34,000 each. Commercial fishing was always a gamble, not only with money, but your life. I was glad to walk away from this season with both.

As soon as I was done spotting I needed to head right for the Italio and get ready for the sockeye season. There was a permit for sale, and I told Harry that he should buy it and we could fish together as a team. He was all for it. I even told him he could use my brother Greg's cabin to fish out of, which was a real benefit to him because it would have cost him a lot more if he were to buy someone's camp or build his own. Harry bought a permit from one of the Bensen brothers. I used my 206 and made multiple trips for him to get his camp set up. I had to haul my own supplies as well. I made about eight trips from Haines to the Italio to get ready for the season.

Now that Greg was gone it was going to be tough being there without backup. Even though Barry would be fishing with me, he could not even hold a candle to Greg. Yakutat was a small village that was very prejudiced against what Alaskans call "outsiders." This town in particular was very hateful even toward Alaskans. If you did not have native blood in you, then most people from Yakutat shunned you and would not have anything to do with you. They would not even pee on you if you were on fire. Regardless, I ended up making a few allies.

Iron Mike Ivers had Gulf Air Taxi there and we had become friends from the minute we met back at Ernie's shop. Mike was also the one that so-called "broke my cherry" while flying the 206 that I bought with my set net permit. At the time I had most of my time in smaller airplanes. It was quite the experience the first time that I flew the 206. When I bought the Cessna 206 from the Millers, it was hangared in Yakutat. I flew over from Haines to pick it up. I went over the plane with a fine-tooth comb several times and read through the operator's manual. I asked Mike if he would take a flight around the patch with me and give me some pointers. He had already given me a good talk about flying the 206 and its operating procedures, so I fired it up and we taxied out for takeoff. There was a fifteen-knot wind out of the east so I lined up on runway 11 and poured the coals to it. I was amazed at the amount of torque and power there was. You had to apply a lot more pressure on the right rudder to keep the nose straight down the centerline of the runway. We went airborne quickly and flew about 500 feet out and away from the runway, then made a big circle around, came back in, and landed. Mike yelled out, "We cheated her again!" Meaning death.

"You are good to go, George. Just remember what I told you about flying through the mountains." At that point I was on my own. There is a certain fear, or even panic that you experience when being left alone to solo in a new aircraft, but overcoming the uneasiness is the most exhilarating feeling one can have. To live my lifestyle I was always pushing myself and overcoming obstacles even in the most adverse situations. A person would not advance very far in this unforgiving environment if they did not have the fortitude and willpower of a warrior.

I ended up moving to Yakutat lock, stock, and barrel. Majestic Air was an air taxi in town flying commercial fishermen. One of my good friends, Chuck, was flying for them. I asked Chuck if he could do a DC-3 load from Haines to the Italio for me. He cleared it with the office and said sure thing. I got a storage unit in the old World War II hangar in Yakutat and we loaded up the DC-3 in Haines. Debbie, the boys, our two Chesapeake Bay retrievers, and our worldly possessions were flown to the Italio, and we unloaded everything we needed to homestead our cabin. What was left got flown from there to Yakutat. We put the rest of everything into storage. When we did find a place, we would then have our household wares nearby to make our home cozy. We had everything we needed at camp. One thing I loved about Haines was that there were wild raspberries, but at the Italio we had salmonberries and acres of wild strawberries. We even brought out supplies for starting a garden. We made planters and Debbie planted a variety of lettuce and potatoes, which grew well down there.

Our fishing and flying operation was running efficiently, and on the closures we had really good subsistence fishing. Debbie and I smoked and jarred fish. During the openers, I fished and flew fish to town with my 206. Everything was going as planned. Helen came down and started helping me fly fish, and she actually helped me commercial fish. You have to be a really talented pilot to fly off sandy beach strips with heavy loads of fish. Most of the time there were severe crosswinds and downdrafts. The runways ranged from 800 to 1200 feet long where you absolutely had to get the plane off the ground. There was no aborting takeoff. You either got the plane off the ground or you crashed. The last thing I wanted was for that to happen.

In October we were wrapping up the fishing operation and got our seasonal moose. While we were closing our camp, I started to realize that Helen had developed an infatuation for me. We were good friends and spent a lot of time together, but I had never given her any reason to believe that I had any other kind of feelings for her. Admittedly, I knew she had a crush on me. Even though I was married, I was used to having girls give me the eye. A lot of girls are attracted to men like me who are tough, rugged, handsome, and can fly an airplane. Her infatuation developed into something a little more intense. Helen approached me and asked me to leave my wife. I had no desire to leave Debbie, as the infatuation was one sided. Helen turned jealous and protective of me. She threatened that if I did not leave my wife, she was going to take the planes away from me. She already had my logbook in her possession because she was supposed to sign off a lot of flight time that we had done together, which only a certified flight instructor could do. She even went so far as to threaten to keep my logbook if I did not accept her sexual advances. I told her she was completely unprofessional and unethical, and she would never get away with that. I also told her that by her actions I would never have the urge to have anything to do with her. I told her I thought it would be best if we severed our partnership and came to an amicable agreement. We had a business meeting in Juneau, and agreed to a pact that ended the partnership that we had in the airplanes. She kept the PA-18 and I kept the 206, and we called it even. She eventually gave me back my flight log, but she never signed off on the time that we flew together. Flight instructors charged a pretty penny for that time. If I were to pay an instructor for all of the hours that I could have had in my logbook, it would have cost me thousands of dollars. By then I was just happy that she had decided to leave town and did not cause me any marital problems. I loved my wife, and the last thing I wanted was to have Debbie think I was unfaithful.

Harry went back to Haines. During the season I had made friends with the owner of Leonard's Landing Lodge. Leonard's Landing used to be a cannery on the waterfront that had gone out of operation and came up for sale. Old man Leonard bought it and turned it into a sport fishing lodge. Since it was shut down for the winter, and Leonard needed someone to take care of it, he gave us a great deal on the bunkhouse that had numerous bedrooms, a nice living room, a bathroom, and a telephone. We had the whole building to ourselves, and that was where we spent our first winter in Yakutat.

Leonard's Landing was a few miles out of town and we kept to ourselves. I did have the occasional run-in with some of the locals. There was a local fishing guide named Hank living out there in another building. He and his wife were always having problems. She was always out running around, hanging out in bars, getting drunk, and cheating on him. In short, they would get in crazy fights. One evening his wife came running to us all beaten up. She asked us for help and said that Hank had beaten her. I confronted Hank and told him that he shouldn't beat women. He told me to mind my own business. I really didn't want to get involved, but I didn't like seeing a woman get hurt, even if she was cheating on him. Hank was known as a rough character that had actually gotten 86'd for life from the Glass Door Bar for stabbing someone. I think he did a little jail time for it, but Yakutat was a lawless town and people got away with quite a bit. Hank was an ex-army sniper, but I was not afraid of him. I've had confrontations with worse and tougher people than him. We ended up having only the one confrontation and stayed out of each other's way the rest of the winter.

I asked Debbie that winter if she would like to stay in town with the boys at the lodge. That way they could go to school instead of being homeschooled, and she would have a comfortable place to stay with running water instead of the rustic commercial fishing cabin with an outhouse. She thought that would be a good idea, so we made plans to enroll the boys in school. By the time I had to get camp ready for fishing, I found out that old man Leonard had unexpectedly gotten sick. We had been working on a deal to use the lodge for a place to live and to run some of my own sport fishing trips out of there. It was not long after we had found out that he was sick that he suddenly died. When he died, his family immediately took over the lodge and it turned into a mess. I stayed out of it, looked around town, and found out that Gary Grey had a house for rent. I called him and asked him if his rental house was available, and he said it was, so I snatched it up.

Debbie was happy, but a little sad because of old man Leonard dying. She also enjoyed being down at the camp living the subsistence lifestyle. Both of us knew it would be a lot more comfortable for her and the boys. I could bring her fish from the river to jar, and there were also plenty of places around town to pick berries to make homemade jams and jellies.

CHAPTER 19

SKIPPY-JACK-JAKE

I WAS GETTING MORE AND more into sport fishing. There were a few cabins put up by the forest service for people who would fly down with Gulf Air Taxi. They would rent a cabin or set up tent camps to go sport fishing. Most of the time guys would need help, so on the closures I ended up helping some of them out, taking them up the river in my jet boat. I had secret spots up the Italio and Akwe rivers where no one else dared to venture. There were some amazing cutthroat trout fishing holes up there. Some guys from town decided to build a cabin to rent to sport fishermen, also known as sportys. They bought an existing cabin site to use that was an old fish-buying station and got a sport fish cabin site user permit. They fixed it up and turned it into a rental cabin. The partnership was between two guys and the son of one of the partners. We ended up nicknaming them Skippy-Jack-Jake.

Skip Byman was the station manager for Yakutat Alaska Airlines. Jake owned the hardware store in town that we called the "Buck Stops Here," True Value. We called it that because everything was so expensive. When you needed anything, such as lumber or supplies, your money came to an abrupt stop there. Jake had a son named Vince, but everyone called him Tiger. When Jake introduced his son to us, the son had a hat on his head with a fake pile of crap on the bill, and he said, "This is my son, shit for brains." I laughed my ass off. I thought, *What a strange way to introduce your son to people.*

In the winter prior to the sockeye fishing season, the Akwe had been eroding and the whole river was moving west. It ended up eating its way through the dunes and eventually moved so far that it made its way to the Italio. It started flowing into the Italio instead of the ocean.

From my cabin I had to cross the river on my ATV to get to the Italio to fish. I could only do this at low tide. I had to make a new trail, and then I built a tent camp at the confluence of the river where it was flowing into the Alsek. I called this my Italoway camp. It took Harry and me weeks of work to get the trail to where it was good enough to haul fish on. The original trail was an existing bear trail that we called Bear Alley. The bears had beaten a path through the alders and they had created a sort of tunnel. We cut it out big and wide enough to drive our ATVs and trailers through.

The Department of Fish and Game closed the mouth of the river and put the regulatory marker one mile up the river. There was a 6:00 a.m. opening and we thought everyone was going to be down at the mouth marker, fighting for the front sets. We were kind of worried, because there were people who had already claimed the front sets and there was no room for us to fish. We decided to make our sets up river and found some good holes where some fish were holding. We were working our nets and all of a sudden here comes Mortensen, who we had nicknamed Morten Snookie. He had always fished the upper holes of the river. He came up to us on his ATV. He looked mad. We never had any disagreements before because we never fished near each other. Now that we had to fish the upper river he was not too delighted to see us. He was the chief pilot and check airman for Gulf Air Taxi. Mortensen gave us his two cents, and then headed up the river to find a set with some fish in it. Unfortunately, there were always going to be confrontations in a competitive fishery.

Besides having disagreements with commercial fishermen, we were having a dispute with Skippy-Jack-Jake. They did not like it that our fish hauling trail went past their cabin. We had already had a few words about it, but we did not have any other alternative. We had to get our fish from the river to my airstrip, and the only place we could make a trail was past their cabin.

It was very early in the morning. The opener started at 6:00 a.m. Harry and I were heading from our Italoway camp to my main cabin. We were not hauling fish yet. We were driving slowly, less than ten miles an hour. We were cruising along and I was in front. All of a sudden I felt something like a wire across my neck. I quickly grabbed the wire and pulled it over my head, and I came to an abrupt stop. Harry was right behind me. I got off my ATV and inspected the wire. Someone had tied a metal wire across our trail at the head and neck level. We had been fishing and knew where everyone was. If any of the commercial fishermen were the culprits, they would have had to go past us to be able to do this. The only people who could have done this were Skippy-Jack-Jake. I told Harry to stay at the wire and guard it while I took off for Jake's cabin.

I came to a spot in the trail where there was a dune that you had to drive down. Something did not look right. I slowly pulled up to it. Someone had spent the night digging out the bank so that if someone would have driven off it, they would plummet straight off a fifteen-foot cliff bank instead of driving down a natural slope. If I would have driven off this cliff bank, especially with a load of fish, I could have been seriously injured or killed. I found a way around the dangerous bank. By then I was almost to their cabin. There was a logjam that had formed with huge beach logs. Earlier that summer, Harry and I used two chain saws to cut our ATV trail through the logjam. When I got to it, I realized the dirty rats had created another obstacle. It looked like at least two people had moved huge logs around so that they were blocking the way to my cabin. I was already infuriated, and by the time I got to the logjam and saw what they had done, I was on the warpath. I had a lot of adrenaline built up. I got off my wheeler and threw the large logs out of the way like a bear. It seemed effortless at the time. I moved enough logs to get through the trail and raced up to Jake's cabin. Down here you can hear wheelers from pretty far away, so I thought that Jake could probably hear me coming. Sure enough, when I got to the trail that went past his yard, he was standing there holding his .41 Magnum pistol down at his side. I looked over at the cabin and in the window his teenage son Tiger, who was fourteen, had a rifle leveled on me.

I yelled at Jake, "Are you trying to kill us? You could have killed us with those crazy booby traps you set! What if my family had been on the trail? You could have hurt my wife or kids!" I was enraged. I asked, "Do you think this is the Old West?" By then I had my hand on my holstered .44 Magnum and challenged him. "Draw, Jake, draw!" I drew my pistol and Jake froze there shaking. I commanded, "Drop the pistol and tell Tiger to put the rifle down or I'll blast you into HELL!"

Jake dropped the pistol and yelled for Tiger to put the rifle down. I told Jake that I was going to go to my cabin and call the troopers on the radio to come down. I left and headed down the trail another two-and-a-half miles to my cabin. I got on my marine VHF radio and called the marine operator. The downside was that when you talked, whoever was on the channel could hear you transmitting. At this point I was so mad I did not care who heard. I got a hold of Ken Peepgrass, a state trooper. We called him Snake in the Grass, because we had caught him sneaking around in the tall beach grass spying on us. Peepgrass said he would be on his way down to investigate.

In the meantime, Harry was guarding the wire. He was in the alders next to the wire with his .375 H&H Magnum. Jake thought he would be sneaky, and while I was at my cabin, he raced down to the wire to try to get rid of the evidence. Harry stepped out with his .375 and told Jake that he better turn around and wait for the troopers to get there, because no one would be touching anything until they got there. Jake turned around and went back to his cabin.

I was waiting for Peepgrass at the airstrip when he landed. I took him to the logjam first, then I showed him the cut bank, and then the wire that was strategically placed at head level for someone riding on an ATV. Ken told me that the charge for doing this type of vandalism was called reckless endangerment. He asked me to take him to Jake's cabin so he could speak to him and Tiger. I was told to wait in the yard and he went inside. They were in there for about thirty minutes. Harry had followed me on his ATV since there was no need to wait at the scene of the crime. Ken had even put police tape on the wire and took photos of it and the cliff bank. The logjam was more of a prank than a real danger. Ken came out of Jake's cabin shaking Jake's hand. Ken walked up and asked me to give him a ride back to the plane.

On the way to the plane, I was informed that Jake had blamed the whole thing on someone else and said if his son was involved, he was not aware of it. He said there wasn't any proof that they had done anything. Even if we were sure they did it, Tiger was only fourteen and would not really get into trouble. Jake was a smooth-talking attorney that was for sure. Ken told me his hands were tied. I told him that what they did could have really hurt someone, including my wife and children who came down to my camp and used the trail as well. He assured me that if they were involved, they would not be putting anyone else in danger by playing reckless pranks.

I was thinking that this was a bunch of bullcrap, but he was right, there was not enough proof.

Later, during the sockeye season, we ended up building a barge out of some old dock pieces that we found on the beach. This barge allowed us to cross the river on our ATVs when we needed to, instead of only being able to cross at low tide, which was very inconvenient. We even had foldout ramps that would allow us to drive safely on and off the barge.

It was a good season money-wise, but work-wise it was pretty tough. We covered our walls at the Italoway camp with clear Visqueen. We used a clear material because there were so many brown bears down there that we wanted to be able to see out. Bear Alley was a beaten down bear highway. There were always fresh bear tracks on the trail every time we drove it.

I was fishing my custom-built 16 ft. aluminum skiff and Harry was fishing my 16 ft. wood skiff. We pulled the skiffs up to the bank. Harry got out and walked up the bank. He parked closer to our trail up the bank and I parked on the other side of him. I leaned down and was bailing some water out of the skiff when I saw him out of the corner of my eye turn around. He had a weird, scared look on his face. Not much scared us, so I knew right then it had to be bad. I figured it was probably a bear. All Harry could muster up to say was "BEAR." I turned around and Big Red, the 1500-pound monster brown bear, was standing ten feet above me on the cliff bank. I reached for my .375 H&H. As I picked up my gun, I looked at Big Red. Where he was standing he could have easily pounced on me and devoured me in a heartbeat. Our eyes met. My heartbeat raced. I did not want to have to shoot him. Big Red paused, slowly turned around, and lumbered up the trail. Larry had his gun leveled on him as well, just in case he decided to attack me. I was glad it did not come to that.

That season we went to the East River to fish the peak of the sockeye run. We got flown down, and set up camp about a mile from the river where we kept the boat parked. I had a brand-new three-wheeler flown down later. During the first week we were down there, it blew up. I could not afford to buy a new one so we had to walk from the river to our camp every day while we fished. It was all sand flats down there and not really easy walking. After the peak fishing died down, we headed back to the Italio and Akwe rivers. During the time in between the sockeye and silver salmon runs, we smoked our subsistence fish in my smoker that held about thirty fish at a time. We also did our annual tradition of putting up cases of fresh pack salmon. We worked on our gear, fixed our nets, and did maintenance on our skiffs, outboards, and ATVs to get ready for the upcoming silver run that usually started in late August. We fished hard all season and were looking forward to moose hunting.

That fall I invited the Turners, friends I had crabbed for, to come down to go moose hunting. They flew their own plane out at the end of the season and we had a fun party. All of us ended up getting a moose. Harry had already bailed out and went back to Haines. After working all season together, we were always ready to get away from each other.

CHAPTER 20

WHITE FLAG
THE BREAKING OF SKIPPY-JACK-JAKE

THE NEXT SPRING I CAME back to camp to get ready for the season. Summer came pretty quickly. I was having more run-ins with Skippy and Jake. They were giving me dirty looks and making snide remarks to me. I was getting really fed up with these guys. They were even calling the authorities on me. They even called the Department of Fish and Game and the Forest Service on me. I found out that Jake and Skippy had become friends with these people, and over the winter Jake held a poker game every Friday night at his house. They tried to get me in trouble for crossing the river with my ATV. They claimed I was ruining the fishery and damaging the spawning grounds. Most of the time when I crossed, it was a dry riverbed, or I was using my floating barge. I did not see a crime in that.

I found out from Mike that they had called the Forest Service and were having the officer flown down to inspect the so-called damage I was doing to the environment. I checked the runway and Skippy and Jake were nowhere to be found. I decided to stay and meet the officer. Mike landed with the officer and they got out of the plane. Mike came over, said hi, and shook my hand. Acting like I didn't know why he was here, I asked the officer what was going on. He told me that he was just coming down to check things out and was going to walk to the river. I told him that I could give him a ride. He answered, "That would be great." I said goodbye to Mike, and James got on the back of my ATV.

On the way to the river I got a chance to tell James everything that these guys were doing, including the shenanigans they had pulled. When we got to the river, Skippy and Jake were standing there sport fishing. They were never at the river sport fishing. It looked pretty strange to me. James got off my bike. Skippy and Jake acted so phony, I could see right through

131

it. They shook his hand and said, "Fancy seeing you down here!" James looked a little awkward.

He nervously replied, "Oh, yes, I am just coming down to check on things, not a big deal."

I told them that I was going to leave and I took off back to my cabin. I was happy that I got a chance to tell James my side of the story. I believe that Skippy and Jake were not there to meet the plane because they did not want me to think that they had anything to do with James being down there. As if I were that ignorant and would not have figured it out. They were acting so juvenile, I felt like I was back in high school.

The rivers on the Lost Coast are always changing and eroding. Sometimes the river can move up to a quarter of a mile. Mostly they move west. Jake and Skippy's cabin was close to the riverbank. Their cabin ended up falling into the river where the bank had been eroding. There was nothing that could be done when Mother Nature decided to move. Their cabin got washed away. Could it be karma? They got the permits to build a new camp and ended up building a costly deluxe cabin up the river. They did not have much choice but to rebuild, since they already had reservations for people coming down to the camp and the other cabins were always booked up during this time of year.

Skippy and Jake kept tormenting me. They were still giving us hateful looks and calling different government agencies trying to get me in trouble. They even went so far as to start a petition to shut down commercial fishing on the river. When I found this out, I became unhinged. I was going to end this feud once and for all. I devised a despicable plan. My brother Barry had been fishing with me that season. He had a severe problem with alcohol. He would start drinking and could not stop until all the alcohol was gone. He would drink everything we had. If we had a half gallon, he would drink the whole thing. One night Barry had ordered some alcohol from one of the air taxi pilots and the pilot flew the liquor down on one of the fish hauls. We cracked open the bottle and I had a few cocktails, but I quit early. Barry stayed up and drank until the alcohol was gone. He got a wild hair and decided to go mess with Skippy-Jack-Jake while I was asleep. The next thing I knew I heard gunshots. I got up and lit a lantern. Barry was nowhere to be found. I saw the empty bottle and got worried. I looked outside and one of the ATVs was gone. I thought, *Wonderful!* I heard more gunshots. It sounded like a big bore rifle. I looked around and noticed that my .460 Weatherby was gone. The only thing I could do was wait. There was no way I was going to get involved. Whatever Barry was doing, I was going to let him take responsibility for it. I decided to go back to bed and try to get some sleep. Barry eventually came back to the cabin. I was going to wait until the morning to talk to him since he was really drunk. I talked to Barry the next day after he sobered up. He looked pretty hung over. I asked him what he did. He told me he drove to a sand dune near Jake and Skippy's cabin and hunkered down with the .460 and shot bullets over their cabin to mess with them. I told him how stupid that was. I told him that with all the trouble that they were causing, it was not a smart idea to be shooting at people. I told him that unless we were in danger, we did not shoot at people, and that I knew of a more strategic way to torment those guys. My brother was not the sharpest tack in the box. He was always acting foolish, especially when he was drinking. I think he might have been overcompensating with the drinking for having to give up drugs to fish with me.

I told him my plan. First I got my backup Briggs and Stratton generator out of storage. B&S generators are notorious for being very loud. I even cut the muffler off the generator to make it louder and more obnoxious. I set up a tent camp pretty close to their cabin with a stereo system that had very big and powerful speakers. When I was at my camp during closures, I would crank up my stereo and I could hear the music way out in the yard while I was working on gear, so I knew that they would be loud enough to get under their skin. I even used plywood to build a makeshift lean-to, so that if it rained, my stereo would not get wet. I hooked everything up. I brought the loudest rock tape I had, which was AC/DC. I started up the generator and played my AC/DC tape as loud as my stereo would go. I could hear the music at my Italoway camp miles away, so I figured it must be pretty loud at Jake's camp. I pointed the generator right at the cabin. I ran it twenty-four hours a day. I made sure it stayed filled with gas and kept playing AC/DC over and over. I bet it was driving them crazy. They even had guests at the time. I am sure their trip was probably ruined. The next thing that happened really turned the tables on Jake.

I went to check my skiff and decided to check the runway while I was out. Jake and Skippy had flown out. They had left their ATV at the runway, and while they were gone a bear had attacked it. The bear tore the seat and shredded the tires. Bears for some reason like things like seats and tires to chew on. The bear really did a number on their bike. It was even flipped over. I figured they would be back at any time, so I went back to my camp and thought how funny it was that Jake's ATV got attacked by a bear. It could not have happened to a better person. I could hear a plane off in the distance. It was probably them. This was my chance to really get those guys good. I decided to take off for the runway. I knew they would have to walk to their camp after being dropped off. I found a good place to hide along Bear Alley. I could hear the plane coming closer. I could barely contain myself. This was going to be great. The plane landed. I could not hear them talking, but I am sure Jake was not happy. I could hear the plane start up and take off. Now all I had to do was wait.

Finally, I could hear footsteps. I waited until I thought Jake was about ten feet away. I had my .375, and my .44 Magnum pistol. I propped my .375 up against a tree, and had my .44 on my right side. I jumped out of the bushes. It was almost dark. Jake screamed and practically jumped out of his skin. He already had his .41 Magnum out of its holster. He was probably already scared to death of being attacked by a bear after what had happened to his ATV. He had to walk down Bear Alley, which was a narrow corridor peppered with fresh bear tracks, all by himself. I thought he might have even peed his pants. He was shaking. He said in a panic-stricken voice, "What are you doing here, Davis?"

I said back to him, "Just wanted to check up on you."

He asked, "Did you do that to my ATV?"

I told him, "No way, a bear must have done it. How would I be able to make bear bites in your tires and seat?"

He asked again, "What do you want?" He sounded scared. His hand that was holding the pistol was shaking.

I asked, "Are you going to draw on me, Jake?" He did not answer. He just stood there shaking. I said, "Do you think this is the Old West? If you want to draw on me, Jake, go ahead. If you think this is the Old West, go ahead and DRAW!"

He said, "I do not want any trouble, George."

I said, "Oh good, because I do not want any trouble either. I want all of this to be over with here and now." Jake nodded his head up and down in agreement.

He said, "I think you are right; I want all of this to be over too!"

He asked if he could get by. I stepped aside and let him pass. I kept my eyes on his hand holding the gun the whole time. He walked past me and toward his camp. I got on my ATV. I wanted him to get where I could keep my eye on him. I did not trust having my back to him. He got to where I could drive and not have him behind me. I took off and went to my cabin. I was pretty satisfied. I believed this last conversation might very well end the war.

I was by myself because my brother had flown to town for the closure to party with some friends. He was supposed to be back tomorrow to get ready for fishing. I went to bed with a gun by my bed and a .44 under my pillow just in case Jake wanted to try anything fishy. I did not trust him for anything. The next morning I put some coffee on and got ready to pick my brother up. When I got to the runway and the plane landed, I saw that Skippy was onboard along with my brother. When I walked up, my brother had already heard what had happened to the ATV from the pilot. Jake came down on another wheeler they had at their camp to pick up Skippy. We did not speak to each other. I got my brother and his gear, and Jake got Skippy and his gear. When we took off, they stayed and talked to the pilot. At the cabin I told my brother what had happened on the trail. He laughed really hard. He said he wished that he could have been there to see it in person. I asked him how it went in town. He said he had a great time and had met a native princess named Sunshine partying at the Glass Door. He said they hit it off and slept together. He said he really liked her and hoped he would see her again. I told him that I hated to burst his bubble, but that she was well known around town to be really promiscuous and a party ho. Barry said, "Perfect! My kind of girl!" We both laughed.

The next day we got our gear ready for the opener. We headed out to go fishing. We set our net out, fished hard, and got the fish hauled back to the camp. We went back to button everything up and when we passed Jake and Skippy's cabin, we saw they had made a makeshift flag pole and was flying a white flag. We slowed down. We thought this might be a trick. The door opened and I told my brother get to ready. Jake and Skippy walked out of the cabin waving white handkerchiefs. This was a sight to see! We looked at each other, but were still a little wary and did not trust them. They waved at us to come over. We decided, what was the harm? We went over to see what they had to say.

Jake and Skippy told us that they had a long talk and thought it was in everyone's best interest if we called a truce. Barry and I looked at each other in disbelief. I said, "Can we trust you?" They both nodded and said that they truly wanted a ceasefire, and did not want to cause us any problems. They did not want any more hassles from us in return. I agreed and said, "Let's shake on it." We all shook hands. Jake and Skippy said they had some good Scotch and cigars and wanted to know if we would join them. We were still a little wary, but we wanted to make amends so we decided to join them. I will never forget that day. The day we broke Skippy-Jack-Jake. The rest of the fall we did not have any more problems with them.

My brother and I went fishing and moose hunting after the season. We had gotten a moose on October 15, opening day. My ignorant brother almost ended up shooting me during the hunt. He had borrowed a gun from me and I was in front of him on the trail. I saw a moose, but my gun failed, so I asked him to hand me his gun. In the process, his glove got caught in the hammer and when he handed it to me, the gun went off right at me. I was outraged. I yelled at him, "You almost killed me!" He apologized up and down, but I was in shock at how negligent he was. Not only did he almost shoot me, but he had become in general a liability at camp. He was always getting drunk and doing thoughtless things. He got drunk one night, and while I was asleep, he took an ATV out in the dark and crashed it. He could have broken his neck or drowned. I found him the next day passed out by my damaged ATV. He was lucky he was my brother and did not have anywhere else to go, or I would have gotten rid of him. None of my other family would help him out. I was hoping that the more time he spent around me he would start acting a little more maturely. High hopes, I suppose. Some people just can't be helped.

CHAPTER 21

DREADLOCKED WEIRDO

THAT WINTER I WAS GOING to Florida. I found out that Barry was pursuing Sunshine during the season on the closures by flying to town. He had plans to move in with her after fishing was over. I was happy that he had found a mate that had his same interests of drinking and doing drugs.

I had been talking to my brother Ben in Orlando. He had an 18-year-old son named Jason Quinn. I told Ben that if Jason wanted to come up for the summer, he could stay with us and learn how to work hard, and live the Alaska bush life. Canneries were always hiring young people to work for the summer, and I thought it might be best if he started work at the local fish processing plant. I knew that if he worked hard, he could make pretty good money. Ben said he thought it would be a good opportunity for him and would talk to Jason about it. Jason was interested and I spoke to him about what the job entailed. I told him the honest truth. He would be expected to work twelve- to fourteen-hour days cleaning fish on what we called the slime line. Salmon have slime on them that workers remove by sliding a knife against the grain of the fish scales. The fish then moves down the line to the person who fillets it. A cannery more or less works like a factory. There are all kinds of jobs, from standing out on the dock to meet tenders and fishing boats to running forklifts and freezers. The first job they give people with no experience though is on the slime and filleting line.

Since Jason was still in high school, he said that he could not afford to buy his plane ticket, and Ben was not able to help him at the time. He asked me if I could get his ticket. I told him he could borrow the money and make payments to me. Jason had a best friend named Kenny who always wanted to go to Alaska. Jason asked if Kenny could come so they would motivate each other. I thought it would be a good idea. Besides, they were competitive and I thought that would give them determination. It was set. After I got my camp open and sockeye season was underway, I was going to get both of their tickets and told them that they could pay me back. They were excited to be spending the summer in Alaska.

That spring when I came back to Alaska from Florida, I found out that a drifter had come into Yakutat. He was tall and blonde with dreadlocks down past his butt. All that winter and spring, locals and law enforcement had tried to run him out of town. He got around Yakutat Bay and the islands with a kayak, where he would find a place to camp and squat. When he would come into town, we would see him around in some of the stores. On one occasion while I was shopping in the grocery store with my wife, we smelled the most awful stench. I wondered if there was something rotten in the store. Come to find out it was this dreadlocked weirdo. We did not even know his name, but that is what he was known as. He smelled so bad we had to cover our noses. That was one reason why they were trying to run him out of town, but mostly because they thought he was just bizarre. He was seen at the local dump eating and rummaging through the trash right alongside bears. Everyone was surprised that he did not get mauled and eaten by the bears, but my theory was that he smelled so bad that the bears did not want anything to do with him.

The man would carry a .22 rifle, even around town, which was not against the law, but the locals did not like it. He even got busted for shooting a duck out of season with the .22. The trooper wrote him a ticket and gave him a date to show up at the courthouse. Instead of showing up, he went to the store, got provisions, and headed out in Yakutat Bay. He eventually ran out of food and came back to town to get some food at the store. When he was spotted, he was arrested on a warrant for missing his court date. We heard that he really freaked out, especially when they transported him to Juneau. In time, we saw him around town again. He must have worked something out to get his freedom back, but the locals were not happy to see him back in town.

Sockeye season was about to start so I flew my family down to my Italio camp to help me open it up and get ready. Then Harry and I flew down to my Akwe camp, which I had constructed the previous season. I had a 12x16 ft. cabin with four-foot walls and the rest was a frame that I covered with tarps. It resembled a wall tent, but with a wood floor and plywood walls. I even constructed a door for it. I also made a beach runway to fly my fish off the spit. This saved me a lot of time and money instead of having to haul my fish back to the Italio River.

Harry and I landed on the runway and secured the plane. I had flown down there the day before to check on it and everything looked normal. Where the camp was, out on the dunes, the wind blew sand like snow and caused drifts to form. Every season I had to shovel my camps out from underneath the sand drifts, but that was all just part of the lifestyle. The day before I made sure I had my shovel sitting there ready and waiting to dig. I had inspected everything and nothing had been disturbed. When Harry and I walked up to the camp, I noticed something very strange. There were human foot tracks. Not only human, but also barefoot human tracks. That was really creepy. Besides that, my shovel was missing. I told Harry that I was just there yesterday and this had just happened. We got the skiff out and put the outboard on it. Then we got the boat in the water immediately. I was going to find out what the heck was going on.

We followed the foot tracks down the river and we could see a makeshift camp set up with a tent and a tarp. We saw the silhouette of what looked like a naked person with their back to us. Whatever it was, it had long blonde hair. Harry right off the bat thought it was a naked girl. I told him that I thought that it could be that drifter everyone called the dreadlocked weirdo. As we got closer, the person went inside the tent and then came out with just pants on. It was the dreadlocked weirdo and we called out, "Hey!" He said hi back and we asked what was going on. We could see that he had his kayak with him. He told us that he had kayaked from Yakutat and came in from the ocean, then up river to get out of the thirty-five- to forty-knot winds. I asked him if he had my shovel. He said he did borrow it and then he grabbed it. I told him that around here if you borrow something, you should bring it back. He apologized and said that he was going to bring it back later that day. I asked him what his intensions were for being down here. He told us about his stay in Yakutat and that he had gotten threats, so he thought it was best that he left town. He said he was going to kayak to Juneau and maybe even further south from there. I said that all the locals fish down here on these rivers, and that it was best that he did move on because people down here did not like outsiders, especially drifters. He agreed and said he was going to make his way to Juneau for sure, and that he did not want any trouble. Harry and I told him we had work to do shoveling out the sand that had drifted and buried my camp, and that we would be around getting ready for fishing. We left and went back to my cabin.

When we got back to camp, Harry asked me if that guy was all right in the head. I told him what I had heard happened in Yakutat. That people said they had seen him eating garbage with the bears at the dump, and that he was camping out on the islands. Harry said he did not really trust him, and I did not really trust the guy either, but he seemed harmless enough. He was on foot and said he did not want any trouble. He was working on leaving the area and was on his way out. I asked Harry, "Would you want to tangle with us?"

He said, "No way!"

We decided to keep our eyes open and watch out for any issues. I left Harry there and I went back to the Italio cabin. When I got back, I told Debbie and the kids that the dreadlocked weirdo was camping on the Akwe and what had happened. Debbie kind of felt sorry for him. She asked if he had sufficient gear for the journey he was going to attempt. I told her that I thought it looked marginal. Debbie insisted that we put together a care package for him. She put together some food, special berry preserves, and some jarred fish. We also had a fresh, large king salmon that we had caught. She talked me into bringing the care package and piece of fish to the dreadlocked weirdo. We did not even know his name. He was a very soft spoken and seemingly nice guy, just strange. Debbie and the kids were curious about him so they asked to come with me. We flew down to the river with the supplies. When we approached his camp, there were fresh hooligans everywhere and it smelled like fish. Hooligans are a surf smelt, similar to a sardine. They are one of the first fish in the river in the spring, and a lot of people harvest them and use them for making oil, and frying up to eat. He came out of his tent when we walked up. He greeted us pleasantly. I told him, "I see you caught some hooligans." He laughed and said that he did, and that they were very oily. I told him that Alaskans actually call them candlefish because there is enough oil in them that you could burn them in a lantern. He laughed. I asked him how he was cooking them since I did not see any kind of stove or a fire. He told us that he was eating them raw. Debbie and I gave each other a look. My kids got excited and said they would love to build a campfire. He said that sounded nice.

Jason and Adam jumped right in gathering beach wood and building the campfire. Debbie told him that we had brought him a care package for his journey, and that we also had a fresh piece of king salmon that we could cook over the campfire. He was so grateful, I thought he was going to cry. He told us that this was the nicest that anyone had treated him since he came to the area. I told him not to take it too personally and that people in the Yakutat district for the most part treated people badly, and that they were a hateful bunch of people in general. He thought that was unfortunate. If you were not from there, or didn't have something to offer, most of the locals were spiteful, vicious, and wretched. I told him he was doing the right thing by leaving town and that nothing good was going to come of him staying there. He thanked us for the hospitality and we all enjoyed the salmon. The boys played while I explained to him how he should proceed on his route to Juneau. Since I had flown the coastline for years I told him the best way to go. He was really grateful for that information. It was getting late and I wanted to get the kids back to camp. We said our goodbyes and we wished him luck.

The sockeye season started the third week in June. Harry told me he needed to fly to town for some supplies and asked me if I had any flights going in. I told him that I had to pick up Jason and Kenny and he could ride along. Barry stayed at camp. Harry told me that he was going to spend the night in town. I said to call me tomorrow and we would fly back together. I went home and had to pick up Jason and Kenny at the airport the next day. I picked the boys up and took them to the cannery, where I had already secured them jobs. I told them that I had to get back to my fish camp, but I would be checking on them. The canneries have a bunkhouse for their workers to stay at out at Leonard's Landing. They were also provided meals while they were working for the cannery. A portion of their pay was taken out to pay for this room and board. The boys started work immediately, and I went back home to wait for Harry's call.

Harry called me, and I picked him up at one of his friend's house. When he got in my truck, he had a smirk on his face. I asked him what that was all about. He asked me how serious Barry and Sunshine were. I told him they lived together and as far as I knew were exclusive. He told me that she was not acting very exclusive last night. I got a sinking feeling. I said, "Harry, what happened?" He told me that he was out partying at the Glass

Door, and that he got to talking to Sunshine and she was really flirting with him. He asked a few guys around the bar what the deal was, and they told him that when Barry was out fishing, she would sleep around, and that it was no big deal. So I figured what the heck. It would just be some other guy anyway, might as well be him. I did not know what to say. He went on to tell me that she was so horny, she led him out to the parking lot and they screwed on the hood of a car. All I could do was shake my head in disbelief. Then I got to thinking about it. After all the things that I had seen, I knew now that anything was possible. I told him that I would not say anything, but if Barry found out, I was staying completely out of it. Harry just smirked.

I flew Harry back to his camp, and then went back to my cabin where Barry was waiting for me. I could barely look him in the eye when he picked me up at the runway. I knew I just needed to get it out of my mind. I had too much going on to worry about any drama between the newly formed love triangle. We had fishing and I had a lot of flying to do. Now I had my nephew and his friend in town to worry about.

I had gotten Jason and Kenny super saver tickets. I ended up loaning each of them $1000. This included the tickets, rain gear, and some warm clothes. Since they lived in Orlando they did not have much to wear that would keep them warm and dry in Alaska. I knew the manager of the cannery and had secured their jobs before they arrived. I was excited to have my nephew up. They were eighteen and said they were ready to work hard and make some money. Jason was a strong, strapping, and handsome young man. My brother had named his son Jason, and Debbie and I had named our son Jason as well. We wanted to nickname him something so that they knew which one we were talking to. Since his middle name was Quinn, I called him JQ from then on out. Later I ended up calling him Quanto for fun. Out in the Alaska bush we were always teasing each other and calling each other names.

After the opener I flew to town with a load of fish and decided to go check on the boys. When I found them, they said that it was hard work but they were making money and were happy. I thought everything was going well.

A month later I got a call from my friend Caroline who worked at the cannery. She was one of the people who drove the cannery truck out to the airport to meet planes full of fish. Workers would load the totes onto the truck and then she would drive them to the cannery. She said she heard that Kenny and Jason had quit, and were at the airport about to get on a jet back to Florida. I was beside myself when I heard this, and flew my plane to the airport to see what was going on. I got my plane parked and tied down. I went in to the Alaska Airlines terminal and saw them there. They looked scared when they saw me, as they should have been. I told them to come outside and have a talk. I asked them what the hell was going on. Kenny spoke up and told me that he had gotten into a disagreement with the boss and quit. Since Jason was his best friend, he quit too. They said they were afraid to tell me because they had not saved enough money to pay me back and they did not know what to do.

I told them that they should have let me know what was going on and not just run out of town. For goodness' sake, Jason was my blood nephew. I asked them what they had planned on doing about paying me back, as I was out $2000. They said they did not know what to do about owing me the money. The jet was on its way and we did not have much time to work anything out. I knew Kenny had a pistol. I said that I would take his pistol as partial payment on the money he owed me. He agreed and gave me his .45 semiautomatic. He was really ashamed and told me that he felt pretty bad about letting me down, and then he went inside.

I was outside alone with Jason. He told me that he really wanted to stay, and that he wanted his dad and me to be proud of him. He did not want to go back to Orlando a quitter.

As we were talking Kenny came back outside and walked over to us. I looked at his face. He had tears in his eyes. He was actually crying. He said that he did not want to leave and that he wanted to make it right somehow, and asked me if there was anything he could do. I came up with an offer and presented them with a deal. I could not afford at the time to pay them cash to work as crew members for my set net fishing operation, which is why I did not have them at my camp in the first place. All my fishing partners had their own permits and we did not hire crew members very often if we could help it. We did as much of the work that we could ourselves to keep expenses at a minimum. That is why I did most of my own flying and hauling of fish and supplies. I could make a lot more money doing that myself. During these years of set netting, I did not do much work in the winter and my earnings from the season needed to last me through the winter.

My proposal was that they could come down to my set net camp and work the rest of the summer to pay off their debt to me. If they did a good job, they would get a bonus at the end of the fishing season. They walked off to talk it over, then walked back over to me. They said it was a fair deal and they would do it. We shook hands and they went back inside and retrieved their luggage. I was proud of them for coming clean and manning up to work off their debt. They had better work hard. Teenage boys eat a lot and they already owed me almost $2000, minus the gun that Kenny traded me.

Since I was already in town I decided to make a trip out of it and ran into town for some supplies. We got back to the airport, loaded up, and took off for the Italio. As soon as we got to camp I immediately put the boys to work. I was going to make sure I got my money's worth out of them, especially since they had already tried to skip town.

Although JQ and Kenny were best friends, they sure did fight a lot. They argued about everything. They were always in each other's faces and almost coming to blows, even pushing each other around. Kenny lasted a week at camp and then he came up to me and said he wanted to go back to Florida. He appreciated the offer I had given him, but he was just not cut out to work in the wilderness away from town, phones, social life, and girls.

I told him I was disappointed he did not stick it out, but understood. While Kenny was packing, Jason came up to me and said that he was staying to fulfill his obligation, and that he liked it out here. I flew Kenny to town and waited with him while he called his dad. His dad was very mad and displeased. He was so mad that he helped Kenny get a ticket to Seattle, but told him he was going to have to ride a Greyhound bus from Seattle to Orlando. Kenny was not too excited about that, but there was not much he could do about it. He did not have any other options.

JQ was happy to stay and worked very hard for me all summer. He did anything I asked him to do, and did things without being told. He stuck it out for the rest of the fishing season and made me proud. He learned a lot about the wilderness and hard work. I gave him a bonus at the end of the season and he went home with a life lesson and a little cash in his pocket, as well as a taste for Alaskan adventures. He told me that he would love to come back and work again if I needed a crew member. I told him that I would keep it in mind. I had plans for next season and would more than likely need his help.

I had always wanted to get a floatplane. I had been looking for one in *Trade A Plane*, a newspaper dedicated to pilots, and featuring aircrafts for sale and anything under the sun when it came to airplanes. I found a really nice 185 on amphibious floats. This plane was so nice. It was what pilots would call "cherry." I was going to research more thoroughly on getting my own air taxi certificate in the year to come.

CHAPTER 22

YAKUTAT FISH WARS

THAD BEEN TALKING WITH MY friend Iron Mike about an air taxi. He wanted me to put my 206 under his certificate and fly commercially for him. I had a wonderful friendship with Mike and I liked flying Part 91. I could fly my own plane and fly fish and freight, and even charge for the flying. It was against the rules to fly passengers and charge them for flying under Part 91, but I did not need to worry about that because I kept plenty busy flying fish and freight just for my own, and whomever I was fishing with. I did have an interest in an idea we had been kicking around about getting my own single pilot air taxi certificate and us having separate companies but working together, not in competition. This way we could keep our businesses separate.

Every season was an adventure. A person never knew who and what was going to show up. Coincidentally, a female pilot that I knew from Haines, Gayle Ronson, had found a set net permit for sale and bought it. She was a divorced single mom who had been flying for air taxis in Haines since I could remember. It seemed my family was not the only one taking note of the set net fishery and flying opportunities in the Yakutat District. After Gayle got the permit, she brought her family down along with her boyfriend Jake. Everyone called him Jake Ronson because she obviously wore the pants in the family. Jake was an A&P mechanic, and was certified to work on airplanes. Gayle hooked in with Mike and started flying for him. She was ambitious and wanted her own plane. They made a deal to buy a Cessna 185 that we called X-Ray. The N numbers off the plane were how we identified different planes. We always had to do this when calling flight service and landing at the airport, but we also did it when flying along the coast as well. There was so much flying going on in the area that we would identify ourselves and our intentions of landing at the different bush airstrips by our N numbers as we would at an airport.

The deal was that Mike would help with the financing and Gayle would do the flying that Mike gave her from Gulf Air Taxi. She in turn would not compete with Gulf Air. That deal did not last long. Gayle ended up being a little more enterprising than Mike had expected. After she got settled in, and started her fishing and flying operation, she got her own air taxi certificate. She got in with all of Mike's fish hauling customers and started undercutting Gulf Air Taxi's prices. There was not much customer loyalty when it came to prices, so she got a lot of business by doing this. When this started happening, Mike was furious. He helped her get the plane and now she was competing against him, not helping him. When Mike told me what had happened, I got pretty agitated about it, too. Mike was my friend, and we were very competitive in our fishing and flying businesses. So now not only did we have to compete on the river for sets, we were fighting over the flying with Gayle. This meant war, not only in flying, but also when it came to fishing.

I was the kind of fisherman who would travel around to different river systems to fish the peaks of the different runs. Some people would stay in one place. A lot of people with Yakutat district permits would fish the Situk. The Situk River was thirteen miles from town and you could drive to it. The cannery would even send out trucks with totes of ice and pick up fish. To pick up fish off of remote rivers the canneries would bring in DC-3 aircrafts that would haul up to 7,500 pounds. A lot of times the pilots would go light on fuel so they could haul more weight, and would put up to 10,000 pounds of fish in the plane. Sitka Sound Seafoods used an air taxi called Methow Aviation. They would set up an office at the airport and bring up a DC-3 every year to haul fish. Even though the cannery did this, the DC-3s could only haul fish off big runways. They needed a solid four thousand feet. There were areas that we fished that those planes could not fly in or out of. That was where the air taxies made a lot of income flying for these remote camps.

The canneries would also help fishermen by hauling fuel and supplies for the fishermen, but everyone always relied on the air taxies for flying in and out of camp, food, some freight, and fuel. The DC-3s were very busy just hauling fish when the fishing was going on, so if we needed any other items flown, including passengers, we relied on the air taxis. Mike, and now Gayle, would accommodate fishermen by even checking their mail, grocery shopping, or running to the hardware store to get parts. It became even more competitive when Gayle came into the picture. This allowed the fishermen to continue fishing and not have to leave to go all the way to town to pick up a part or some groceries. Air taxies would even pick people up at the airport for you, run you around town, and do all other kinds of nice things. This was all, of course, to get your flying business, but it was nice to have people bend over backward for you. The nice thing about competing air taxies was that the customers always made out like bandits.

I loved having my own plane because I could come and go as I pleased and did not have to wait around for a flight. It would have driven me crazy if I had been without my own plane, because during the busy times, people were always at the mercy of the air taxi and their schedule. There were times when people were given precedence over others. The kind of service you got depended on how much money you spent with an air taxi. The more money you spent the higher priority your flights became. Having my own plane also made me money, instead of it being an expense of fishing. It was income since the air taxi charged by the pound, and flights for freight and supplies cost money. It was an expense most fishermen paid out of the cost of doing business. The drawback of doing my own flying was the danger of hauling out max gross loads of fish and freight off short, sandy, and primitive runways. Besides that, I had to do most of my flying in marginal weather. It was dangerous, stressful, and a lot of extra work. When I did the math on it though, I always decided it was worth it to do year after year.

I did not like to stay in one place, especially when the fishing slowed down, because I was out to make as much money as I could. It was not as comfortable, because I had to set up makeshift camps, but it was worth it to make the extra money. Other people built nice set netting cabins on remote rivers as a base and did not travel very much to other systems.

One family in particular had a really nice setup down at the East River, but fished other rivers in the district. The Shumacker's were really intimidating and no one messed with the sets that they claimed. I knew that they fished up the Alsek River and heard they did quite well. I had even heard a rumor that Gayle's son Steve was up there fishing near their set and he claimed that he heard bullets whiz past him. He got very frightened, and he turned around and left that part of the river alone. I was not intimidated by them, but I respected them since they had been down there a long time and they ran a pretty tight ship. Old man Shumacker had a Bering Sea crab boat that he fished in addition to his Yakutat set net permit. They had everyone convinced that if you went fishing up the Alsek, the Shumackers would shoot you. I had even heard that one of his crew shot holes in a helicopter that had been buzzing over them on the river.

While Mike and I were trapping the Alsek Valley the winter before, we started talking about the upcoming fishing season. We decided we wanted to fish up the Alsek, and we were going to show everyone that we were not afraid of the Shumackers. Another reason that we wanted to go up there was that they were now doing all their flying with Gayle. Mike had a cabin on the Alsek about five miles from where we would be fishing. It was called the Dry Bay Camp. Dry Bay was a place on the coast where the cannery had set up a buying station. They had a 4,000 ft. runway that was hard-packed sand so that the DC-3 they brought up there could haul fish out. From Dry Bay you could drive a trail all the way to the East River that was about five miles away from there.

From Mike's cabin to the mouth of the Alsek was about five miles. The river turned into a maze of sandbars and narrow channels. There was a group of guys who had a camp at the mouth and fished there. From the fish hauling Mike and I did, we saw that they had been doing pretty decent fishing there over the years. We thought we would give it a try, so we tried fishing down at the mouth. We found out that it was not worth the gas that we burned going back and forth, plus it was very dangerous and not easy to navigate the sandbars. The worst part was the advection fog that always seemed to be lying on the mouth of the river like thick soup.

Mike and I thought it was time to make a move on the upper Alsek near the Shumackers. We loaded up the skiff with the net and headed up there. We found a nice spot in the river where some fish were schooled up. While we were fishing, we did not see anyone for a while. All of a sudden we heard a four-wheeler. When they got close, we noticed it was Vern Jr., old man Shumacker's son. He pulled up and asked us what we were doing up there. We answered, "We are fishing. What does it look like?"

He got a funny look on his face and said, "Well, this is our territory up here and there is not much room for anyone else. The fishing is only good enough to support our nets."

To be honest, it was not that great. We did not get the reaction we had expected, but we were glad they did not retaliate with threats or violence against us. We fished the rest of the week there since we were already down there, and then decided that it was not worth staying to eek it out. There was better fishing at our other spots along the coast. We were pleased though that we made an impression that we were not afraid of them. We did not want a war, but we did not want to be told where we could or could not fish. After that week I got my skiff out of there and took it to the Akwe to fish the rest of the sockeye peak. When the fishing on the Akwe slowed down, I would take my skiff down to the East River when it started hitting its peak. I usually did this for about four weeks.

Mike went back to mostly flying for the air taxi, and I brought my brother down to help me fish. We got our camp set up at our usual location. We had been fishing for a week or so now. We went down to the river on our ATVs to see where there would be a good place to set the net. We had a spot marked off as our designated set, but we liked to run the river and look for other good places to set. The river was glacial and would change often, so the places we would set and where fish would school up would change as well. We cruised the riverbank and saw that Vern's set was open and no one else was fishing it. His set was full of fish and I just could not resist. I told my brother we should mop up the fish. He was kind of worried because there was not only Vern Sr., Vern Jr., and another brother Virgil, but also maybe a few other guys helping them. It would be at least three or four guys against just the two of us if there happened to be a confrontation. I told Barry not to worry. Traveling around the different river systems, I have had run-ins and confrontations with most of the families that fished. It was pretty much inevitable if you were competitive like I was. I would not let people bully me, so sometimes it led to disagreements. In the end, I gained respect for not backing down. It was just a matter of time before I was going to have a run-in with the Shumackers down on the East River.

We set our net out in the hole where all of the fish were schooled up. Of course as soon as we were fishing, here comes someone on an ATV.

When they got close enough we saw that it was Vern Sr. When he got closer we could tell he was mad. We were in the process of pulling in the net full of fish when we stopped to talk to Vern, who had pulled right above us on the riverbank where their net was sitting. I told my brother to let me handle the talking. I pulled the skiff up to the riverbank so that we could get out. Vern had a mean look on his face and so did we. We were prepared for anything. After hearing the rumors that the Shumackers had shot at people fishing near their sets, I could only imagine what they would say or do to people actually fishing the set that they had claimed as theirs. The first thing that came out of his mouth was, "You know that is my set right?"

I yelled back, "I did not see anyone's name on it, and this is an open fishery where we can fish where we want. The only rule is that we have to set 100 yards from another net."

He said, "You know how it works down here, Davis. We all have certain sets that we claim and you are fishing my set!" I said back to him that no one was around fishing and we wanted to catch some fish.

Before Vern had gotten close to us I had told my brother to let me do the talking, and I also told him to beware of Vern pulling a gun on us. He was known to carry a snub nose .44 in a holster across his chest. Sure enough when he had gotten off his wheeler, he had his hands under his rain gear like he had a gun.

Then Vern said, "Well, it sounds like I am going to have to bring my crew of hit men out here from my Bering Sea crab boat."

I said, "Go ahead, but just so you know we belong to the AFA."

Vern looked confused and asked, "What is the AFA?"

I replied in a really serious tone, "Assassins for America."

With that Vern said back, "Well, Davis, you do know that I am well known to be the fastest draw in the West." He said this as he was pushing the barrel of his snub nosed .44 out of the side of his rain bibs.

We were standing very close to each other, and with one swift motion I grabbed his hand and shoved the gun in his throat and said back to him, "Looks like I am faster." I asked him if he thought this was the Wild West.

With a gun pressed against his throat he kind of coughed and said, "Oh, Davis, I did not mean anything by it. I was just trying to scare you guys. You know how protective we are of our sets. It's how we make our living." I told him that he should not put his hands on his gun unless he intended to use it, and that this was not a game. He said, "You are right, Davis." With that I let go of his hand and stepped back. I had a .44 on my belt and I was ready to draw if necessary.

Vern said, "Davis, I have to tell you, I think that took balls, and I respect you. I just ask that you guys not fish my sets, even if no one is around."

I said back, "All right, Vern, I agree, and we will not fish your sets to keep the peace."

With that Barry and I got back in our boat and finished pulling the net full of fish in the skiff. Vern got on his wheeler and drove off. We never turned our backs to each other until he was out of sight. My brother was shaking. I could tell he was scared. I would not be surprised if he had wet himself. If it were not for me, he never would have survived out there.

We had been taking notice of where Gayle and Jack had been fishing. They had a set about a mile up the river. It was in a spot that had formed a nice hole where the fish would hold in a school. We also noticed that Gayle and Jack had not been at their set for the openers that were usually at noon. Since we had just come down to the east for the peak of the season, and they had stayed there and had a camp, we did not take the set when it was available. The night before this particular opener I had been contemplating where to fish and told my brother that if we went up there and the set was open, we were going to take it. My brother questioned me and I told him that if she wanted to fish and fly, she was going to have to play with the big boys and by the big boy rules. I told him as Greg would say, "It is tough all over."

We got a good night's rest and when we got up, we had coffee and breakfast. It was nice that the opener was not until noon. It gave us plenty of time to get started. We got in the skiff, got the net loaded, and headed out. I ran the skiff right up to Gayle's set. Sure enough, at noon no one was around. *Ha*, I thought. There was a huge school of sockeye piled up in the natural hole in the river. I was excited to see if anyone else would show up.

If I took this set, it would mean about 300 fish, which averaged about $3,000. That was a pretty good set in my book.

We milled around and tried not to spook the fish. I told Barry that I would give Gayle a fighting chance and wait thirty minutes before I would make my move. I was watching the time closely and looking intently to see if anyone would show up. Gayle was fishing with Jack, but since the permit was in her name she had to be there before they could legally set out the net. I would have left the set if Jack would have showed up, but he or Gayle were nowhere in sight. At 12:30 p.m. sharp I said, "Let's set!" Barry looked hesitant. I said, "What's wrong?"

He replied, "Well, are you sure you want to do this?"

I told him, "Absolutely!"

We started setting out the net. This was going to be good. I wished Mike were here to see this! He was going to laugh his ass off when I told him what I did. We got the net out of the boat and into the river. The net started filling up and was sinking from all the fish hitting. I love seeing this. I made a few circles in the river with my jet boat and even more fish hit the net. "Oh, baby!" I yelled.

At about 1:00 p.m. we started picking up the end of the net. We were picking out fish when we looked up and saw Jack Ronson walking toward us. I would describe it more like strutting toward us, sort of like a rooster. It was a sight. I could not help but find the humor in it. He looked pretty mad. As he approached all he could say was, "Gayle is not going to be happy when she gets here!" He was pacing back and forth with his hands behind him on his hips. He truly looked like a strutting chicken.

I snapped back, "Well, that's what she gets for not being here. Where is she?"

Jack said, "She is flying."

Just then we heard her fly over. She flew low enough that we could see her face in the window of the plane. I looked at my brother and started laughing. Gayle landed and headed straight for us. We kept picking the fish out of the net and pulling the net in the boat. Jack was still strutting back and forth along the top of the riverbank with his hands on his hips.

It was raining out. We could see Gayle getting closer. When she got close enough for us to see her face, it was a sight! She had mascara on and the rain made it run down her face. It was frightful. She yelled at us, "George! What are you doing stealing my set?"

I said back, "You weren't here."

She said, "That should not matter; you should know that this is my set."

I laughed and told her, "Gayle, you know the rules and how it works down here. If you are not here at noon and the set is open, it is up for grabs. I was nice enough to wait until 12:30 before I put my net out."

She was not amused. I got my net all the way into the boat and told her that if she wants to keep her set, she would have to be on time. I told her that if she wants to play with the big boys, she is subject to all the same rules as everyone else. She let us have it. I just laughed, and as I was pulling out in my skiff, I said, "Okay, you can have your set back." In my mind as I was looking at her, she reminded me of Tina Turner in *Mad Max Beyond Thunderdome*. When we got out of sight, I told my brother about Gayle looking like Tina Turner and he laughed so hard I thought he was going to collapse. We went up the river to look for more fish and another set. We hoped we would find a set that we did not have to start a war for. I couldn't wait to tell Iron Mike about this. Gayle was so mad at me that she really lost her temper and was furious; in the end she just threw up her fists at me. I was completely satisfied and yelled out to Gayle, "It's tough all over!" laughing as I gunned the throttle of my outboard and peeled out.

I was the first one to have a higher-grade product by taking care of my fish better than anyone else. By producing a better product, I got paid extra per pound. Most everyone else did not take care of their fish very well, and sometimes they were all smashed up and covered in sand. I kept my fish on ice from the time they came out of the water until the time they got pitched into the cannery truck that would meet me at the airport. This made for better fish and the cannery was willing to pay me extra for it.

I believe as a fisherman that you should take pride in the fish you are selling to people and take care of it as if it were going to be served to your own family. I use that as an example because that is how I took care of my fish, as if it were my own. Some of the locals were animals and did not take care of their fish. Some of the people in Yakutat were disgusting. They took care of their food in a way that you would think would kill them, but maybe they became immune to the bacteria on rotten food.

The opener ended and I told my brother that I was going to fly to Yakutat to get supplies. I got to the airport and went over to the Gulf Air Taxi building. At the front of the building was a nice office. There were hallways with freezers and then a corridor that let back to the hangar and shop. In the hangar was an upstairs with apartments for pilots who were there flying for the season. I went into the office and was greeted warmly by Mike's wife. I spoke with her briefly and asked if Mike was around. I saw the planes were outside, so it was likely that he was there, but pilots are very busy in the summer, always running around and getting parts or supplies for the air taxi and the customers. Mike had pilots and mechanics working for him. Marie said, "Yes, George, you are lucky. Mike is in the back."

"Great. Thanks, Marie. See you later," I said as I walked back toward the hangar.

I got to the shop and hangar and saw Mike and Kurt working on the 207. I walked over to them and said, "Mike, you have to hear what I did to Gayle!"

He got a surprised look on his face and said with a smirk, "What did you do, Davis?"

I started laughing. "Nothing too bad. Pretty comical, really." I told him the story and they got a pretty good laugh out of it, especially the part of calling her Tina Turner from *Mad Max Beyond Thunderdome.* "She got what was coming to her and she should have gotten more." I told Mike it was all in fun and that I was not planning on terrorizing her too much, unless she wanted a war. I do not think she wanted a battle with me on her hands, especially after the Skippy-Jack-Jake incidences. Since then, I had gotten a reputation for being someone you did not want to tangle with. Mike told me that he wished he could have seen the whole thing in person. We talked for a bit about fishing on the river.

He said, "Sorry to cut you short, George, but I have to get back to working on the plane. You know how it is."

I said, "No problem, Mike, I am busy myself. I have tons of work to do as well. I am like a one-man army. If I did not stay on top of things, nothing would get done." Even though I had help, I was the main person in the operation.

Mike laughed and winked at me. He was the same way. He had employees, pilots, and mechanics, but without him staying on top of everything I am sure it would fall apart. His wife, Marie, ran the office and without her that end of the business would be non-existent. Running the air taxi was a full-time job for both Mike and Marie. We were one in the same when it came to work. That was why his nickname was Iron Mike.

As I was walking out of the shop and back to the office, Mike yelled, "So, when are you going to come fly with me, Davis?"

I turned around, laughed, and yelled back, "When I can get someone to replace me on the fishing grounds? Until then, I have fish to catch. See you later, Mike. Stop in at camp sometime for dinner."

He replied, "Okay, in my free time!"

I knew Mike would be too busy until things slowed down at the air taxi, but I wanted him to know he had an open invitation. Heck, you never know, pilots have been known to get weathered-in for the evening.

CHAPTER 23

ADVENTURES IN
FISHING AND FLYING

OVER THE NEXT FEW YEARS I had many more exciting adventures. A lot of them were with pilots. One pilot in particular who had a set net camp near me had more than a few screws loose. While I was fishing down on the East River, I had noticed a new plane flying around the area. It was a really exceptional Cessna 170. What made it unique was that it was an all-aluminum plane with pinstripes. Harry and I were fishing together at the time and we had the misfortune of our wheeler breaking down. We were hiking back to our camp from the river when a stranger pulled up on an ATV. He got off and introduced himself as Kirk Kirkendal, but his nickname was Sparky. He asked us if we needed a lift. We said sure! We got on and went to our camp. He had some beers with him and we joined him for one. I asked him if he was the owner of that 170 that I had seen recently. He told me yes, that was his, and that he had bought a Yakutat set net site and was going to be down here fishing. In my mind this could be a blessing or a curse. If we befriended him, it could benefit us, but it could also go south quickly, especially in the wilds of Alaska. We got a lot of fly-by-night idiots down here and usually they partnered up with a local, learned everything from him, and then stabbed you in the back. I figured what the heck, better to have an ally than an enemy. I got a good feeling from him, so I decided to befriend him and give him the benefit of the doubt. Harry and I pretty much told him that we were already in a partnership and that we kept to ourselves. We explained that we could be friends and help him out if we could, but out here you are pretty much on your own.

Things went pretty well for the rest of the season. After the openers Kirk would invite us over for dinner and beers. I hit it off with him, being a fellow pilot. He was an amazing aerobatic pilot and while we were fishing we would see him fly by doing maneuvers.

I thought it would be best to get to know Kirk for the season before I would do any partnering up with him. I would keep it in mind for next season though. After a few weeks, I approached him about working together next season. It would take a lot of pressure off of me if I did not have to do most of the flying. If I could share the flying part of the operation with Kirk, I figured we could have a more streamlined operation.

Kirk explained to me that he was pretty much a tail wheel pilot. My plane was a nose wheel and had considerably more horsepower. My Cessna 206 had a 300 hp engine. Kirk's 170 had a 140 hp engine. I figured with his 15,000 plus hours of flying time, he would pick up flying my plane pretty easily. Over the summer during the fishing closures, Kirk and I would fly in his plane together. He went over acrobatic maneuvers with me and had me perform a lot of techniques in his certified aerobatic Cessna 170B. This really honed and improved my flying skills. We did a stall called a falling leaf, which helps a pilot learn how to prevent a spin. This is where you hold the yoke or stick all the way back in a full stall, power back to idle, and every time the left wing stalls, you apply full right rudder keeping the ailerons neutral. Then when the right wing stalls, you apply full left rudder so you are falling out of the sky flopping back and forth like a falling leaf. We did spins, several barrel rolls, and snap rolls. I was having a great time learning all of these acrobatic maneuvers, and getting a really good feeling about having him do some of the fish hauling next season.

I did have one concern in the back of my mind. I noticed on landings that he did not have very good directional control. I thought that flying a nose wheel might alleviate some of that problem because it takes a lot more directional control to land and take off on a tail wheel, especially in a crosswind. It was a concern, but I did not give it too much thought because he was such a good pilot. I have flown with a lot of pilots and can usually tell if a pilot has a natural ability or not. His nickname was Sparky. I assumed he might have gotten it from doing some kind of electrical work, but I nicknamed him Cappy Kirkendal. One of the funniest things about him was that he always brought his dog flying with us. It was hard to believe that a dog would be comfortable flying around during those aerobatic maneuvers.

The beginning of next season rolled around. Harry and I decided to partner up with Kirk. He had gone back to Haines for the winter and came back to town in May to get ready for fishing. Fishing started and as the season progressed, I was getting more and more annoyed with Harry, who was slacking off and being lazy. I hate having to get people up out of bed, and it seemed Harry was sleeping in more and more when there was work to be done. We were partners, and even though I was doing 75 percent of the work, Harry was reaping the benefits, too. Besides fishing, I was flying all the time. When we got a good fishing routine dialed in, I decided it was time to get Kirk flying my 206. This would take some pressure off of me since Harry was not pulling his weight around camp.

I asked Kirk to meet me in Yakutat and I would check him out in my 206. This way he could get used to my plane, practicing first on the 6000 ft. runway at the airport. We flew around the patch a few times together with him at the controls. After a few touch-and-goes, I felt it was time to turn him loose. We parked and I got out. I told him that I was going to be at the Yakutat Lodge watching and that he should do a few touch-and-goes by himself. My 206 was a 65 P model, which was known to be very nose heavy. I even carried some extra weight in the tail when the plane was empty to offset the weight up front.

I was freaking out when I saw him come in for the landing. As I watched from the window of the lodge, he landed directly on the nose wheel. In a proper landing you float in and put most of the force on the back two wheels, then let the nose naturally come down. After watching a few of his cringeworthy pancake landings in my empty plane, I could not imagine Kirk being able to land my plane with a gross load of 1600 pounds, especially in the kinds of weather we had to fly in. Today was a perfect day with the wind blowing directly down the runway. Most times flying off the remote runways we had at least a crosswind, if not severe crosswinds. Down at my Davis runway from where I did most of my fish hauling, we typically had a crosswind, and it is only a 1200ft. sand strip where you had to get the plane off of the ground or you would crash. There were no go arounds when you flew in and out of most bush airstrips. A missed approach meant crashing and possibly death.

Cappy landed the plane after doing three touch-and-goes. He taxied over to the parking spot and I walked out on the ramp to meet him and help tie down the plane. When he got the plane shut down and got out, the look on my face probably said it all. He could tell I was not pleased. He said "Sorry, George" with a long face.

I told him, "Well, Kirk, you know I am not one to beat around the bush. After watching your three touch-and-goes, I can tell you do not have what it takes to fly my plane with a full load of fish. If you had landed like that with a grossed-out 206 with 1600 pounds, you would have crashed. You would have torn the nose gear right off. In fact, I would not be surprised if my nose gear is a little bit damaged from those landings you just did."

He replied with a dejected look on his face, "I know, George. I am sorry and agree with you. I have very little time in a nose wheel and I thought I would pick it up faster, but I do not feel comfortable flying your plane."

Since we were in agreement, I told him no hard feelings. The last thing we need is a wrecked airplane. I was a little disappointed, especially since Harry was being a lazy ass. I told Cappy that we should just put it behind us and concentrate on fishing. He agreed.

Things were getting back to normal at fish camp despite the fact that my plans were pretty much toast for getting more time to fish and having less pressure to be a one-man army. I wish there was something I could do about Harry making more of an effort at camp. He had always been kind of a mooch like my brother Barry. I was always doing most of the work while they skated and rode on my coattails. I was down there busting my ass and risking my life constantly flying our fish out so they could make more money, while they were taking me for granted.

We decided to clear the air with the whole Kirk Kirkendal issue by inviting him over for dinner. It is a big blow to a pilot to be told they can't handle the flying, especially someone with his time and experience. Even though we fished for salmon, jarred salmon, and smoked salmon, we never got tired of eating fish, especially king salmon. I had a nice king that I had caught during the subsistence-fishing opener and I was going to serve it with my famous marinated BBQ recipe. Even people who tell me they do not like fish love my special marinated BBQ salmon.

We had a bonfire going and Kirk flew over in his 172, and as always, doing some crazy aerobatic maneuvers. We always got a kick out of his fancy flying. He flew at air shows in the winter. Kirk landed and got his plane secured. I went out on the ATV to pick him up at the strip. Kirk brought some beer with him. I had told Kirk that I had plenty of room at camp and if he wanted to drink, he could spend the night. He said that sounded all right. We got to camp and cracked a beer. We were telling pilot stories and I started cooking the salmon. By the time dinner was ready we had already had at least six beers apiece. We were having a fun time. It was good to cut loose after all the tension.

Dinner was ready and we were pretty buzzed. I had made campfire-baked potatoes along with the salmon. Dinner was delicious. Since it was summer we still had plenty of daylight. After dinner, Kirk was getting his gear gathered up. I asked him what he was doing. He said that he did not really want to stay. He wanted to go back to his own camp. I was taken aback. I knew for sure he had had at least six beers that evening. I confronted him and said, "Do you really think it is a good idea to drink and fly in the same evening?"

He jokingly said, "Ah, Davis, you worry too much! I do it all the time, no big deal."

I thought, *Is this a joke?* Surely he could not be serious. I offered once again for him to stay and said that it was no imposition. I actually insisted that it was not wise to drink and fly. He was just as adamant that he was fine, and sober. He said that six beers was no big deal for him to drink and still be able to fly. I could not believe my ears. That would be typical of someone to say about driving a car or an ATV, but an airplane? I guess he was so complacent about flying that he compared it to driving a car. No matter how talented a pilot is, drinking and flying is not the same as driving a car. I could tell that no matter what I said, he had made up his mind. I told him that I would give him a ride to the strip. I was really disappointed that he would do this, especially when we went out of our way to make him feel comfortable with a place to stay. We got to the plane and I said, "Be safe, and give me a call on the radio when you get back to your camp."

He replied, "You got it."

In my mind I was rehashing what he had said, that he did this all the time. Thank God partnering up with us on flying did not work out. There was no way I would allow a pilot to drink and fly my plane. Little did I know how much this was going to affect my life in the future. It was kind of like the Wild West out here and pilots were like outlaws. We flew in crazy weather and with overloaded airplanes, and a lot of pilots partied and flew the next day. One of the rules of flying is "Eight hours from the bottle to the throttle." A lot of pilots did not adhere to this rule, but this was a first for me to see this brazen drinking and flying.

Kirk got in his plane and I headed back to camp. On the way home I was wondering if I would be the last person to see him alive. When I got back, Harry asked me what I thought. I said, "He did not seem intoxicated, but I would never condone drinking and flying in the same evening, especially since he had a comfortable place to stay."

Even though he did not seem drunk, drinking affects your coordination, and Kirk definitely had a coordination problem with his landings.

We could see Kirk taking off from camp. The first thing he did was take off downwind. As a rule, we learn as pilots to always take off into the wind. We were all standing around the fire when we noticed that Kirk was flying west toward Yakutat instead of going east toward his camp on the East River. I was really worried now. It was getting late. It was just a short hop to his camp, but a 15-minute flight to Yakutat. Maybe he felt like going to town. I had no idea what could be going on in his head at this point. Then we heard him turn around and come back toward us. We could see him coming closer and it looked like he was flying close to the ground, about fifty feet AGL, (above ground level.) As he flew past, he pulled the plane straight back into what looked to me like an aerobatic maneuver, probably a loop. This was insane. I could not believe my eyes. I thought for sure I was going to be witnessing a plane crash. All aerobatics should be done at least five thousand feet AGL. The plane went into the loop. I was saying a little prayer, "Dear Jesus, please put your hand on Kirk's plane and surround him with your angels."

Kirk's plane went up and over into the float part of the maneuver where his plane was upside down, and then transitioned into the next phase of the downward part of the loop. He was upside down and on his way toward us. So far he was executing the maneuver spot on, but was getting closer and closer to the ground. One thing you had to do to pull off a proper loop is not let your airspeed get too fast on the way back down. The exact loop ends at the exact altitude that you started the loop at, which in this case would be at fifty feet. If Kirk did not perform this perfectly, he was going to crash for sure. "Here he comes!" I yelled out.

As Kurt finished the loop with perfection, he flew right past us looking out the window and holding a beer up in his hand. I was completely shocked, to say the least. We had to cheer though. I believe we had just witnessed a miracle.

We had the radio turned up so we would be able to hear him call when he landed and got back to his cabin. I figured that would take him about thirty minutes. I looked at my watch. Just because he pulled off that amazing performance did not mean he was in the clear. He still had to land on his little strip at the river. For most that would be an easy task, but for some reason, while Kirk was amazing in the air, his directional control of his plane on landings and takeoffs was very poor.

About thirty minutes went by. I was on pins and needles. I then heard Kirk squawking, "Italio Camp, Sparky here safe and sound. Over and out."

I came back, "Glad to hear it. By the way, nice loop." I did not want to give him too much praise and encourage him to think he was invincible, or think I approved of his drinking and flying, but it was impressive.

He replied, "Thanks, and that was a great dinner. You guys have a good one. I am headed to bed."

"Goodnight!" I was just glad he was alive. I knew for sure I did not need that kind of stress in my life on top of the stress that I already had. I was going to have to sever my partnership with Kirk and distance myself. I liked him well enough, but this was truly the icing on the cake. I was going to do it soon, too. Might as well not drag it out.

The next day I flew to town. I had to pick up some groceries, supplies, and gas for the ATVs and skiff. I got to the airport and tied down the plane. My buddy Joe, who worked at Alaska Airlines, walked up to me. "Hey, George, how's it going?" I had to laugh. He was going to get a gut ache whcn he heard what Kirk did last night. I told him the whole story. He doubled over and said he could not believe it. Then he said, "Well, I don't think I could top that story, but I do have one for you. Are you still going to fish with him?"

I said, "No way! I am going to talk to him ASAP and tell him that I don't want to fish with him."

He said, "Okay, I have a crazy story to tell you. We were working Alaska Airlines Flight 66 and everything was going as planned. The flight arrived and we got the passengers unloaded, and as we were unloading the luggage, one of the bags had come open from a broken zipper. We were putting the contents back into the luggage and it was a bunch of kinky stuff."

I asked, "Like what?"

Joe was laughing as he said, "Stuff like dildos and kinky women's garments."

I said, "Well, that is funny. So whose bag was it?" I was thinking it would be really amusing if it belonged to some unlikely person like a church lady or someone who worked for the city office. It was going to be entertaining to know who this kinky person was.

He blurted out, "The bag belonged to Kirk!"

I said, "WHAT?"

He replied, "Yeah, the bag belonged to Kirk. Jim and I were working the flight together and we had to put all of that stuff back into the bag. Of course we looked at the bag tag to see whose it was. That is not even the whole story. He brought a guy with him."

I said, "Yes, he has a cook at his camp who he brought up to help him."

Joe said, "Well, I believe they are doing some cooking down there."

Another shocker was coming. This was just getting weirder and weirder. I am not sure I could handle much more. I just stood there stunned and in disbelief. I was already going to distance myself from Kirk, but this really made me glad I had already made the decision to cut my ties with him.

I told Joe I had to run to town and pick up some supplies, and thanked him for the heads up on Kirk. This town was just full of surprises. Those guys at Alaska Airlines were crazy. Joe worked with another guy, Jim Benson, who was one of the main cocaine and marijuana dealers in town. I suppose working for the freight department at the airline gave him the opportunity to easily smuggle drugs into Yakutat. I even heard that if he thought you were bringing in drugs, the drugs would "disappear." Some guys thought they had gotten busted, but nothing ever came of it, and then Jim Benson coincidentally had dope for sale. The guys whose drugs went missing were just happy that the cops had not busted them, which was one of their first assumptions. I presumed they were not going to report their "stolen or missing" freight.

I raced into town and picked up some grub, gas, and beer for the camp. I got back to the airport, loaded the plane with the freight, untied the plane, and taxied to the aviation fuel pump. I topped off my fuel tanks that held a total of 84 gallons of avgas, which I mixed with auto gas in my jugs for some very high-octane fuel that burned a lot cleaner than straight unleaded. I was ready to get back to camp. One day in town was enough for me. With my newfound information I was ready to get home and then straight to Kirk's. I wanted to let him know we were done. I taxied out for departure and flew to Italio. I called the camp from the marine VHF radio that I had in the plane. I also had an aircraft radio. All of the planes that flew regularly in the area had both aircraft and marine VHF radios to communicate with set net camps. I had Harry meet me at the strip with an ATV and trailer. I got out of the plane and Harry drove the ATV close to the plane to make for an easy offload. I siphoned fifteen gallons of avgas out of the wings into jerry cans. As we were unloading, I told Harry what Joe had told me at the airport. He busted out laughing and then kind of looked disgusted. I said, "My feelings exactly."

He said, "We have a pair of butt stabbers down here?"

I replied, "Looks that way, but at least they are at the East River and we don't have to work with them."

"Agreed!" Harry piped up.

I told him I was going to fly down there right now and tell Kirk that it was over. Harry said, "All right, see you back at camp. Give me a call and I will come back to pick you up."

"Will do," I replied.

I was happy to get this over with, so I got in the plane and took off for the East River. I landed, and Kirk was there to meet me. Kirk said, "So, do you want to come up to camp?" I told him that I was in a hurry to get back for dinner, and that I had been running around town all day, so no thanks. I did say that I had flown down there to tell him something in person. He got a worried look on his face. He asked if there was anything wrong.

I answered, "Well, there kind of is something wrong. I went into partnership with you thinking you were going to be doing a lot of flying for our team, but since you can't fly the 206, I am going to have to do the same amount of flying with or without you. I think it's best if I just keep the same program I had last year and we just not team up."

He let that sink in and then said, "Well, sorry to hear that. Is there anything I can do to change your mind?"

I told him there was not really anything he could do to change my decision. I said, "Nothing personal, just business." This was the truth. I said, "I don't mean to be so short, but I really need to get going."

He said, "Well, don't let me hold you up."

I replied, "Good luck for the season, and stop by sometime." I really did not mean it, but wanted to end it on a good note.

I got in the plane, and Kirk drove off. He looked kind of sad. I was not sad, just very disappointed about the flying, and glad it was over. I got close to camp and called on the radio so Harry would be there when I landed. He was waiting with a cold beer for me. "Thanks, Harry, I could use a cold frosty beverage." Even though Harry had been slacking, he had his moments.

Fishing and flying went on for the rest of the season. We all did our part. Mike was doing more and more flying. Kurt and his brother Shaun stayed busy at Gulf Air. Sometimes in between the fishing and flying I would see the pilots and catch up on all the latest scandals. I think most of us pilots have something in common. We love to fly, and affording the opportunity to fly, we sometimes have to make compromises for it. You can work a nine-to-five job and maybe get some time once in a while to fly, or be a commercial pilot and fly all of the time, but you give up a part of yourself in return.

Kurt would always say that being an air taxi pilot was a thankless job. In a way he was right. Sure, people appreciated you, and looked up to you, but a lot of people were clueless about how stressful and taxing it was to fly heavy loads in and out of small, short bush strips, especially in bad weather with high winds and low visibility. A lot of people sometimes put extra pressure on pilots to fly. They would say things like, "I really have to get back to town. I have to get back to work, can't we just put one more cooler in the plane?" An so on. Your life is not worth losing just to make it back to work on time. People also pressure air taxi pilots to put more weight in the plane than is recommended. Pilots sometimes cave in to these requests so as to not disappoint people. That is when complacency kicks in and pilots crash.

Besides being a great pilot, Kurt was an ace mechanic. He and Mike worked together on keeping the planes in tip-top shape. He had his own Cessna 185. His brother Shaun flew for Methow Air, out of Washington state. They only brought their planes up for fish hauling for the cannery, and mostly flew the C-47/DC-3's. I will never forget when Shaun was flying over my camp in a Pilatus Porter, a single-engine beast of a plane that can carry loads of up to 1800 pounds. As he was flying over, my son Jason and I heard a loud explosion. Then we watched the plane fall out of the sky. Shaun crash-landed the plane in a tolerable place where the plane would probably be damaged, but he had a good chance of not being injured too badly upon crash landing. I immediately took off on my ATV to the crash site. When I got to the scene, Shaun was a little shaken up, but he was all right. The plane was wrecked, but salvageable. I told him he was lucky, and that where he landed was a lot better than most places to go down. The first thing a pilot is trained to do is to always be looking for a place to land. Alaska's coastline can be very unforgiving. It is mountainous with a lot of water, swamps, and rivers to fly over. The area I fished had a lot of sand flats and dunes, which had some areas that were good for landing in an emergency. I told him he could come back to my camp and call the office for a pickup. We got on the radio, but did not say much as the whole town practically stood by on the radio. We called Gulf Air and asked for Kurt to come down. Kurt flew down and we went to inspect the airplane. Kurt flew Shaun back to town so he could tell his office about the engine failure and that he had to land the plane in an emergency. He added that the plane was unfit to fly. I told Shaun that I would take care of the plane and help them salvage it to get repaired. Just goes to show that you can be the most careful pilot, but never know when a catastrophe might occur.

CHAPTER 24

CHERRY BOMB

THERE WAS A GROUP OF Tlingit Indians fishing Yakutat. Tlingit was the main native Alaskan tribe in the area. There were Tlingits in Haines when I was growing up. I would have to say that the Yakutat area natives were different. They were known to be a warrior tribe, and had a reputation for being mean and hostile. They would give you dirty looks, gang up on people, and try to intimidate people. They even tried to gang up on my son when he was ten years old. They did not know I was watching and I overheard a gang of local kids taunting my son. I came out from behind the house and told the rat pack of kids to pick their toughest, meanest, baddest kid, and that he could fight my kid with me supervising. I told them that I would make sure that it would be a fair fight. They huddled up and agreed to the challenge. They said they picked Situk to fight Jason. This kid Situk was two years older and a lot bigger than Jason. I knew Jason was not afraid, and that he was as tough as nails from growing up in the wilderness. I had already been teaching him karate. Jason was a natural. Even at a young age he was muscular. He was kind of short for his age, but as tough as a wolverine.

The kids formed a circle around the two boys. They started the fight buy pushing on each other, and then Situk threw a punch. Jason avoided the punch and came back with a wicked counterpunch to Situk's gut. I could tell it hurt him. Situk pulled his fists tight and brought his elbows in a little. Since he was so much taller, his stomach was a weakness that Jason was going to take advantage of. Situk threw another punch that landed on the side of Jason's head. It did not even faze him. Jason hunkered down, went in, and attacked Situk's body with punches. He gave him about ten hard punches and Situk fell over. The kids were yelling and screaming for Situk to get up, but he was done.

Jason raised his hands like a boxer who had just won a championship. I grabbed his fists and patted him on the back. I was proud of him for standing up to the town bullies. The kids helped Situk up, and they quieted down. I said, "Hey, kids, this was a fair fight and Jason won. Is there anyone else who wants to fight?" They all looked at each other and shook their heads no. I said, "Okay, then it's done." One of the kids asked if Jason wanted to play and he looked up at me. I knew Jason could take care of himself and I had a feeling they were not going to mess with him any longer, so I thought it would be okay for him to go. I said, "Sure, Jason, make sure you call me if you need me." He said he would, and ran off to play.

That was the good thing about growing up when boys could have a little fight and afterward the beef was over. Usually if you beat up the toughest kid, all the other kids followed suit. I do not believe in babying children. Most parents do not let their kids stand up for themselves. There are always going to be bullies, but not much is usually done about them except calling their parents, who don't do a damn thing, much less discipline them.

My other son, Adam, was two years younger than Jason and much different. Jason was tough and had always been mechanical, whereas Adam was more kindhearted, soft spoken, and a mamma's boy. He would not be the kind of kid to fight, even if he were being bullied.

Things were changing at the rivers. People were getting more competitive. It was pretty much an all-out war zone down there. One local native I knew, Burt, had a very nice camp and cabin up the beach from me on the Italio. He fished hard and always made good money. He was usually partnered with a clan of Tlingit Indians. He had a big family. His brother Kenny had a permit and fished with another crew of Indians. I was in fierce competition with these guys. They were always testing me, trying to push me around to see if I would back down and let them have my sets that I worked very hard for. I never caved in. I always stood my ground.

There was one group of guys with the last names of Smokestack and Remis. They were already crazy, but this particular season, besides being fueled by gallons of whisky and beer, I heard that they had gotten hold of a large amount of cocaine. They would stay up all night partying. We could hear them from our camp. A lot of times they would shoot guns off and we would hear bullets whizzing past our camp. By the end of the season I was getting pretty fed up with their mischievous ways. When I saw them on the river, I could see coke rings around their nostrils, and they were obviously as high as kites. They tried to act tough, but I never backed down. Burt's crew even brought down a Lurch-looking person to come after us and try to intimidate us. They claimed he was a hit man. We had to build a wall out of beach logs for protection because of the bullets they kept lobbing were coming near our cabin. They were really trying to scare us, and could even have killed us. The troopers and police never did anything to stop people from tormenting each other out here. I suppose they thought we would work it out amongst ourselves. The only thing I saw the troopers do was harass people, including me.

The crew of natives had illegal nets that were made of monofilament line that we called bingo nets. They also fished with extra nets that were not allowed. You could only fish one net per permit, but these guys had extra nets out to catch more fish. We had a tactic of getting fish to hit our nets. Some might consider it herding fish, which was against the law, but everyone was doing some kind of herding. We would drive our jet boats up and down the river looking for schools of fish. When we found one we would chase the fish toward our nets so that we could catch them. It turned out that the natives had spies on the riverbank, taking pictures of me in my skiff running the river like I always did. They thought they could turn me in for herding fish and get me in trouble. If I were guilty, it could mean a ticket, and some offenses had jail time as well.

I saw them taking pictures of me, but I did not think the pictures could prove much. Everyone ran the river in their skiff and checked their nets. Unless a trooper actually saw you and caught you herding fish into your net, just being near your net in your jet boat was not against any laws. It took quite a bit to get pictures developed from the river. They would have to get the roll of film to town and have someone mail it off to get developed, and then get the pictures back in the mail and back down to the jokers who were trying to get me in trouble. Weeks went by and these guys were getting worse and worse. I suppose when you stay high on cocaine and booze for weeks straight, it might affect your personality, especially when their personalities were not that great to begin with. Every time I saw those guys they had what looked like coke rings on their noses and acted high. I just continued working and fishing hard. They kept putting out their illegal bingo nets and herding fish, and in the meantime catching a lot of extra fish. In my mind they were being very unfair.

One day I was on the river fishing, minding my own business as usual, when I saw the trooper plane fly over. I could tell it was going to land. It was normal for troopers to check on us. There were a lot of things a trooper could do to give you a ticket. One thing in particular was that nets had to be 100 yards apart. Sometimes in a war over sets we would pace off exactly the footage from the other person's net. This usually infuriated the other person to have someone fish that close to them. Another violation that troopers were looking out for was fishing over the boundaries set by the Department of Fish and Game. You were in big trouble if you were caught over the line. I thought that finally the troopers would catch the Indian clan doing any one of the numerous illegal acts they had been getting away with.

The trooper came toward me. I said hello. I could tell by his look that it was not good news. He actually had a smirk on his face. He said, "Davis, I have a ticket to give you."

I exclaimed loudly, "For what?"

He replied, "For herding fish."

I said, "This is a bunch of bullshit! Did you see me herding fish?"

He replied as he handed me a manila envelope, "It shows in the evidence that you were herding fish." He got a wicked grin on his face as I ripped open the envelope.

Inside were blown up pictures of me in my skiff running toward my net with fish jumping in the air. There was also a ticket and a court date.

"This is ridiculous!" I yelled.

He said, "Well, if you want to fight the ticket, I will see you at the hearing."

I replied, "Oh, trust me, you will be seeing me at the courthouse to fight these false charges!" He turned around to leave and I said, "By the way, if you want to catch the real violators, you should go up the river and look at all the hidden monofilament bingo nets those guys have set out. I bet if you go up there right now, you will actually catch them in action."

He got a concerned look on his face and said that he might look into it. I thought that he should, because I was not doing anything wrong. The only thing the picture showed was me running my skiff toward my net. How else was I supposed to check my net? I have to go toward my net with my skiff to pick my net up and pick the fish out. He told me that I would have a chance to explain myself in court. I told him that I would be there.

I was enraged! I could not believe these guys would go this far to try to get me in trouble. In fact, I believed that people in glass houses should not throw stones. They were up there fishing illegal bingo nets and had what I assumed was at least a kilo of cocaine in their fishing camp. They were the last people who should have been turning someone in to the cops considering all of the shooting they were doing toward my cabin. As I had already learned though, it is what you can prove. I could not prove it was them shooting at me, so there was no use in even bringing it up.

I saw those guys later on and they asked me if I got my present. I said, "Oh yeah, I did, and you are going to get yours, too."

They laughed and said, "Yeah right, Davis, we have the troopers on our side. Haven't you learned anything by now? You will always be an outsider and we can get away with what we want, because we are local." I told them that we would see about that.

I kept fishing and gathering my own evidence for the hearing. I snuck up the river and got pictures of all of them herding fish into their nets. I was going to fight fire with fire. There was no way I was going to just lay down and take my chances. I was going to battle. I not only got pictures of them herding fish, I got pictures of them with their bingo nets. They messed with the wrong guy.

The date of the hearing was coming up and I had my pictures and my testimony all thought out. When I got to the hearing, I was pleasantly surprised that besides the trooper, the guys who turned me in were actually there to testify against me. This was going to be great. I gave copies of the pictures to the judge and to the trooper. The judge called the hearing to order and we were all sworn in. The trooper was allowed to present his case.

He called the first witness, who looked as high as ever. He actually had coke in his black mustache, which was unbelievable.

The trooper handed him and the judge a picture of me in my skiff heading toward my net and asked him what I was doing in the picture. As he looked at the picture he said, "Mr. Davis was herding fish into his net."

Now it was my turn to question him. I asked him if running a skiff in a river toward your net is herding. He had to answer truthfully. "No."

I asked, "How can you tell if a person is herding fish?" He stuttered and tried to say that he just knew that I was herding fish and that is why he took the pictures. I handed him and the judge the picture of him running a skiff upriver toward his net and asked him if he were herding fish.

He said, "Definitely not!"

I asked how could he prove it? He just said that he did not break any laws. I tried not to laugh.

While the trooper was up on the stand I asked him the same questions. I asked him if he had personally witnessed me breaking any laws. He said, "No." So I asked the judge to consider the trooper's testimony hearsay, which meant that I believed the pictures did not show enough, and that without the troopers actually seeing me do anything wrong, the charges should be dropped.

The judge asked if there was anything else to add from either party, and the cokehead spoke up and said in a crazed voice, "JUDGE, LET ME MAKE YOU UNDERSTAND!"

Everyone in the courtroom was shocked by this extremely bizarre behavior. The judge looked pissed and said that would be all, but the cokehead kept yelling, "JUDGE, LET ME MAKE YOU UNDERSTAND!" The judge yelled at the cokehead and slammed his gavel.

"One more outburst and I will have you locked up! You are lucky I don't have you locked up just for showing up to my courtroom obviously high on something!" The cokehead shut up and sat back down. The judge gave his decision. He said, "I find Mr. Davis not guilty of herding fish, and court is adjourned."

Thank goodness. I was relieved. If the judge had believed that bizarre guy's story, I could have been fined and given a jail sentence. The Yakutat crew scurried out hurriedly, probably afraid of being busted. I would not be surprised if they were crass enough to be holding drugs. They were so convinced they were invincible. They finally got a reality check.

This gave me the perfect chance to approach the trooper with the pictures I had of the guys and their bingo nets. I handed the trooper the envelope and said, "If you want to catch the real bad guys, here you go," and walked off. Whatever he decided to do with the evidence was up to him. I think he was going to have to catch them in person though, so that would mean I would be under scrutiny as well and would have to be very careful not to break any laws. I had not broken any laws anyway, but there was always a fine line when it came to fishing. I was so glad this was over with.

The troopers in the fishing area were sneaky. We had nicknames for them like Spying Brian, Dickless Tracy because she was a female, and Snake in the Grass because his last name was Peepgrass. They would sneak around to bust people for illegal activities. I hoped this particular trooper would investigate these guys. They had it coming for trying to get me in trouble. They wasted my time fighting the ticket by making me come into town, going to court, plus missing out on valuable fishing time.

The guys who turned me in seemed pretty disappointed, especially when the trooper flew over where they had their bingo nets out. The trooper then went up the river and caught them red-handed. This was a more serious charge than herding fish. Now they had to go to court and explain themselves. I heard they all got tickets and suspended jail sentences. People who live in glass houses should not throw stones! It is my policy not to deliberately cause people problems. I like to keep to myself, work hard, and make money. When people intentionally set out to cause me problems and mess with my living, that is when I retaliate. I strike back to win, and usually do so in a way that they never want to mess with me again.

I had a big end-of-the-season surprise for this crew. I brought my own henchmen down to the river for the closing weeks of the fishing season. It was October and getting cold out. I actually really enjoyed this time of year. I liked the smell in the air and the crisp frosty mornings. Even better, it was moose and duck hunting season. My Chesapeake loved it. The Italio had a great duck-hunting place I developed that I called Quack a Duck Swamps. I set up a few blinds and had really good wing shooting there. It was the perfect location on the coast where most species of ducks would stop on the flyway. We shot mallards, widgeon, pintail, gadwall, teal, and geese. I did not care for goose meat that much. Filbert, my henchman, was a hoot to have at camp. He was a survivalist and dressed in all camo. He was a large mean-looking guy, and he had all kinds of assault rifles that he brought down with him. He had an H&K 308, a Ruger ranch rifle mini 14 equipped with high-capacity, thirty-round clips. He would even paint his face in camouflage just to freak these guys out. They believed he was a Navy Seal who was now a mercenary for hire. For all they knew he could have been. He definitely looked the part.

Filbert would hang out behind the bunker we had built and lob bullets over toward the Smokestack and Remis camp to give them a little taste of their own medicine. They were so stoned on coke and booze they were probably scared to death. Besides, Filbert's antics were an even better surprise for the end-of-the-season bash I knew the guys would be having. They had been partying all season, but since the end of fishing was coming up, I knew they would have an extra huge party. I went to town to get my own party favors. Filbert loved to bake, so I bought a bunch of baking supplies so he could make his famous turnovers. I bought a case of seal bombs at the hardware store, which is like an M80 times two. I also bought boxes and boxes of .223 ammunition. I had my own Ruger ranch rifle with high-capacity clips. This was literally going to be a BLAST!!

When I got back to camp and showed Filbert what I had bought, he busted up laughing. My plan was to wait until the guys were nice and wasted. So in the meantime, Filbert and I had a few beers. I cooked us up some steaks and spuds, and he made some turnovers for dessert that were delicious. It was about 10:00 p.m. and I told Filbert we should get our gear ready. We had four thirty-round clips loaded, one hundred and twenty .223 rounds. Filbert loaded two thirty-round .308 clips. I brought out my .460 Weatherby cannon with three rounds and my case of seal bombs. We dressed in all black and painted our faces black.

We drove over and then parked far enough away so they could not hear our ATVs. As we walked up to their camp armed to the teeth, we could hear them partying from quite a distance away. They had their generator going and loud music playing. They were hooping and hollering. We could even hear them talking about us, plotting their next attack. Little did they know that World War III was about to break out.

They had a wall tent camp with a wood stove. I snuck up to their wall tent and threw a seal bomb into their stovepipe. Then I ran to where Filbert was hiding. BOOM! The seal bomb blew up and exploded inside their tent. I could see the door front door of their wall tent fly open, and burning embers flying out of the door of the wood stove that had blown open. Everyone screamed and ran outside. As they ran outside we proceeded to fire off multiple rounds of .223s, and Filbert was firing off his .308. For kicks we fired off the .460 cannon. Then we threw some seal bombs toward them and they exploded. This was great!

They were screaming in fear and yelling, "PLEASE! Don't shoot us!"

We ceased fire for a minute. I yelled out, "Hey, guys, it's me DAVIS!"

They yelled back in a shaky voice, "Please don't kill us."

I told them that Filbert and I were spying on them and heard of their plots to cause us more problems.

They called back, "We are sorry, please don't hurt us. We promise, we just want a truce! It was a mistake to mess with you!"

I yelled back, "I don't think I can trust you guys. I think you want a war."

They replied, "We were mistaken. We don't want a war with you. Please, let's just have a truce!"

I said, "Well, I have to talk it over with Filbert and see what he thinks. He's a professional." We looked at each other and smirked. They had no idea where we were exactly, so they could not see us. They were all huddled outside of what was left of their tent. They had a big bonfire going so that was where they were gathered. I asked Filbert if he thought they had had enough.

He said, "It's fun to torment these guys, but yes, I think we scared the shit out of them, and I don't figure they want to keep playing war games with us."

I told Filbert that I agreed. It was fun, but I believed a truce was in order. I yelled at them, "Okay, I am going to come out and I want you to shake our hands for a truce, and don't try any funny stuff or else. We have a sniper in the woods with a bead on you."

They said, "We promise no funny stuff. We want peace!"

I said, "Okay, I am coming out!"

I came walking out with my ranch rifle with a full thirty-round magazine. I approached the fire where the gang was standing. The leader of the crew came up to shake my hand and he promised the war was over and no more shenanigans. I shook his hand back and said, "I hope not, because the next time I am not going to be so forgiving."

They said they were going to go repair their wall tent stovepipe, which had exploded, and clean up. They asked us if we wanted to have a drink with them. I said, "No, I am just going to go back to my camp and hope not to hear any more racket coming from you guys."

They promised that they would keep it down and behave themselves. I turned around and walked into the woods where Filbert was waiting. We got out of earshot of their camp and it was all we could do to hold in our laughter. That was one of the funniest things yet! Filbert said this was one of the most amusing and enjoyable fishing trips he had ever been on. We got to our ATVs and drove back to the cabin. We got in and cracked a beer, had a good laugh, and we both agreed that we had done an outstanding job of winning that battle.

We wrapped up the season and buttoned up the cabin for the winter. I had plans on doing my usual trapping expeditions with Iron Mike. I had a ton of stories about my adventures to catch up on since we had both been so busy all summer.

Winter trapping went by fast and we did pretty well. We got to fly all winter and made a few bucks doing it. I think at this point, we were happy if we made enough to pay for the gas and a little pocket money.

I made pretty good money fishing so I was able to live all winter on the money I made during the summer. I was glad that I did not have to go crabbing again. Crabbing during the winters in Alaska is a brutal job. I had much more fun flying around with Mike in his ski plane, trapping Alaska's

Lost Coast. Spring came fast and before I knew it, it was already time to get ready for commercial fishing. I was excited to see what this season's adventures would bring. There were always surprises in store for me.

I had been helping Mike during the winter in his hangar with his air taxi planes. This was a great experience to work hand in hand with ace mechanics. I learned a lot about working on airplanes and how to do a lot of my own maintenance. Even though I did not have an A&P license, I could work on planes as long as I was supervised during the maintenance. The A&P mechanic signed off in my logbook any maintenance that I did. I liked to work on my own plane. This saved me a lot of time and money, and the anxiety of having someone else work on my plane. I had been around so many mishaps that I felt more comfortable being the one doing the work, or at least be there helping while the mechanic was doing the work. Pilots have a saying, "If something were to go wrong, it was usually after the annual."

CHAPTER 25

KANAE!

I FLEW DOWN TO MY cabin and started getting ready for the season. When I opened up my cabin I had no idea what to expect. Sometimes varmints ate their way into the cabin and would make nests out of sleeping bags, and a mess with their droppings.

I was outside getting my nets and totes out of the shed when I heard a wheeler approach. There were other people down here getting ready for the season, like the Hansons. The Hanson, Smokestack, and Remis clan were part of the group that I had had a war with the season before, but it was a quiet winter and I did not expect any problems from them. If anything, they might just be trying to be neighborly. When I could see someone coming up on the ATV, it looked like a fellow named Burt. Burt had a really nice cabin up the way from me and always ran a first-class operation. He did like to party, but he was not part of the group that I had had a war with. He had a brother named Kenny who ran with the Smokestack and Remis clans, but I do not think they got along that well. When Burt pulled up, he looked friendly, so I smiled and greeted him graciously.

He said, "Hi, George!"

I replied, "Howdy, Burt! How goes it?"

He said, "Pretty good. I spent the winter down in Baja, Mexico. I have a little trailer on the beach."

I said, "Wow, that sounds nice. I had a good winter trapping with Mike."

Burt replied, "I brought back some marinated carne asada from Mexico that is to die for. I was going to BBQ some up tonight if you would like to join me."

I said back, "That sounds great. What time should I come over?"

He replied, "How about around six." I asked if I should bring anything and he said, "Nope, I have everything, even some beer and Crown Royal!"

I said, "Great, see you then!"

Burt started his wheeler and drove off. I thought, *WOW, I had a crazy war with practically the whole native clan, and now I am being invited over to Burt's for a special carne asada dinner. Sounds interesting.*

I kept working on my gear and then started getting ready about five. I got to Burt's cabin around six. He was already having a Crown on the rocks. He asked me of I would like a Crown. I said, "Sure, sounds outstanding." Burt poured me about four fingers in a glass with ice. When Burt showed up at camp, it was like Christmas. He brought down two 206 loads of groceries and supplies. He brought all kinds of food, liquor, beer, and wine. He liked to camp in style. We had a toast to being friends.

Burt confided in me that he kind of felt that the guys he was fishing with were taking advantage of him, and partying too hard. He said, "Don't get me wrong, I like to have a good time, but I like to work hard and make as much money as I can during the season. Those other guys would party so hard that they would be too stoned to check the nets and be late setting out our nets on the openers." He told me that he noticed that I was always there early and ready to fish, and that I fished hard the whole opening. He even saw how hard I worked on the closures mending my nets, and putting up smoked and jarred fish. He asked if I was interested in partnering up for the season. I told him I thought it was a good idea and that we would make a good team. He said, "Let's have a toast, KANAE! (Ka Na`)."

I said "KANAE!" back and then took a drink. After I got my drink down I asked Burt what kanae meant.

He laughed and said, "Tlingit for F'n A!"

I Cheered "KANAE!"

We worked together really well, alternating fishing in the bay and the Italio and East Rivers with Burt's big 21 ft. Bay skiff he had suitably named *Kanae*.

We were making good money. During the closures I was doing my annual subsistence fishing, and smoking and jarring my king and sockeye salmon on the Italio River. I was very meticulous about the way I put my fish up for the winter. When I made smoked fish, my process was very lengthy and a lot of work was involved. First I have to catch the fish. Then I keep it on ice, being careful when I handle it so as not to bruise the meat. After that, I fillet the fish and clean it well. For smoking, I cut the fish into strips and leave some of the fish in whole fillets. I use a special brine that is one pound of kosher salt to two pounds of brown sugar in about three gallons of water, or for a bigger batch I use two pounds of kosher salt and four pounds of brown sugar in five gallons of water. One of the tricks to the brine is that you have to use enough warm water in the beginning to dissolve the sugar and salt. This takes about a gallon. After the sugar and salt are dissolved, the rest of the brine is cold water. I brine my fish for twelve hours, stirring the fish so it gets an even marinade. When I take the fish out of the brine, I use paper towels to dab off excess liquid and slime. No matter how well you clean the fish, there is always some slime from the salmon skin. I place the fish on my racks to air-dry overnight. I built my smoker at the Italio River. It was 6x8 ft. and seven feet tall, with a shed roof. It was built to hold about thirty to thirty-five salmon.

When I did a batch of fish it was serious business. After the fish dried overnight then it was time to build the fire. I have a fire pit in the bottom of the smoker with a cast iron skillet that sits directly on the fire and is covered by a stainless steel plate. This is so the drippings from the salmon don't put the fire out. I use alder that I chopped down, and I actually peel the bark off and age it. Seasoned dry alder makes the best smoked salmon. Hot and sunny weather makes for the best conditions for smoking salmon.

I started a fire in the smoker and began the process. All together from start to finish it is a three- to four-day procedure. The end product is so delectable I can barely stop myself from gorging on it once it is finished. That is one reason I have to make plenty of it. Most of my friends and family would prefer my smoked salmon as gifts instead of store-bought presents for holidays and birthdays.

It was evening and we were all exhausted. We fished a seventy-two-hour opener, nonstop, and then we immediately put the subsistence net out and worked nonstop on the batch of smoked fish. I got the fish in the smoker to a point where I could build a small fire with some alder wood in the cast iron skillet and left it in the bottom of the smoker to lightly smolder all night. I could finally get some rest. I slept like a boulder. I was assured my salmon was going to be perfect and that I could even sleep in. Even after the salmon was smoked it would need time to cool off before the next stage of processing.

During the night I heard the dogs barking in the distance. I just figured they were chasing off a bear, which was normal for this time of year. Bears were thick down here, especially with the temptation of a smokehouse in the yard. My Chesapeake Bay retrievers were great at keeping unwanted visitors out of my yard. Since the ruckus was so far in the distance, I was not worried that anything was bothering my smoker. I looked out the window and did not see anything. I was exhausted and just wanted to go back to sleep, so I went back to bed and fell asleep as soon as my head hit the pillow.

The next morning I woke up and put the coffee on. I went outside to do my morning business and saw something I did not like. The double doors to the smoker were wide open. I had a pretty good latch on the doors, as bears were an issue on this area of the river. If it had been a bear attacking my smoker, I can't believe that I did not hear anything. Maybe I was so tired that after I fell back asleep and something came back and attacked my smoker. I walked up to the smoker to investigate. My fish were totally ruined, not to mention the big mess of scattered, half-eaten fish covered in sand.

As I further investigated, I was getting more enraged by the minute. The tracks in the sand were not the tracks of a bear, but those of a dog. I thought, *I know my dogs would not attack my fish.* They had never done it in the past. I fed them well and they were not mischievous in that way. I called my dogs and they came to me. They looked guilty, I believe, because they knew something was wrong, but when I inspected their faces and paws they had no signs of having gotten into my smoked fish. If they were the culprits, they would have had fish oil and smell all over them. I put the dogs in the house because I was going to track down what had done this. The tracks that were around the crime scene were that of a wolf or a very large dog.

I got on my Honda Big Red three-wheeler and started following the tracks. Off in the distance I saw that someone had set up a tent camp near the mouth of the river about a mile away. The tracks were headed straight for it. Whoever it was, they must have come in on the evening tide with their skiff and set up camp. When I got closer, I could see remnants of my smoked salmon. I could also make out drag marks near the dog tracks where the dog had dragged my fish back to this camp. When I pulled up to the camp, I yelled out, "Hey, you in there!"

I could hear someone getting ready and they came out. It was a small, skinny guy. He said, "Hey, what's going on?" Then he looked down and saw the fish carcass lying there and said, "Oh, I wonder what that is all about?"

His dog was nowhere to be seen. I asked him if he had a dog. He told me that he had a large husky. I asked him, "First of all, what are you doing down here?"

He told me that he was from Kotzebue, had bought a Yakutat set net permit, had a custom made fiberglass 21 ft. Wegley, and ran his skiff thirty miles from Yakutat into the mouth of the river and set up his camp last night on the high tide.

I asked him, "So you plan on fishing here?" He told me he did. I said, "Well, I think we are going to have a problem. For one, your dog broke into my smoker and destroyed thirty sockeye and five king salmon that took me three days to prepare. Two, there is a limited fishing area, and since there had been no one else fishing the mouth, I was setting my nets upriver. If someone starts fishing the mouth, then they are going to be intercepting my fish. By the way, what is your name?"

He told me his name was Jim and that he had no intention of infringing on my fishing areas. He apologized up and down about his dog breaking into my smoker and ruining my fish. He immediately offered to pay for any damages and said he had his checkbook in his wallet and would write me out a check. He asked me what I thought was a fair amount. I told him $350 was fair. Jim went back into his tent and brought out his checkbook. He asked to whom should he make the check out to. I said, "My name is George Davis." He handed me the check. I told him that this solves the first problem. Fishing the mouth of the river is the second issue. I went on to explain that to effectively fish the mouth, you needed a two-man crew, which I had. Secondly, it was technical and dangerous fishing this area, and since he was new to the area it was not a good idea for him to be fishing the mouth by himself.

I proposed a solution. I told Jim that I would be willing to help him out and that we should partner up. I said that he should let my brother and me fish with his new Wegley with a new 60 hp Johnson in the river mouth, and he could use one of my three-wheelers and my 16 ft. skiff to fish the upper river. I explained to him that it would be in his best interest to take the deal for safety reasons. He agreed and thought it was fair to partner up and take the deal. After we fished two openers together, he told me that he was going to pack up and take his camp to the East River. I told him, "Good luck, Kotzebue!"

CHAPTER 26

SPORTYS AND SPANKERS

LATER ON THAT WEEK WHILE I was fishing, we saw a plane flying over. It looked like a Gulf Air Taxi plane and was circling around above us. I looked at Barry and said, "Probably dropping off some more sportys." We heard the plane land. When we got done fishing, we went down Bear Alley. It was getting dark and I could see two silhouettes on the trail that looked like two people. I said to Barry, "I wonder what this is all about?" I had recognized the plane that had flown over to be one of Mike's. As we approached the two men, I slowed the three-wheeler down. One guy was very tall, about six foot four. I pulled up to them and noticed they did not even have a firearm. They definitely were not cops of any sort. I yelled out, "What in the heck are you guys doing down here?"

They looked at each other and answered, "We are down here to go fishing. Gulf Air dropped us off and we are going to camp out for a few days."

I asked, "Do you guys have a gun?"

They looked dumbfounded and said, "No." I looked at Barry and we both started laughing. The tall guy asked, "What is so funny?"

I replied, "Well, I just happen to call this trail Bear Alley for a reason. Look around you; this trail was made by bears. Look down in the sand beside the ATV tracks."

"Holy shit, I did not even notice those were bear tracks!" exclaimed one of the guys.

"Yeah, buddy, let me tell you. I have driven down this trail and bears have been right on it. Besides that, after I have driven to the river, checked my net, and was on the way back from the river, and bears had walked on

189

top of my ATV tracks. Being down here without a gun is very risky. Even being down here with a gun is dangerous."

The more I looked at the two guys the more I noticed the tall one looked exactly like Clark Kent from *Superman*. He even had the same glasses. I looked at Barry and looked at the guys and said, "I am going to do you guys a favor. I am going to show you a good place to camp and loan you a shotgun with bear loads, 00 buck. Can one of you handle a firearm?"

Clark Kent answered, "Yes, I can. I used to go hunting with my dad."

I said, "Good." I told them that I was going to go to my camp and get another ATV with Barry so that we could give them a ride with their gear to my camping spot. I was also going to grab my loaner shotgun. I told them I would be right back. Barry and I took off back to our cabin to get the other wheeler.

Barry asked, "So, George, what do you think about these guys?"

I said jokingly, "City boys," and chuckled. Barry laughed too. I said, "Hey, Barry, does that guy look like anyone you know?"

Barry replied, "No, not really."

I said, "I think he looks just like Clark Kent from *Superman*!"

Barry cracked a grin and said, "You know what, George? Now that you mention it, he does!"

I grabbed my Mossburg twelve-gauge, three-inch Magnum with a pistol grip. I took out the shells and made sure it was loaded with the slug in first and then with three 00 buck. Barry got on the other ATV and we were on our way back to pick up Clark Kent and his friend.

We pulled up to them and I asked, "So what are your names anyway?"

Clark said, "My name is Rich," and the other guy said his name was Robert.

I said, "Okay, Clark Kent and Robert."

Rich got a funny look on his face and said, "What?" I started laughing and asked him if anyone had ever told him that he looked like Clark Kent from *Superman*? He said no.

I said, "Well, maybe not to your face, but yes, you do." Barry busted out laughing. "Get on the back of the ATVs, you two," I told the guys.

They hopped on and I took off to where their gear was dropped off. We loaded the gear into the trailer I had hooked up to the back of my ATV. We went to my Italoway camping spot. This would be a perfect place for them and very close to the fishing. I asked them if they were taking home any fish. They told me they were staying for two nights and if they got some fresh ones the day they were leaving, they would bring them home, but they were mostly fly fishermen who were going to be catching and releasing fish. I told them that would be better, especially because of the bears. The guys thanked us up and down. I told them that we were going back to our cabin to have some dinner and then get ready to go fishing tomorrow. I handed Clark the shotgun and told him only if need be, to shoot to scare the bear off, or if the bear was going to maul them. We don't just kill bears for no reason. This is their home and they eat fish, so only if you are being charged, use deadly force. Clark reassured me that he understood and that he would not shoot a bear unless he was being attacked.

I told him to show me that he knew how to use the shotgun before I left. He opened the breech and pumped out all of the shells. He then placed them back in how I had loaded it and put on the safety. I said, "Great job, and only chamber the gun if you are going to shoot. Do not walk around with one in the chamber. That is how accidents happen." He promised me that that was the way he was taught by his dad. He did not walk around with chambered guns.

Barry and I took off and went back to the cabin. I felt better that they were camping in a safer spot, and now they had a gun to protect themselves if they got into a confrontation with a bear, or even scarier, a sow and cubs. We were tired from a long day of fishing and taking a few hours to help these guys out. We ate some dinner and crashed.

We got up early the next day and headed for the fishing grounds. While we were fishing we saw Clark and Robert. They looked like they were doing fine and catching some fish. After we were done, we went over to check on them. They had a campfire going and were having a Scotch. They offered us a drink and we accepted. They asked us how we ended up here and I told them how I grew up in Haines and that my brother and I commercial fished together and trapped in the winters. I explained how it was getting more crowded, and how my brother had found this set net permit for sale out here in Yakutat, so I started flying out here and checking it out. I had found my own permit, with a cabin gear and Cessna 206. I asked them what kind of work they did and they said that they were attorneys from Anchorage. They said they had an attorney friend who had his own plane and liked to sport fish. I told them that we were seeing more and more sport fishermen down here and that it was like the Wild West when it came to commercial fishing. They thought we were armed to the teeth because of all of the bears, and I told them that bears were not the only things a person had to worry about out here. I said the local natives were crazy and told them a few stories of our encounters with the crazy Indians from Yakutat. I even said that we had run-ins with the owner of the True Value hardware store who was white and a retired attorney, and that he, his son, and partner almost killed me. They were in awe about the lawlessness that was going on out here. I told them they did not have anything to worry about, and if you left the commercial guys alone, they left you alone. I explained how I had had it out with all of them and that we all made truces. They looked comforted after I told them that generally if they were with Gulf Air and stayed low-key, they would be fine, especially if they stuck with me, because they all respected my space as I did theirs. I thanked them for the drink and told them I wanted to get back to my cabin. They said good night and we left.

The next day was the closure and I was going to fly our fish to town and pick up some supplies while Barry worked on the boat and gear. It took me a few trips to get the fish flown out, and on the back hauls I brought ice so that we could keep our fish iced down and in top condition.

A few weeks later while we were fishing on the river, a plane we had never seen flew over us. Then it started circling. It looked like they were looking for a place to land. It was not unusual these days to see strange planes land and set up camps, or even fish for the day. We were seeing more and more sport fishermen fly down with Gulf Air Taxi and people flying their own planes up to Alaska. I identified the plane to be a Citabria. It flew low enough for me to see that the guy was alone. After a few go-arounds, I could hear the plane landing on my strip in front of my cabin. I told Barry that I wanted to check out what was going on. We left the net and headed over on the three-wheeler to investigate.

I stopped at my cabin first. I parked the wheeler and we went in. My dogs in the yard started going crazy and we went out to see what was going on. A guy was standing at the edge of my yard with my dogs keeping him at a distance. I called the dogs off. The guy looked harmless. Nonetheless we could never be too careful. Since we had just come off of the river we still had our guns on us. I had my .44 in my holster on my hip and my .375 H&H on the rack of my ATV. Barry had a ten-gauge shotgun on a sling with a strap full of bullets like a Mexican bandito. As I walked out to talk to the guy, I could see he was holding a piece of paper. It did not look like he was trying to serve me anything like documents, but he looked kind of nerdy. He was kind of skinny and had glasses. As I got closer he said, "Hi! My name is Jerry Barker. I'm a friend of the attorneys you helped out a while back from Anchorage."

Barry and I looked at each other and I smiled and said, "Oh yeah, Clark Kent and his friend. How's it going?"

He said, "Great. After they got back they told me they had a good time and that you helped them out. I love to fish and I have my own plane, so I wanted to come down here and check it out. They drew me this map and said I should come find you."

He handed me the piece of paper. It was a map to the airstrip, my cabin, Bear Alley, and the river, with a note saying: "Find the Davises. They are heavily armed commercial fishermen. They look mean but were pretty nice to us." I laughed.

"Okay, Jerry, we can help you out. A friend of Clark Kent is a friend of ours. First off, where did you park your plane?"

He said off the runway. I told him to get on the three-wheeler and that Barry would follow us over with a wheeler and trailer for his gear. I showed Jerry where I had an extra tie down and he moved his plane. We unloaded his gear. I told him that he could not camp in my yard or stay at my cabin because of Forest Service regulations. He said that Clark had told him about that and he knew that he had to camp out. I said that my Italoway spot was a nice place to camp and was right by the fishing, so he would be fine. Jerry told us that even though he had to camp out, he brought down steaks and cocktails and wanted to know if we wanted to have dinner. I told him that I thought that would be great. We would drop him off and go pick up our net, and then be done for the evening. By the time we were done, Jerry had most of his camp set up.

We picked him up and headed to the cabin. Jerry brought some nice big steaks and a bottle of Tanqueray gin. He asked us if we wanted a cocktail. We said that sounded good, so we had a few gin and tonics while I was getting the grill ready. I threw some potatoes in the oven for us, too. Jerry was all ears when we started telling our crazy commercial fishing stories about the fish wars and battles we had to go through to get our spot on the river. We had a great evening and a good steak dinner to boot. We had a nightcap and then Jerry was ready to go back to his camp. He said his friends mentioned that we let them borrow a shotgun and asked if I would lend him one since he did not bring one. I said sure and handed him my loaner Mossberg. I asked him about gun safety and if he knew how to use it. He showed me that he could, so I felt better that he had some bear protection. It was dark. We took him back to his camp and came back to the cabin and crashed out.

I had a big day of flying tomorrow, getting our fish to the airport so that the cannery could pick it up. They came to the airport in a truck and loaded the fish, and then drove them to town. They also brought ice for me to take back to fill my totes. I drove into town to pick up a few things and then went back out to camp. I was always happy to get back out to the river. I did not care too much for town. My place was in the wilderness.

When I got back to the cabin I checked on the gear. Barry had been going through the nets on the rack, looking for holes to mend. The less tears and large holes meant more fish could be caught, so it was important to mend them. We checked the cork line, which was imperative to keep in top condition as it was what kept the net floating when it got a bunch of fish caught in the web. I had a nice weed line below the cork line that helped keep nasty kelp and weeds out of the net. If you did not keep your net clean, it would detour fish from hitting your net. They would swim right around it.

After we got our chores done I told Barry I was going to go check on Jerry and asked him to stay at camp. I wanted to go by myself. People working and living together all summer need to take breaks from each other. I headed up to the Italoway camp. There was Jerry fishing away. I pulled up, got off the wheeler, and asked how it was going. He told me he was having a great time. I said, "I bet I could make your trip even better. Let's get in my jet boat and I can take you to my secret cutthroat trout hole, but under one condition. I have to blindfold you." I said it really seriously and Jerry actually believed me. I cut up laughing. "I am just joking, Jerry!"

He said, "You looked so poker faced, I was convinced you were serious."

I replied, "If you come here without me and give my spot away, we are going to have a problem."

Jerry looked at me and said, "Honestly, you are one person I would never want to cross, George."

I told him to get his trout flies and bring the salmon rods, too. He went into his tent and got his gear. We got in my jet boat and headed up the river. It was a nice day and we got up river where I had found a sweet cutthroat hole. Even though I was a commercial fisherman, I loved to sport fish and came here by myself to get away from camp and relax. I could see the handwriting on the wall. If commercial fishing ever went in the dumps, sport fishing could be a way to make money. I told Jerry that trout love eggs, but you can catch them on top of the water with dry flies like stone flies, caddis, and mayfly patterns. Jerry decided to tie on a common mayfly pattern and cast it where I told him, right under a tree overhanging a bend in the river where a stream flows out into the main confluence producing a back eddy. The bait swirled around and a nice cutthroat hit his fly. He was stoked and the fish fought pretty hard. I helped him gently land it in the boat. I actually had a small landing net with me. It was a nice three-pound cutthroat trout. In inches that would be about a twenty-four-inch cutty.

Jerry kept fishing his mayfly pattern and said he was having the most fun he had had in a long time. After about six fish the bite slowed down and I told him I had another spot to take him, but before we left I wanted to try something. I had some eggs with me that I had cured in salt. I asked Jerry if he had any egg patterns with him. He said he did and I told him to tie on an orange or red egg. I got a handful of eggs out. When he got his fly tied on, I told him to get ready to cast. I threw a handful of eggs into the back eddy. The water was crystal clear and you could see really deep into the hole. Cutthroats came out of the abyss and started gobbling up the eggs. I told Jerry to cast out the egg. He did and caught another trout. He was as giddy as a schoolgirl. I was tickled that he was having such a great time.

I wanted to show Jerry more places to fish on the river so we ran the boat to some holes where the sockeye were schooled up. We had a great rest of the day and caught Dolly Varden trout, more cutthroat, and a lot of sockeyes.

I told Jerry we should head back. He put his gear away and we headed back to his camp. I dropped him off and he thanked me up and down about how great of a time he had. He actually said it was the best day fishing in his whole life. I told Jerry I could come back and pick him up later if he wanted to come over for dinner, and he thought that would be great. I went back and got Jerry on the ATV a few hours later.

I had taken one of the fresh sockeyes and marinated it in the special marinade that I had learned from Burt. I told Jerry he should fly back down in September for some slamming silver salmon fishing. He said if it was anything close to the fishing that we just did, he would come back for sure. I told him that silver fishing was a lot more fun than sockeye fishing because they are on the bite a lot more than sockeye. Sockeye can be tight lipped and not bite anything you throw at them, whereas silvers are voracious eaters. There are times when silvers can be difficult to fish too, but usually caused by water conditions, such as clear low water. If a school has been fished hard, they can be hard to catch, but typically there are fresh schools coming in the river often, and in big numbers. I told Jerry after dinner and a nightcap that I would give him a ride back to his camp.

On the way he could not stop thanking me again for taking him up the river. He said he had to pack and get back to work so that he could come back in September for another adventure. I told him I would come over and get his gear and take it to the plane for him. He said that would be great and would see me in the morning.

I got up early and went over to help Jerry. He was already packed and ready to go. I took him to the plane and said that I had to get going to get ready for the next opener. Jerry shook my hand and slipped what felt like money into my hand. I said that it wasn't necessary. Jerry insisted on helping with the gas money. So I accepted and put the money in my pocket. I could use the cash to replace all the gas had I used. When I drove off and got back to my yard, I looked in my pocket to see how much money he had given me. It was $500! Wow, that was great. It was worth meeting him, and besides the camaraderie and fun we had fishing, I was able to pay for the gas I used. My mind started racing on how lucrative it could be if I could get my guide license and permits to host sport fishermen. I could not use my cabin for guests, because the law forbade me from having anyone but commercial fishing crew members or my immediate family stay at my cabin.

I could see that there were more and more people flying down here to sport fish, and if I could make extra money on the closures, it would really help. We had some down time in between the end of sockeye season and the start of the silver season. When the silvers started hitting the river, we went back to fishing. This was usually around the end of August. I had told Jerry he should come back in late fall, around the end of September.

Some openers I would partner up with Burt. He would move around quite a bit. He would come down to the Italio during the peak runs and we would hammer down and fish hard, and party hard. Burt loved to party, cook, and have a good time. He always brought good food, Crown Royal, wine, and beer with him. After the opener we always had a big party. When he would get to drinking he would yell out, "Kanae!" When it was good fishing in Yakutat Bay, we would go out in the *Kanae* skiff, and fish a seventy-five-fathom bay net. We usually did really well fishing the ocean.

I was back at my cabin in between openers, when I saw Jerry's plane fly over. I was happy to see him. We had such a good time and really hit it off on his first visit. After working hard all season, I was looking forward to having some fun and doing a little bit of sport fishing. Jerry said he would be bringing some steaks and I was looking forward to that, too. I met his plane with my ATV. When Jerry got out he shook my hand really hard and said how happy he was to be back and to see me. I told him the same. I helped him unload his plane. I saw that he had brought out the steaks, a half gallon of Tanqueray gin, and a half gallon of Stoli vodka. After we got the ATV loaded and were on the way to set up his camp, he told me that he had a really special surprise that he was going to bring over to the cabin.

After we got his camp set up we headed to my place. Jerry had seen that I had a fly-tying vice and that I knew how to tie flies. He was into tying flies as well. While in Anchorage before he flew down, he stopped at the fly shop where they had some new tying materials that had just come out. He pulled the materials out of his bag and handed them to me. I looked at the package and it said Flashabou. It looked just like Christmas tree tinsel. I started laughing. I asked him how much he paid for this stuff. He said too much and laughed. I told him that I had a package of Christmas tree tinsel in my wife's storage that I would sell him. He laughed and said the fly shop guy said it was the latest, greatest thing. I told him we would give it a try. I was known to be an innovator and on the cutting edge.

We poured cocktails and I started using the materials he brought to create flies that I had a feeling would be deadly for slamming some silvers. He also brought some other new material that I had never seen before. It was called Ice Chenille in colors called chartreuse (fluorescent green) and hot pink. I already had some traditional materials that I had been using for flies, such as rabbit tail and marabou. I made silver flies with hackle, too. These new materials he brought looked like Christmas tree decorations to me. That night I created my own fly, but I did not know what to call it yet. I was going to see how well it worked first. Jerry made his own creations. While we were tying, Barry was getting wasted. He got hammered drunk and ended up passing out. Jerry and me had a blast trying flies and eating our steak dinner. I took Jerry back to his camp and we were both very excited to try my new creation the next day.

In the morning Barry was too hung over to even get up. I was glad because I did not want him to come with us anyway; he was not into sport fishing and would be a third wheel. I got my flies and gear and picked up Jerry. We hit the river in the skiff, and I took Jerry to a place where some fresh schools of salmon were holding up. He said, "After you, Davis. I want to see your fly in action." I decided to tie on a chartreuse Ice Chenille fly with a Flashabou and rabbit fur tail. One cast and a few strips and WHAM! The salmon nailed my fly. I fought the fish and we landed the big buck (male) coho, then released it.

I said, "Go ahead, Jerry, you give it a go."

He said to hand him one of my hot pink Ice Chenille flies. One cast, strip, strip, and WHAM! Another fish. I yelled, "These flies are spanking the fish!" We caught fish after fish on the two flies until they were shredded to pieces. We moved to another hole and put new flies on, and spanked the fish until we were tired.

I pulled up to a sandbar and parked the skiff. I asked Jerry if he felt like having some lunch. He said that would be great. I gathered some wood and built a campfire. I kept a nice, bright silver and grabbed it out of the boat, along with my kit for making a salmon shore lunch. I had packed tinfoil, peppers, spices, and onions. I gutted the fish and stuffed it with the fixings, then I wrapped the fish in foil and threw it on the campfire. I had paper plates and a couple of forks. In about twenty minutes the salmon was ready to eat. We pulled the fish out of the coals, sat on a log, and devoured our lunch.

While I was sitting there I had a genius idea. I told Jerry that I knew what I wanted to call my fly. He said, "What are you going to name this creation?"

I said, "Well, Jerry, since my fly spanks the fish, I am going to name it the DAVIS SPANKER!"

We started laughing, and Jerry said, "That is a perfect name!" I told him the pink one should be called the "Lady Spanker," and laughed, and he agreed. That is how my Davis Spanker came to be.

Jerry had a great time the rest of his stay. He kept using my fly, and actually doing comparisons with other popular flies that people were using for silvers. Jerry said hands down my spanker out-fished every other fly in his box at least ten to one. I was excited that I had created a fly that was that effective for catching silver salmon. Jerry told me he was going to tell all his friends and the guys at the fly shop. I am sure it would help them sell the new ridiculous-looking fly-tying materials, knowing they had been field-tested. Jerry flew back to Anchorage and told me to stay in touch. I told him I would, and if I needed an attorney, I would be calling him up. He said I could call anytime but hoped I would stay out of trouble and not need his services as a defense lawyer. We both got a laugh.

I told Jerry he should plan a trip to come back next season and he told me to count on it. He was hooked on the area and was going to make it an annual tradition. I was sad to see Jerry go, but I had serious work to do. Besides commercial fishing, I was going to work on pursuing the sport hunting and fishing line of business.

Overall we had a pretty good season. I did notice a difference in prices. It seemed like the price they were paying for fish was getting lower and our expenses were getting higher. There was a huge change in 1990. It was actually one of the worst commercial fishing seasons. The prices had plummeted because in my mind the Asians, who were our biggest market, started to come to the United States and were buying out all the canneries. Then us fishermen assumed they started price fixing. We went from getting $3.60 a pound for red sockeye salmon in 1988 to ninety cents a pound in 1991. The price of everything was going up, and the price of fish was plummeting.

CHAPTER 27

FAIRY GARY

I WAS GETTING APPROACHED MORE and more by big game guides and sport fishermen who wanted my services. The big game guides in the area wanted my help setting up camps and transporting guides by ATV and skiff. I was also well known for my expertise in knowing where the best fishing and hunting areas were. These skills and knowledge were very valuable to big game hunting guides. Learning the best fishing areas was already helping me get my foot in the door for my sport fishing operation, Alaska Gulf Coast Adventures (AGCA) that I was developing.

Two guides in particular, Jim Treeline and Gary Gray, had been asking for my help in the spring and fall. During the winter Gary had asked me if I would be interested in helping him with a few projects that coming spring. He told me that he wanted to prefab a cabin and haul it to the Akwe River come breakup. He also wanted me to help him retrieve a skiff that he had stored fifty miles east of Yakutat up on the Doame River, and to help open up his hunting camp on the Alsek River. I told him that I would do it.

I got the materials packaged together for a 12x16 ft. cabin. Instead of eight-foot walls he wanted it built with six-foot walls, and a 5x12 ft. pitch gabled roof. That winter I pre-cut everything and had the materials staged in his hangar so that in the spring everything would be ready to be flown to the building site. This involved cutting 4x8 ft. sheets of plywood in half lengthwise and other dimensional lumber to fit in the plane. Once this was done the plane could be loaded. All of the seats had to be taken out, including the passenger seat. The only seat in the plane would be for the pilot. When it was all said and done, I figured we could get this accomplished with three 206 loads.

In the spring, I got my backpack ready with my sleeping bag and gear. I had to pack light so I just brought the necessities. I asked Gary about food

201

and he said he had it covered. Even against my gut feeling, I decided not to pack any snacks for myself. I usually would have brought things like dried smoked salmon, moose jerky, dried fruit, and nuts. I did not bring anything for myself. I was trying to pack light and assumed Gary would bring our needed food supplies.

We watched the weather and picked a time frame that would allow us to complete the daunting task that we were about to embark upon. The goal of the mission would be to get dropped off, open Gary's camp, get his ATVs and trailer out of storage, then head up to the East River. After that we would go up to the Doame River to recover a skiff that he had loaned to Gayle.

To accomplish this we would have to cross a freezing cold river on an ATV without swamping the wheeler and ourselves. Then we would have to pull the skiff out and get it into the water. After that we would have to load it on a trailer and take it to the East River, then to the Alsek. Easier said than done. My crew and I had done this numerous times, but it is very difficult and dangerous. Having someone like me to help is a real asset to an operation. It takes a special kind of person to pull off these tasks and survive.

Once I got the skiff, ATV, and trailer to the Alsek, we were going to have the cabin materials flown down and unloaded, and I was going to build the 12x16 ft. cabin.

When the weather conditions seemed in our favor, Gary and I decided to make a go of it. I met Gary out at Mike's hangar at Gulf Air Taxi. We had everything we needed to get the cabin opened up. We loaded up and flew down to the Akwe runway. We told Mike we would stay in touch over the marine VHF radio. Mike had a huge antenna installed on a building that could reach miles east and west to anyone who had a VHF antenna set up on their cabin. That is how we communicated with the air taxis when we needed flights or supplies. If you had a good handheld, you could talk to the planes as they flew over because most of them had marine VHF in them. The air taxi would stand by on certain channels. Each camp had a handle and we usually had an agreed upon general channel. We also had secret channels to talk to our friends or fishing partners. The bad thing was that when new radios came out with scanners, we could put the radio on scan and it was like a police scanner. We would find each other's secret channel, so having a secret channel did not do us much good. Some radios came out with scramblers. This was nice because when you turned that on, to anyone who did not have the special frequency the conversation sounded like a foreign language. Another way that I communicated was with my handheld aircraft radio. This was in case of an emergency. I could call for help to any aircraft flying by. Since I was out in the middle of nowhere most of the year, communication was very important, especially since the work I did was very dangerous.

Cabins sitting over the winter usually had sand drifts against them, where even the doors had to be dug out with shovels. Instead of snowdrifts, sand would get blown against the cabins because they were, for the most part, built on sand dunes. Gary's cabin on the Alsek was set back from the beach in the trees, so we were lucky not to have to dig away sand. Some cabins were literally a few feet from the beach on the Gulf of Alaska. Right away I got the cabin opened and headed straight for the heater. This particular cabin had an oil-burning stove. This in itself was an undertaking. They were sensitive to begin with, especially from sitting over the winter, and were known to be hard to get lit and going. This certain stove was finicky and was known for getting sooted up. I was an expert though and got the oil stove blazing and the cabin heated up. Next we had to manually pull out the four-wheelers and get them started. It could sometimes be a difficult task to get the ATVs running after sitting all winter without being started in the damp environment.

We knew that getting the skiff would be an all-day job, so we straightened up around the cabin and got the trailer out. We greased up the bearings. We made sure everything would be ready for tomorrow's challenge. I started to get uneasy about the food situation when it came to fixing dinner. I asked Gary what we were having for dinner. He said, "Look in the pantry. I am sure there is something we can fix."

I looked around and found some old cans. It is not good for canned food to sit and freeze over the winter. Most of what he had in the pantry was old looking with moldy labels. I knew that as long as the can had a seal, it was supposedly safe, but it made me uneasy to eat canned food that had been out here for God knows how many years. I found a canned ham that looked fairly safe and some rice that had been kept in a Tupperware

203

container. I got the rice pot out and the frying pan. If I had known about this food situation, I definitely would have brought my own food. I could have thrown some moose steaks in my pack and we would be eating that right now. I guess it didn't bother Gary, but it did me. Heck, he didn't even have butter. He had a tub of margarine that was who knows how many years old. When I asked if he had brought any butter, he said, "No, but there is some margarine in the pantry, and that stuff never goes bad."

I rolled my eyes and thought, *Well, I don't really like eating something that "never" goes bad.* That can't be good for you. If that is all we had, then so be it, we were stuck down here. I checked the margarine. He was right, not one spot of mold. I cooked a pot of rice and fried up the canned ham. I was as hungry as a grizzly so anything would do for now. I noticed he also had peanut butter and jelly in the pantry. I checked the jelly. There was some mold on it and he told me to just scrape it off. I had a feeling this was going to be tomorrow's lunch. I hoped he had brought some bread, but at this point I was too annoyed to ask.

After dinner we were pretty tired and had a big day ahead of us tomorrow. We decided to hit the hay. We woke up bright and early and I asked Gary where the coffee and coffee pot were. He told me that there must be some instant Folgers in the pantry and to just heat up some water. I had been on trips where I had some crappy food and coffee conditions, but I never would have thought a big game guide would operate like this. I know he was a commercial fisherman and a lot of commercial fisherman had meager food and coffee, but this was ridiculous. If I had had any idea it was going to be like this, I would have definitely brought my own supplies. I was kicking myself for not doing so. I heated up the water and found the Folgers crystals. At least it had caffeine. I was going to need some for this upcoming expedition.

It was eight miles to the East River from Gary's cabin, then another four miles to the Doame River where the skiff had been stored. We got up to Gayle's cabin, which just happened to be out in the middle of the river on a sort of sandy, flat island. I suppose it was built for the convenience of using the skiff to haul the fish to the runway, and then flown out. We would have to cross the river on the ATVs to get to the cabin so we could get the skiff on the trailer.

I found a good place to cross. It was sort of deep, but not deep enough to swamp the ATV. If you went off the trail, you would definitely put the wheeler deep in the water and risk swamping the bike. I got across first with the trailer and Gary followed. We found the skiff. We store skiffs upside down and so we had to turn it over and wench it on the trailer. We had a 50 hp Mercury for the 16 ft. custom-built, all-welded aluminum skiff. I got on the ATV and started to make my way across the river with the skiff in tow. Gary was supposed to be behind me. When I got to the other side and got the skiff and trailer up out of the water, I turned around to see Gary down below where I had crossed in the middle of the river. He messed up and drove into a deep hole. I could barely see the handlebars on the four-wheeler. The bike was swamped and had quit running. He was off the bike and being swept downstream, trying to hang on to the ATV and pulling it toward the bank.

I immediately got off of my bike and unhooked the trailer. I was going to have to walk out into the river because I could not risk getting my ATV swamped. I waded out to Gary and it took both of us, with all our might, to pull the bike to the bank. We were completely soaked from the freezing cold water. It was March and fifteen degrees outside. The wind chilled us to the bone. We both tried to get the ATV drained and started. There was water in the oil, which was not a good sign. I told Gary, "Forget this for now. If we don't get warm, we are going to get hyperthermia and die." He agreed. We both got on the other ATV. I said that maybe it would be better to find a cabin out here to get warm and dry off in rather than try to make it back twelve miles in the freezing cold to the camp.

"Sounds good to me," Gary replied.

We searched around the area for some of our fellow commercial fishermen's cabins. We found a few, but they were boarded up really well. We came to the conclusion that most of them would have oil stoves, and most people did not leave much for supplies at their camps. Everyone usually brought in their oil when they opened up. I said, "This is not going to work. We need to get back to your cabin pronto! Hang on!" I peeled out and poured the coals to the four-wheeler. Dang, it was cold. The faster I went the colder I got. At least Gary had some protection. He was riding behind me and had me for a shield. I had to stop midway. We did jumping jacks and I wanted to warm my fingers, which were turning into icicles. I placed my hands near the exhaust of the bike. We just had to make it back. We were both shivering uncontrollably. After a few moments we got back on the ATV and I hauled ass back to the cabin. All I could think about was getting back to a warm cabin and out of the freezing cold.

We pulled into the yard and ran to the cabin door. I flung it open. I could see my breath. I could not help but blurt out, "What the heck? Why is it so cold in here?" I looked at Gary and he had a weird look on his face. I looked at the heater. It was shut off. I asked Gary, "Did you shut the f'n heater off?" He looked guilty, and said he did. I asked him, "Why?" He said to save fuel. He did not think it would be that hard to just light it up again when we got back this evening. I yelled, "You cheap bastard!"

Instead of staying on that topic, I immediately started taking off my wet clothes. I told him we had to get this thing going or we could die. I put some dry clothes on, but was still shivering. It was fifteen degrees outside and only eighteen degrees in the cabin, not much difference. The stove was flooded and sooted up. I had to take it apart to get it going. After about twenty minutes of dickering with the stove, I finally got a light. Thank God! I was so cold that I was about to build a campfire in the middle of his cabin floor. I told Gary that I was going to get in my sleeping bag and rub myself around in it to get some friction to try to warm up. I got as close to the heater as possible. Gary did the same. I was so mad at him. First the food, then the ATV, and now this. What a disaster. We eventually stopped shivering and were getting warmed up.

As soon as I could muster up the energy, I put on some water for some delicious Folgers crystals. I found a few packets of hot cocoa to add to the water. I could barely talk to Gary I was so livid. We could have died over a couple of gallons of stove oil. Gary offered to make us something to eat. I snapped, "Oh great, some delicious pantry food from 1970!"

He replied, "I am really sorry for all this, George."

I apologized and said that I was just grumpy. I told him that I would have brought some food if I had known that this was what we were going to be eating. I told him that I am very particular about my food. Gary promised he would make it up to me. I believed he would. Even though he was cheap, deep down he was a good guy. He did say that he was frugal and was always trying to cut corners to save money, but he just learned that when it comes to out here, cutting corners was not safe. I totally agreed. That is why I always keep my equipment in top-notch shape, and if I can, I have new or like-new outboards and ATVs. Even though I keep my stuff in great condition, I like to sell my outboards and ATVs and buy new ones every few years.

Gary fixed us dinner, and afterward we were so exhausted we passed right out. We had another big day ahead of us. We had to go back and get the ATV running, and tow the skiff to the Alsek River. We had to put it in the water, load the ATV in the skiff, run the boat down to the mouth of the river, and then find a landing place good enough to beach the skiff, then unload the ATV. I would then have to make another crossing to put the trailer in the skiff and unload it so I would be able to tow the skiff sixteen miles down the beach.

We got a good night's rest and woke up early. We got our gear ready and the tools to fix the ATV. I also brought what I could find for emergency survival gear. The one important thing that I learned from this situation was to never depend on anyone else for proper food and survival gear. I had an extensive pack that I ALWAYS carried with me, but in this situation I thought I needed to go light on gear because Gary was a professional big game guide. I just assumed he had sufficient gear.

We left the yard and got to the ATV where the skiff and trailer were parked. I immediately started taking apart the ATV and got it running. I hooked up the trailer and got the skiff loaded on the trailer. Now we had to get the skiff almost ten miles to the Alsek River. We were on our way. The wheeler Gary was driving seemed to be running well. I was glad. We got to a place in the trail where there was a fork. One way was a trail back to his lodge, the other a trail to the DC-3 strip. This is where the DC-3s would haul fish off the river, on the 3800 ft. runway. The trail to the big strip was about five miles long, and then another mile north from there was his lodge with a smaller strip for smaller airplanes. As we approached the fork, he rode up beside me and yelled for me to slow down and stop for a minute. I assumed it was a problem with his ATV. We both came to a stop. I asked, "What is wrong?"

He replied, "Oh, nothing is wrong with the wheeler, but I have to get back to town. The plane is on its way to pick me up."

I was in shock. I could not believe he was going to abandon me and leave me to do all this work by myself. I asked Gary when he decided this. He told me that he did not plan for the mishap, and that it was already arranged for the plane to be down to pick him up. I was still in shock that he did not call the air taxi to get them to come down a day later so he could help me with the skiff and trailer. He apologized and said he would make it up to me. I explained to him how dangerous it was going to be for me to do what he was asking of me. He said the plane was already on its way and that he knew I had done it before by myself, and that I could handle it. He said, "That is why I needed someone like you!"

I just shook my head and said, "All right, go catch your plane. If everything goes as planned, I will be at the Akwe camp location by this evening so you can plan on sending the plane down tomorrow with a load of lumber. And by the way, if you want me to stay onboard here, have my wife put a care package of some decent food and coffee for me on the flight, damn it!"

He said, "Great, will do, George. I knew I could count on you!"

Gary took off up the trail to meet the plane. I despondently started making my way to the Alsek River where I knew I had my work cut out for me. It was five miles to where I was going to put the boat in the water. I got to the bank and found a good place to back the skiff into the water. I got it secured and then unhitched the trailer. I was going to load the ATV into the skiff first and then make a landing on the other side where I could unload the ATV. I would have to come back across for the trailer and load it into the skiff and make another crossing. After that I would unload the trailer then hook it up to the ATV. I would pull the boat out of the water and make the sixteen-mile journey to the Akwe camp building site, which was a raw piece of property.

I had two rough-cut 2x12 ft. heavy-duty planks that I used to load ATVs in and out of these high-sided commercial fishing skiffs. The planks had two 2x4 ft. boards countersunk and bolted to the bottom of the planks so that it could be secured on the rail without sliding. I still could not believe Gary left me to do this by myself. Yes, he was right, I had done this before without any help, but it was very dangerous and I would have preferred to have had assistance. I anchored the bow and stern to the beach so it didn't push out as you drove on to it. I set up my planks on the side of the boat and drove the ATV into the boat perfectly. I designed the planks so that as I drove the ATV up, the planks acted as a teeter-totter and went down to the bottom of the boat deck on the other side and stood up and out enough to back the skiff out of the boat when I got to the other side. I pulled in the anchors, and pushed the skiff out into the river far enough for me to put the motor down and get it started.

I was about a half mile from where the river dumped into the Gulf of Alaska. If anything went wrong, I could easily get swept into the treacherous currents of the Alsek River mouth to the breakers, and then out into the Gulf of Alaska to meet my maker. I got the Mercury 50 hp outboard going and headed across the river. I was about halfway across when the outboard started sputtering and died. I was alarmed, but had to keep my composure. I had a five-hundred-pound ATV in the skiff and was half a mile from the river mouth with large waves breaking on a sandbar. If I got swept out without power, and by some act of God made it past the crashing waves without getting flipped over, the next stop was the Gulf of Alaska. I immediately went for the anchor, which I had ready in case of an emergency like this. Throwing the anchor would stop me from getting swept out of the mouth, but if I did not get the motor started, I would still be stuck in the middle of the river and have to try to get to one side or the other by hook or by crook. I took the cowling off the motor and started troubleshooting. After a few adjustments I put the cowling back on, said a prayer, and let her rip. She coughed a little bit and came back to life. "Praise Jesus!" I was relieved. I pulled up the anchor and bolted across the river.

I shoved the boat firmly on the beach, and then got the boat in a position that would allow me to back the ATV out of the skiff. I got the ATV unloaded successfully and parked it up the beach a ways. I positioned the planks back in the boat so I would be able to load the trailer. Even though I was worried about the outboard, I knew that I had to get back over there to get the trailer so that I could get the skiff down to the Akwe camp. I got back in the boat, shoved off, and fired up the outboard without a hitch. I got safely across and got the trailer loaded. I headed back to the west side of the Alsek bank where I had the ATV positioned. I got the skiff beached and the trailer unloaded. I hooked up the trailer to the ATV and backed it down into the water. I then had to get back into the boat and run the skiff up on to the trailer, jump out, tie it off, and get it ratcheted up on the trailer. Thankfully, it was hard-packed sand and a shallow slope bank so I was able to get the skiff up the bank without getting stuck.

I was so relieved to have that stretch of ordeal over with without dying, but I still felt as if I had one foot in the grave during this entire operation that Gary goat roped me into. I got far enough up the beach to feel good about taking a break. I needed to catch my breath. Now I had to get the skiff and trailer sixteen miles west to the building site. I thought I was ready, so I took off for camp. The condition of the sand was fairly hard and I did not run into any more snags. I was worried about hitting patches of soft sand and getting stuck, but thank goodness I got to camp without any more predicaments. I had already been through enough difficulties and did not know how much more I could endure.

When I got to the camp building site, I wanted to get my tent set up right away and get a campfire going. I asked Gary before he took off if he had any supplies he was going to leave me to set up the camp. He said he thrown some food in the skiff. I got the pack out and found cans of tuna, a jar of peanut butter, and some jelly, along with some Sailor Boy Pilot Crackers. Wow, how thoughtful! I was really disappointed. I am glad I mustered up Folgers coffee from his cabin before I left.

I gathered some beach wood and made a campfire on the double. I got my two-man guide tent set up as fast as I could. I got my coffee maker out and made myself some Folgers. I was so exhausted that I just made some pilot crackers with peanut better and jelly on them. Luckily, the flight should be coming tomorrow, and I knew that Debbie would put together a good care package for me with goodies and my coveted real ground-bean coffee.

I slept like a rock. I had to sleep with full arctic long johns on and a wool hat to stay warm. As long as I stayed in my twenty-below-zero arctic bag, I was warm, but as soon as I got out of my bag, I had to get moving to stay warm.

I had plenty of work to do. First, I had to dig holes for the foundation posts. I kept my hot water cooking on the campfire. As I was busy gathering logs for the foundation, I could hear the plane coming. Thank goodness! It was Iron Mike flying down the first load. He was able to land fairly close to the cabin site. I met him with the ATV and trailer. He helped me unload the plane, and the lumber that would not fit on the trailer we piled next to the runway. I would have to make multiple trips to get it staged in the yard. Mike told me that he had a box for me that Debbie had brought out. I told Mike about the whole ordeal from start to finish. He said, "That is unfortunate but, not make light of your struggle, it is kind of comical." He chuckled.

I said, "Looking back it was dangerous, and I'm glad to have lived through it, but I don't think I'm going to work with Gary after this cabin is done." Mike said he did not blame me. I told Mike about Gary wanting me to fly his Cub for the hunting operation and he warned me that he was not sure how safe that would be. I agreed that Gary did not keep his plane in tip-top condition, which is what I was used to. I never skimped on safety, especially with airplanes.

We finished unloading the plane and Mike said that he had another planeload of lumber ready to bring down. I thanked him and told him that I would see him later. He told me to be safe and take care. He also said that Gary had informed him that he was going to fly down sometime soon and help me with the cabin. Mike took off and flew back to town. I needed to get to work on the foundation, but for now my first priority was opening my care package from Debbie. I took the box back to camp and immediately tore into it like a savage animal. Oh, baby! Steaks, chops, cheese, bread, butter, and one of my favorite foods, smoked salmon. She also sent down some smoked moose jerky that we had made, and some dried fruit trail mix to snack on. Everything looked so good I did not know what to eat first. I thought I would start with the bacon and eggs.

I got my cast iron skillet out and my Coleman camp stove. I got the stove set up on my folding table. Oh yea, I am going to enjoy this. Debbie was a good wife for putting this together and sending it down. I already had my hot water going for the ground-bean coffee that smelled delicious. She sent down butter and a loaf of her homemade sourdough bread with homemade strawberry preserves. Now this was how I was used to eating! I got breakfast cooked, found a log to sit on, and enjoyed my scrumptious Alaska Man breakfast. After my food settled I could now get some serious work done.

I got six holes dug for my foundation posts for the 12x16 ft. cabin. I got to work on laying stringers on top of the posts, and then got the plywood ready for the floor. Mike flew down a few days later with Gary and another load. His specialty was custom floors, but he was good at framing as well. We made the walls and framed in some windows. We raised the walls and got them tacked off. This was turning out to be a nice little cabin. We notched the stringers for the roof and started putting them up. Pretty soon we would need the plywood for the ceiling. Gary and I got along well, but I did not let on that I was not going to work for him after this. I did not want any animosity while we were working together. I liked Gary as a person, but I just did not like the corners that he cut to save money, such as food and maintenance for equipment.

Gary had a wood stove brought down and some more lumber for bunks and tables. We made a counter, some shelves, and a table with benches. We also got the roof put on. I evaluated the time that I had put in and told Gary that I had gotten a fair amount of work done for what he had paid me. He agreed and said he was more than happy with what I had accomplished. He asked me if I would go with him to look for bears before I left. I told him that I would take him to a few spots where I had seen some monster bears.

After I had showed Gary a few good bear spots that I knew of, I told him that I needed to get back to town. He was thankful for my help and asked me if I would be staying on to help him until I needed to get ready for fishing. I was kind of vague, but more or less told him that I would be busy and probably did not have time to stay on and help him with the guiding operation. I actually had all the work I could want helping Mike and my friend Kurt in the Gulf Air Taxi hangar. Mike had given me a standing offer of working for him anytime I wanted to earn some extra money. Gary thanked me and said there were not many people who could do what I do and that he really wanted me to work for him. If I changed my mind, he wanted me to let him know. I told him that I would. Gary got on the radio and called the office for a charter. The charter would be here soon, so I gathered my things and we headed to the strip. I got my pack loaded in the plane and shook Gary's hand. We said good-bye, and I was on my way back to town. Thank God I had "cheated her again!"

CHAPTER 28

FIST FULL OF DOLLARS

WHEN I WAS IN TOWN, I hung out in the Gulf Air Taxi hangar quite a bit. I got to know numerous pilots over the years, most of whom are now dead. There is a saying up here in Alaska; "There are old pilots and bold pilots, but there are no old bold pilots." This rings true. One pilot that I really had a bond with besides Mike was Kurt. Mike had hired him at Gulf Air as a pilot and mechanic. He also owned his own Cessna 185. I had worked under him doing all kinds of aircraft maintenance, including stripping and painting three planes one winter. He was an incredible mechanic and could rebuild an airplane from the fuselage to the engine. He also did outstanding paint jobs. Kurt did a lot of ski plane flying, but he was an all-around ace pilot. His brother Shaun was a pilot as well and happened to be flying the Pilatus Porter that my son and I witnessed crashing near my camp on the Italio River

When I got back to town, I started to get my gear ready to go to my own camp. I went out to the hangar to get my plane ready for its annual inspection. I went over to Gulf Air and saw Kurt working on his plane. He yelled out, "Hey, George, good to see you, buddy!"

I said back, "Same here! How goes it?"

He said, "Pretty good. Mike told me you had a hair-raising adventure with Gary."

I said, "Yes, that is putting it mildly, and nicely. I don't think I will be doing too much with him unless I really need the money." I laughed and said, "And I pray to God it won't come to that!"

Kurt asked, "Was it that bad?"

I said, "Well, if you consider almost dying, then yes, it was that bad." He looked surprised. I told him about the whole thing, and how I was abandoned and left there to do it by myself.

Kurt said, "Well, at least you were able to pull it off. Not many guys could do what you did and live." I agreed. Kurt told me he had to get ready for a flight and asked if we could catch up later over a cocktail at the Yakutat Lodge, the pilot haunt. I told him I looked forward to sharing war stories.

I finished getting my plane prepared for the annual and then walked across the tarmac to Yakutat Lodge to wait for Kurt. Shortly after I got settled in, I could see Kurt landing and putting his plane away. He made his way toward the lodge and walked in. He was kind of a small guy, about five foot six with wavy shoulder-length black hair. He was a handsome guy as well. He sat on the perch next to me. I told Kurt it was good to see him and I asked, "How goes the battle?"

Kurt said back with a shrug and a big sigh, "Air taxi flying is a thankless job." The bartender interrupted, and we gave her out drink order.

I asked Kurt if he knew how Jim was doing. Kurt said he was in recovery. I asked him if he knew the whole story of the incident. He said that he did not know much. I told him that I knew firsthand what had happened, and Kurt replied, "I am all ears!"

Jim Steinbeck was flying for Mike. It was fall, and I was silver fishing at my camp when a big high-pressure front had moved in off the gulf. There were clear skies, but north winds roared out of the Alsek and Dangerous river drainages. I had several loads of fish that needed to be flown to town, but was unable to take them due to the severe north winds that produced a direct crosswind on my runway. The forecast said that the winds were gusting up to sixty miles an hour, and it was no joke. I had flown in severe weather conditions to get my fish to town, but there was no way of even thinking about getting my plane off the ground in these conditions.

I heard what I thought was an aircraft engine. I wondered who the heck would be flying down here in these winds. I looked out and it was Gulf Air's 180, 38T, which was Mike's pride and joy. He loved that plane. I got on my marine VHF radio to call the plane to see what was going on. It was Jim, one of Mike's pilots. He told me he was heading down to Dry Bay to the Crow strip to pick up some passengers. I came back to him on the radio and told him he should tell them to meet him at the big Dry Bay strip instead of the little Crow strip, which was only a 1000 ft. gravel runway with trees at the end. This made for a bad downdraft while the severe north wind was blasting. If he could pick up his passengers at the main Dry Bay runway, it would be a safer option because the Dry Bay runway was 3900 feet long and about 100 feet wide. Jim came back and said he was going to go take a look at it. I never heard anything back from him.

About an hour later I heard another aircraft from the west. I looked out and it was one of Gulf Air's 185s. I called the aircraft on my VHF radio. I saw that it was 47L. It was Mike. He told me that there was bad news and good news. My stomach dropped. I had thought something bad could have happened. He said the bad news was that 38T was totaled, but the good news was that Jim walked away with what he thinks is a broken collarbone and other minor injuries. He was on his way to pick up Jim on the Dry Bay strip. I told him that I was glad to hear Jim was okay, but too bad about the plane. Mike asked me if I would be available in the next few days to fly down and help him with the aircraft recovery. I told him that after I got my fish flown out that I could help him. He asked me how many loads I had and I told him about five. He said, "Done deal. I will get down as soon as I can and we will get your fish flown out, and then head down to the Crow strip as soon as these winds lie down."

I said, "Roger that, Italoway camp out."

Two days later the wind dropped down to twenty-five miles an hour out of the north and it was game on. Mike showed up early. As soon as he landed I needed to know what happened. He told me that the plane was totaled. The only thing left was the fuselage. He said, "Jim got flown directly out to Juneau and the report was that he did have a broken collarbone." Mike said that he was lucky to be in one piece. One thing that saved him from being busted to pieces was that he had his shoulder harness on. If not, who knows how bad he could have ended up. He said, "Let's get these fish down to the plane and flown out."

I said back, "Let's roll."

We got the fish flown out in five loads. I did two loads and he did three with his fleet.

Mike had the insurance adjuster at the hangar ready to be flown to the crash site. We loaded up in the plane and the three of us flew down in his 185. We circled over the wreckage at 500 feet and assessed the damage from the air. We then flew over to the main Dry Bay runway where Mike had a camp with an ATV. We landed near his cabin, got on an ATV, and rode the trail over to the Crow strip. There were pieces of the plane scattered everywhere. We went to the south end of the strip to visualize coming in for a landing into a north wind. We could see where the plane touched down, and then we could actually see where green paint from the wingtip scarred the gravel on the strip. We then figured that the plane cartwheeled from the impact of the wing on the strip. From there the plane started breaking apart. The wings were torn off, and the engine all the way back to the firewall of the plane was also torn off. The whole tail was separated from the fuselage of the plane. The fuselage was sitting there completely mangled, but intact. Wearing his shoulder harness probably did save Jim's life. Just looking at the damaged plane made it hard to believe that a broken collarbone was all that he walked away with. Kurt said, "Yes, pilot error, pushing the envelope. Hey, speaking of pilot error, I have a story for you. You know those guys you help out all the time down on the river, the Oregon Rose guys and Bob Wheel?"

I said, "Yes, those guys have always taken really good care of me. I have known them for four years." The first winter after I had helped them on the river, a box showed up at Alaska Airlines around Christmas full of the largest, most beautiful roses I had ever seen. Then a box of grapefruits and oranges came. I was thrilled to have fresh citrus in the middle of winter when it was very hard to get any good fruit in the small village of Yakutat.

One year Bob Wheel came up alone because the Oregon Rose guys were not going to be coming up. Bob called me and asked if he came on his own, would I take care of him. I told him no problem. He came up the last week in August and stayed a week. The day before he arrived I got a call from Alaska Airlines. About 800 pounds of perishable freight had arrived for me and that I needed to come pick it up. I had no idea what it could be. When I went to Alaska Air and received the freight, I saw that it was from Bob Wheel. I opened it and saw that it was cases of fruits, vegetables, cheese, spiral hams, and steaks. Not only twenty-five pounds of porterhouse steaks, but also two prime ribs. My mind was blown. I loved that he was thoughtful enough to send all of this food up. It was so much that I filled my 206 plumb full of food and still had boxes of corn, peaches, cherries, and apples left over. It was so much food I had to give some away. Bob Wheel showed up the next day and we went down to my cabin. I set him up at the Boy Scout encampment. At the end of his trip he gave me a $2,000 tip. It was totally worth it.

Kurt said sarcastically, "Well, Davis, so glad to hear you had such a great experience with those guys, but let me tell you what your friend Bob Wheel did to me."

Kurt explained that they came to Gulf Air with their group of guys. "We got them flown down to the Boy Scout camp. I had loaded my 185 to the gunnel with their freight. I was just going to drop their freight on the runway and they were going to have to carry their freight quite a ways to their camp. When I got down there and landed, Bob Wheel, the big heavy Jewish guy, was back toward the camp waving a fist of what I thought were $100 dollar bills. He waved at me to taxi my plane through the pucker brush and off the runway. I was just going to turn my plane off, but since he kept waving me back and had a handful of money, I decided what the heck, so I taxied my plane through tall grass and small alders to get back as close as I could to their camp. I turned my plane off and walked up to Bob. He handed me a handful of one-dollar bills for a total of seven dollars. To say the least I was furious. I yelled at him and said, "I cannot believe that I taxied my plane back here, and risked my engine and prop for seven dollars! Bob just laughed, which made me even more enraged."

I could not help but laugh. I told Kurt I was sorry for laughing, but could not believe Bob would pull a stunt like that. Kurt replied that he was so mad that he told Bob not to call him ever again. He said that when he got back to the Gulf Air office, he told Mike that he would not turn a prop for those guys, and if Mike asked him to fly for them, he would quit. Mike told him that I meant more to him than those guys, and that he was not going to fly for them. "Like I said, George, flying air taxi is a thankless job. I may as well just drive a school bus. It would be less stressful and more rewarding than this. Every day you are risking your life for $50 an hour.

Most of the customers complain and are always trying to overload the plane."

I told Kurt not to be so hard on himself, that not all customers were thankless, and told him to keep his chin up. He replied, "Hey don't forget about me the next time you get a big tip or a planeload of food given to you!" I laughed and told him that he would be first on my list; everybody loved Kurt. We had a few cocktails, and I told Kurt I was going to go home, and would see him tomorrow. Flying is a dangerous profession, and mixing it with commercial fishing makes it a danger cocktail, that I drank with ease.

CHAPTER 29

ALASKA GULF COAST ADVENTURES

Jim Treeline, a big game guide, saw me at the airport. He walked up to me while I was loading my plane and asked if I would be interested in working for him during the spring brown bear and wolf hunts. He wanted to use my camp as a base, and then set up outpost camps for his main big game guide Scotty. His offer sounded pretty good. The pay would be acceptable, and I also knew that Jim did not skimp on food. It was well known that he went all out on food for his clients, and even in down time he made sure the guides he had hired ate well. I told him that I was interested in working with him and we could go over the details later. I invited him to fly down to my camp the next morning. He said, "See you tomorrow."

I finished loading my plane and headed to my camp. Treeline flew down to my camp the next morning in his Citabria. I had coffee ready, and after a strong cup of joe, I took Jim on the ATV to my Italoway camp. I explained that my commercial fishing camp could not be used for big game guiding, but that I could build an elaborate outpost camp for the hunting operation. I offered to do the cooking and set up the outpost for the hunters. I would also use my ATV for the hunts and the jet boat for going up the Akwe. Jim would supply the food and pay me by the day for my help.

Working with Jim was a lot better than working with Gary. Doing this extra work would help me out a lot, as I was always looking for ways to make extra money. I could also see that the flying part of the industry was lucrative for a person like me who was a pilot and owned his own plane. I was going to work more and more on phasing out commercial fishing and move more into guiding sport fishermen and hunters.

219

This spring I set up the Italoway camp for Jim's operation. Jim had a particular client, Dick, who had been up on five different ten-day hunts trying to get a monster brown bear. He had turned down numerous nine-foot bears, waiting to tag the monster ten-foot bear. Jim put me in touch with Dick and said that Dick was on call if we spotted a ten-footer. As soon as he was notified, Dick would fly immediately up from Utah to hunt the trophy bear.

I had the camp set up and Scotty was in his outpost camp. I was busy scoping out the area for trophy bears when I spotted Big Chocolate, a bear that I had been watching for a few seasons. This was definitely a bear worth calling Dick for. I knew for sure he was a ten-foot square bear. I got a message to Jim, and Dick flew up as soon as he got the call. When he arrived, we had to wait a day to hunt. We decided that in the morning we would take him on a hike from camp down to Bear Alley. The next morning we hiked out to the trail and then circled back to camp. Low and behold, on our way back to camp we discovered that Big Chocolate had walked directly in our tracks. It was actually spooky that he had seemingly been stalking us. It was midday by now, and I told Dick that this time of day was not really worth hunting, because bears like to nap. I explained that the best times to hunt bears are in the mornings and evenings. That being said I told him we should go back to camp, regroup, and get ready for the evening hunt.

I decided to take Dick up to a bend in the river and glass the dunes where I had spotted Big Chocolate. We could glass downwind of where the bear had been hanging out. As we were watching with binoculars, we saw a large brown bear sow heading toward us. Not a minute later we spotted Big Chocolate about half a mile behind her with his head down, stalking her to breed. As they got closer, Dick told me that he wanted to take the shot. I said, "All right, I'll get ready." Dick had a .300 Weatherby and I had a .375 H&H Magnum. The bear turned broadside. Dick had a good rest and he took the shot. The bear dropped like a rock. How exciting. One shot and he got his trophy bear. Dick was ecstatic. After fifty-two days of hunting in the field, he had gotten his ten-foot bear. He excitedly thanked me and I said, "You're welcome, now let's get to work on this bear."

We got in the skiff and went to where the bear had dropped. We got some great pictures and then I went to work skinning out the hide. Dick thanked me over and over. I told him he especially deserved it after putting in all of that time in the field to get his bear. I got the hide loaded into the skiff and then we got back to camp. I asked Dick if he wanted to go fishing for a few days and he said, "That would be great!"

The next three days I took Dick up the Akwe for some killer rainbow and cutthroat fishing. We even caught some steelhead. He told me that this was the best experience he had gotten out of all of the trips he had been on. We had been glassing the bear carcass and getting some very cool eagle pictures and seeing what else might be feeding on the remains. Dick had a wolf tag so he was able to shoot a wolf if we saw one that he liked. We inspected the scene and there had been a large wolf feeding on the carcass. We went out early in the morning to glass the area and saw a beautiful black and silver-tip wolf. I asked Dick if he wanted to take it, and he said he did. One shot and Dick had a trophy wolf on top of his trophy bear. He was on cloud nine. I skinned out his wolf for him and the next morning he flew back home.

I recommended my taxidermist Rick Leach to Dick and told him Rick does phenomenal work. He decided to get his bear and wolf fully mounted with Rick. He told me that he wanted the bear standing up with the wolf snarling beneath it. I told him that I could not wait to see it and was thrilled I could be part of such a deserving sportsman's successful hunt. Dick thanked me again, and then got on the plane back home.

During the winter Mike and I had been talking seriously about expanding the air taxi part of my operation. After mulling over numerous possibilities, we both decided that starting my own air taxi would be the best route. This way I could run the aircrafts as I saw fit and Mike would not have to worry about the logistics of the scheduling. I decided that I would and could put to work a Beaver and a 206 full time during the summer. I found an owner-operator of a Beaver and a 206 pilot. I also found an amphibious 185 that caught my eye in *Trade A Plane*. This would be ideal for big game guides and OAS (government) flying. I could envision the forest and park service using the amphib for a lot of the flying that they were doing.

During that winter I got the air taxi certificate and called my venture Fairweather Air. I secured the Beaver, and the pilot showed up June 1 with his plane ready to haul fish. My amphib was supposed to be ready on March 15, but no later than April 1. With that in mind I started securing some flying jobs for Yakutat Lodge. I would use my amphib to go up to Situk Mountain and Italio Lakes. I also approached Branum, who was a big game guide, and got him to reserve some flying jobs. I also got my air taxi OAS certified so that I would be able to do government flying. I started having meetings with the park service and forest service to do some of their flying.

I was confident that this would be a lucrative venture. I hired a pilot, Chuck Stockton, to fly the 206 and amphib. He would also be my chief pilot and director of operations. The pilot of the Beaver had his own air taxi certificate, which I liked. I was able to have my own single pilot air taxi certificate and have Chuck be the single pilot. I only had a private pilot's license, so I was not able to fly commercially for the air taxi. I could still fly freight and haul fish for my own use while the planes were off-line. Since it was a gray area at the time, I did get some backlash and was always being checked by the FAA. I had the feeling that Gayle might have turned me in for flying commercially without a commercial pilot's license. I think Gayle was angry because in the past she was getting a lot of the fish hauling and government work, and now I was actively going after that business and offering them all kinds of incentives, such as free expediting that she had been charging them extra for. I was having my expeditor Caroline do their grocery shopping, check their mail, and go to the hardware store to get them needed supplies. I could see Gayle was losing a lot of business. Like my brother always said, "It is tough all over," meaning when things are tight, you have to go the extra mile to do what it takes. I was willing to do just that.

While the air taxi business was going on, I was also an assistant big game guide and commercial fisherman, and hauled my own fish. Jim told me my next hunt was two guys from Kentucky, who were car dealers. They paid for a two-on-one hunt. This meant two guys were hunting with one guide, and it usually did not pay as much as a one-on-one hunt. Obviously, it is hard enough for one person to get a trophy bear much less two. But that is the risk you take if you want a cheaper hunt. Besides it being hard on the hunters, it was actually harder for the guide to try to hunt two clients and get them both animals.

While all of this was going on, I was also working with Mike on a much bigger deal. We had built a 12x16 ft. cabin on the Kiklukh River, about 150 miles west of Yakutat. Mike, his son Wayne, and Wayne's fishing partner Tim hauled a skiff and an ATV from the Tsiu River to the Seal River, then had to portage the ATV, skiff, and trailer across to the west side of the Seal. Once on the west side of the Seal, they drove the ATV and pulled the trailer with the skiff twenty miles to the Kiklukh, where we had flown in the lumber to build the cabin. This was a small river nicknamed 8 Mile. This was mainly a silver salmon river but had a good number of trout in it. There was even a small steelhead run in late fall. The silver fishing was spectacular though. We hauled out 55,000 pounds of silvers that previous fall and a lot of them were giant, weighing fourteen to twenty-four pounds.

I had different plans for that river though. I was going to incorporate it into a sport fishing operation that was going to cover the gulf coast. From Yakutat to Cordova, I was going to pioneer these fly-out-only rivers and host the most spectacular sport fishing and hunting trips on the coast. Mike and I agreed that no one else was doing anything like it and that it would be a huge success. Mike was working on securing a hangar and doing flying for Silver Bay logging company out of Cordova. We were even working with Burt because he had a commercial fishing cabin on the Tsiu River from where we could base other specialty trips. Things were getting crowded on the Italio, Akwe, and East rivers. I wanted to move my operations to a more specialized and secluded part of the coast that had little or no traffic. The Kiklukh could be turned into an exclusive fishing area since we already had the cabin secured, and not many folks would be coming out there on their own.

Mike would definitely not be flying anyone out there that was not a guest of my new company, Alaska Gulf Coast Adventures. The Tsiu was a popular river for commercial fishing, but even with all the commercial fishermen, the number of silvers in the river was extraordinary. The fishermen had closures, which would be the perfect time to do sport fishing trips. There was also a system of three different rivers in the same vicinity. The Tsiu, Tsivat, and Kaliakh, hence my name for the area, Three Rivers. With Mike and I working together, we were going to dominate the coastline. We were very excited about the potential of our plan. Mike had secured the DNR permit to build the guest cabins on the Kiklukh. I had secured Burt's commercial fishing cabin and the ATV for basing sport fishing trips out of his camp on the Tsiu. Burt also had a cabin on the Kaliakh, which was going to be incorporated into the grand scheme of things. The Kaliakh was a phenomenal river that could only be fished with a jet boat. Everything was coming together.

I was at my camp ready for Jim's next hunters, Denny and a fellow named Mr. Magoo. These were the guys from Kentucky, the two-on-one. I was not too excited about trying to get two guys trophies, but I was going to do my best. Denny and Mr. Magoo showed up and we started hunting the next day. We hunted hard for a few days with not much luck. During the hunt I was telling Denny of my plans and he was very impressed. Denny expressed an interest in owning his own place in Alaska to come hunting and fishing. With all of my equipment and knowledge, Denny told me that I would be the perfect person to partner up with. I told him that Mike and I were partners in the planes, but the sport fishing lodge and operations were strictly mine, and that besides my air taxi, I had started a sport fishing business called Alaska Gulf Coast Adventures. I was looking for some investment capital, since I was putting everything I had into the start-up. I told Denny that it would be nice to have some investment money. Denny told me that he and his family did investments, and that he would love to be a part of something so exciting. He said to give him a proposal on paper and he would consider it. I told him that I would work on it. The hunt was not much of a success, but it was a blessing to meet someone who had some investment capital. Even though I already had a bunch of assets such as skiffs, ATV's, my own plane, a cabin already built, DNR permits, and loads of camping gear, I knew that it was going to be a real struggle to have the operating money it required to run this kind of business.

We kept hunting and I did my best to find them a decent bear, but I guess it was not in the cards. They were disappointed, but Denny was happy to have met me and was excited about my business venture and my proposal. I told Mr. Magoo that a lot of hunters come to Alaska and do not go home with a trophy. I told him that he should come back and try again. I explained that with my new business, if he came back, we would find a way to get him with another big game guide and out on a hunt for a big bear. I got Denny's contact information and was going to send him a proposal as soon as possible.

In the meantime my businesses kept rolling. I talked to Mike about my opportunity for taking on an investment partner, and he told me he thought it would be smart. He did warn me to make sure to protect myself. I told him that I would. In my proposal I was asking for a $250,000 investment. For that I was including all of my existing assets, such as skiffs, ATVs, gear, and permits. The money would be for purchasing building materials, paying for charters, paying labor costs, and buying an airplane for the sole use of the guide business. After sending this proposal to Denny, he read it over and had a meeting with his family. He called me back way sooner than I had expected. He asked if he could come back and see it all in person. He wanted to physically see the operation on the Tsiu, Kiklukh, and Cordova. I asked Mike if he would help fly Denny around and we would all make a trip out of it. We could have another business meeting in Cordova with Silver Bay, the logging company that Mike would be doing a lot of flying for. They owned a hangar there that we could base the Cordova operations out of, and also house a Gulf Air Taxi pilot in the hangar, which had an apartment in the loft. Having a hangar would be ideal for my operation on the Kiklukh, since it was only a twenty-minute flight from Cordova, instead of an hour-and-twenty-minute flight from Yakutat. Mike said he would help with the meeting.

Denny flew back up with Richard Brown, his attorney, who was also his brother-in-law. Mike and I showed Denny the plan. We landed on the Tsiu, then at the Kiklukh, and then flew on to Cordova. We mapped out the whole plan to them. Denny and Richard were really impressed. They left out of Cordova on Alaska Airlines back to Kentucky, and we flew back to Yakutat. Mike and I had our own meeting. We agreed that we could do it ourselves, but that it would be a lot easier with working capital and another partner to help with the building and managing of the business. Denny and his brother owned a car dealership, so he was a businessman and a salesman. I could see this being a tremendous help when it came to marketing and selling trips. It seemed like a win-win situation. I went back home and started to work on flying and fishing. I had so much going on I was moving nonstop. Mike was also very busy this time of the summer running his air taxi and securing his expansion to Cordova.

It was not long before Denny called me back and told me that he wanted to make a deal. He was going to have Richard draft up a contract and send it to me for review. I was so excited. I couldn't believe that someone would invest $250,000 in cash that fast, at the drop of a hat. Denny sent me an operating agreement and I asked my attorney friend Jerry Barker to take a look at it. He gave me a thumbs up. This was all happening so quickly that my head was spinning. I had just met Denny in May and now in July he was going to invest $250,000 in my company Alaska Gulf Coast Adventures (AGCA). I was euphoric. I got back to Denny and told him that I had my attorney review the contract and I was ready to sign. Denny said to sign it, get it back to him, and look for a company airplane to buy. When I signed on the dotted line, little did I know what was in store for me.

I was very busy commercial fishing and running my air taxi, but found time to search for a 206 to buy for the sole use of my company. I ended up finding a one-owner cherry U206. As soon as Denny received the signed contract, he called up the owners and bought the plane. Denny set up a bank account and told me to start buying the needed lumber and supplies to begin the building project. Even though I was very busy I immediately went to work. I already had the layout of the guest cabins and the cookhouse drawn out. I had the lumber package already figured out as well. All I had to do was buy what I needed. It was a great feeling. I was also getting an immediate salary. The date of delivery of the U206 was supposed to be July 30. I bought two new Yamaha Big Bear ATVs and had them shipped to Yakutat and taken out to the Kiklukh. At the same time I purchased two Tag-A-Long trailers. With lumber I was going to build seats and sides for comfortably hauling sportsmen in the back of the trailer. When completed it would look like a chariot. Everything was coming together like clockwork. It was amazing.

It was getting close to July 30 and I was excited to get my plane to Yakutat and found a ferry pilot to fly it from Cortez, Colorado. I had heavy-duty tires and bought a heavy-duty Landis nose fork to install on the plane. Kurt said he would help me put the mods on the plane as soon as it arrived. These modifications were a must for flying in and out of bush runways and sandy beaches. The Kiklukh had a primitive runway that we carved out by hand with picks, rakes, and shovels in the dunes. The strip looked more like an ATV trail, but with more work it could be improved. The beach runway could be up to a few thousand feet long, and was a bonus to utilize for flying heavy loads in and out. The bad part was that it had to be constantly maintained, because the tides would leave debris or even huge ruts and washouts. I was getting all kinds of supplies staged and ready to be flown out. The lumber was stacked in the hangar, and the ATVs and trailers had arrived.

A few days before the U206 was supposed to arrive the weather turned to drizzle and fog. I was in town fishing with Burt at Ocean Cape with the bay skiff, *Kanae*. It was eerie weather that day and I had a weird feeling in my gut. Low ceilings mixed with drizzle and fog meant bad flying conditions. I always felt sympathy pains for pilots when they had to fly through fog banks with no visibility, from point A to point B. We all flew in fog and marginal conditions, but if it were not for powering through these dangerous conditions, we would definitely not get much flying done. Mike had a ton of flying going on, and I knew he had a group of rafters out that he had dropped up north on the 17th. They were supposed to be picked up by Gulf Air, off the Dry Bay strip near the river on July 27. It was now the 29th, and I knew Mike was getting anxious about them being overdue. I had a feeling that Mike was very concerned about the rafters and would be tempted to fly out to look for them. My intuition was right. Burt, my brother, and I pulled up to the little dock at the cannery to pitch off our catch and James yelled down at me, "Hey, George, you have an urgent message."

I asked, "From who?"

He said that Marie Ivers, Mike's wife, had called to have me call the office immediately when I came to the dock. My gut dropped. I had a feeling that this could in no way be good news. I climbed up the ladder to the cannery and got on the pay phone. I called the office and asked for Marie. She sounded shaky. I asked her what was going on. She told me that Mike had gone out against his better judgment to look for the overdue rafters. I felt nauseous. She said he was late on his flight plan and that they could not reach him by aircraft or marine VHF radio, which Mike had both in his plane. I tried to sound confident despite the deep down bad feeling I had. I told her, "Don't worry, Marie, you know Mike, he is probably on a beach or gravel bar somewhere waiting for the fog bank to lift."

She said, "You are right, George."

I told Marie that I would go out immediately and look for Mike in my own plane. She said that would make her feel better. I yelled down to Burt and my brother that I had to go to the airport right away to go look for Mike. Burt and Barry yelled back that they hoped everything was all right and I said that I hoped so, too.

I found a friend at the cannery to rush me out to the airport. I ran into the Gulf Air office and asked if there was any word yet from Mike. They told me that he had left the airport and was an hour and a half overdue from the flight plan that he had filed, and that they had not heard from him since. I said I would get my plane pre-flighted and be out there shortly to find Mike. I untied my plane and checked my fuel. I had three hours of fuel onboard. That should be plenty of time to search for Mike. I walked back into the office to tell them that I was ready to go. In my mind the worst-case scenario was that Mike might have had a minor incident and had to put his plane down on the beach. I was sick to my stomach thinking about what might have happened to him. Everyone in the office was on edge. We were trying to stay calm, but we could all feel the tension in the air. You could hear a pin drop until suddenly a squawk came over the office radio.

It was Gayle. She was calling over the radio to inform us of her discovery. She had been out on a flight when heard that Mike was missing. She announced, "I found Mike." Everyone froze. I should have been relieved, but I wasn't. I did not feel better at all. With everyone already out there, and Mike found, there was not much more I could do at that point. The room was spinning and my head was in a daze. I had a feeling something more serious had happened than a minor incident. I could not believe that with everything going on, and all of our plans, that everything could come to a screeching halt. Besides that, one of my best friends and mentors could be dead, or at the least seriously injured. I was anxious, tense, and fearful to know more.

There were so many thoughts racing through my mind. My first concern was for Mike's well-being. I started to pray that he was in one piece and safe. My next concern was that my U206 was supposed to be arriving tomorrow and Mike and I were immediately supposed to be starting up operations in Cordova. I needed to keep my mind on building my dream, Camp Kiklukh. Denny was also expected in the next few days with some of his friends, Harold and Donnie, who were going to be helping with the building project. I still could not believe this was happening right now. It seemed like a nightmare that I would wake up from. It was wishful thinking on my part. Unbelievable as this might be, all of it was really happening.

About the Authors

"FEAR IS THE TOOL OF a man-made devil." - Napoleon Hill

George Davis has lived a life of adventure and danger. He has learned to overcome the most grueling obstacles and looks fear and death in the face and laughs.

George left home in 1971 when he was fifteen to pursue his dream of living life in the wilds of Alaska. He has since became a woodsman, commercial fisherman, entrepreneur, builder, high-time Alaska bush pilot, sport fishing guide, assistant hunting guide, wildlife enthusiast, wilderness expert, adventure lodge owner, consultant, and off-the-grid film producer.

He has pioneered the waters of Alaska's coastline from Haines to Cordova. He commercial fished, then built three remote adventure lodges, on the gulf coast and admiringly named it "The Lost Coast." George is an innovator in the lodge business. He also invented his own world-renowned sport fishing fly called the "Davis Spanker."

George sold Alaska Gulf Coast Adventures, Kiklukh Lodge, Three Rivers Lodge, and Icy Bay Lodge. Now Alaska Wild Adventures and Alaska Man Consulting are his passions. His videos document real-life living in the wilds of Alaska, off of the grid. He also consults with clients on anything and everything in Alaska, including, adventure planning, building, living off the grid, and alternate energy systems. His books encompass his exciting life in the Alaska wilderness with the added humor of his interactions with the numerous characters that he encounters.

"SELF-CONFIDENT FAITH IN ONE'S self is both the man-made weapon which defeats the devil, and the man-made tool which builds a triumphant life. There is a link to irresistible forces that stand behind those that believe that failure and defeat are but just temporary experiences." -Napoleon Hill

Jill Davis, Alaska Woman, moved to Cordova, Alaska from Oklahoma when she was seven. She grew up in the woods and has always had a passion for adventure. She hunted and fished with her dad and became a gun enthusiast. Her mother affectionately started calling her Annie Oakley, Little Sure Shot, at a very young age.

After attending college, she pursued her dream of being in the adventure guide business. She became a huge part of Alaska Gulf Coast Adventures, Kiklukh, and Three Rivers Lodge. She then went on to build her own business, Icy Bay Lodge, with husband, George Davis.

Jill wears many hats, but even during her years of building, guiding, and flying, she never lost her enthusiasm for writing. After selling Icy Bay Lodge, she pursued her passion full time with Alaska Wild Adventures, as a writer, and wilderness expert. Jill started her own consulting business, Alaska Woman Consulting. Now she travels Alaska writing, filming, and documenting real-life living in the wilds of Alaska off the grid with her husband. She lives a thrilling life of excitement and adventure, on the cutting edge.

Social Media Links

GEORGE DAVIS ALASKA MAN
Facebook Alaska Wild Adventures- facebook.com/AlaskaWildAdventures
Facebook Alaska Man Page - facebook.com/ManAlaska
Twitter- twitter.com/@alaskamanak1
Instagram- instagram.com/ALASKA_MAN1
Google+ - plus.google.com/+AlaskaWildAdventures
You Tube- www.youtube.com/user/AlaskaWildAdventures
Website- www.alaskawildadventures.tv

JILL DAVIS ALASKA WOMAN
Facebook- facebook.com/AlaskaWildAdventures
Alaska Woman Page- facebook.com/jdalaskawoman
Twitter- twitter.com/jillddavis
Instagram- instagram.com/alaskawoman1
Google+- plus.gogle.com/+JillDavisAlaskaWoman
You Tube- youtube.com/user/AlaskaWildAdventures
youtube.com/jdlostcoast1
Website- http://www.alaskawildadventures.tv

Made in the USA
San Bernardino, CA
04 August 2017